This Land of
ENGLAND

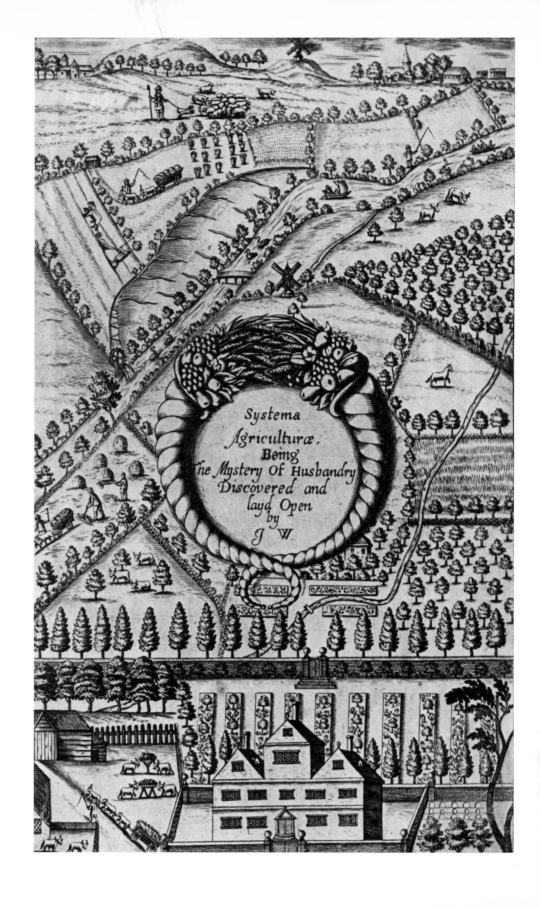

This Land of
ENGLAND

by
David Souden and David Starkey

Photographs by Peter Anderson and David Souden

Watercolours by Pam Williams

MULLER, BLOND & WHITE

IN ASSOCIATION WITH CHANNEL FOUR TELEVISION COMPANY LIMITED

FRONTISPIECE. The title page to John Worlidge's Systema Agriculturae, *one of the most widely-read farming manuals of the seventeenth century. The engraving was accompanied by a doggerel poem, explaining the types of farming, and the loss of sophistication moving back through the picture.*
OPPOSITE, the guide post of much the same date, at Wroxton near Banbury, has hands pointing in each direction, linking the metropolis with the provinces.

First published in Great Britain by Muller, Blond & White Ltd, 55 Great Ormond Street, London WC1N 3HZ.

This Land of England copyright © Mirageland Ltd., 1985

British Library Cataloguing in Publication Data
Souden, David
   This Land of England
   1. Country life — England   2. Natural
   history — England
   I. Title   II. Starkey, David
   942'.009'734   S522.G7

   ISBN 0–584–11128–2

Printed and bound in Great Britain by
Purnell and Sons (Book Production) Ltd.,
Member of the BPCC Group, Paulton, Bristol

CONTENTS

To our colleagues in television, who often ask more searching questions than do our colleagues in history.

PREFACE

Take three men, very different historical figures – two aristocratic, and one very far from it. The first is the last holder of a peerage title, third husband of a seemingly man-eating wife who still dressed and danced like a young girl even in her nineties. The second is one step higher in the league table of peers, and is one of the greatest-ever English book collectors. The third is a farm labourer, living and working most of his life in a single village, and rarely far from dire poverty. In putting together the varied material for this book and the television series with which it is twinned, these three men were all arrived at separately, by quite different routes of historical inquiry. And yet, although they are separated a little in time and in space, there are connections between them all.

The first, who married the astounding woman, was the 6th Viscount Saye and Sele. He died at his wife's ancestral home, Doddershall in Buckinghamshire. Doddershall is in the parish of Quainton, and that is where Joseph Mayett eked out his existence. It was to Doddershall that Mayett went when he had to appeal to the squire for his Poor Law rights, and to the Viscountess' grandson that he had to appeal. And in the great mid-nineteenth century library at Ashburnham Place, in East Sussex, was one of the manuscript collections of the 4th Earl of Ashburnham, the Stowe Collection. If the Earl had cared to read his possessions, he would have found copious details about the inhabitants of Quainton at the time of Joseph Mayett's childhood, and charming watercolours of militiamen in their uniforms, one of whom might have been Joseph Mayett himself.

All three men appear in this book. The connections between them may seem rather forced, mere coincidences: but my researching footsteps have been dogged by such coincidence. These are just special examples of what this book attempts to convey – the astonishing inter-connectedness, the *integrity* of England in the past. Other writers might stress the diversity of landscape, people and history in England. But we look with another perspective. In the 6th Viscount Saye and Sele's own ancestors' home (still lived in by his relations' descendants, as Doddershall still is by his wife's) there is a Latin inscription over a doorcase, proclaiming that "There is no pleasure in the memory of the past." But there is a pleasure, and a necessity, in understanding the past of *This Land of England*.

There will not be many more of these riddles in this book: but the intention here, as in the Channel 4 television series, is to persuade the

"An assembly of fat motherly flat-caps . . . a litter of squad elephants." Billingsgate fishwives, drawn by Thomas Rowlandson, provide one of the many images we examine to show economic reality and regional inter-connectedness beneath the Olde Worlde charm.

reader, or viewer, to re-examine many of the preconceptions (and prejudices) that exist about the pre-Victorian past. The two ventures, perhaps more than most, have been a collaborative effort. David Starkey had the initial idea, which he and John Slater turned into a working idea. Together with Bruce MacDonald, Heather Hampson and myself that was translated into a film medium. Amongst all those people, it is often difficult to pinpoint where a certain idea began, or indeed sometimes where it ended. Much of the detailed research and working historical expertise has been mine; together, David Starkey and I planned this book. He wrote the introductory chapter; we wrote the concluding chapter in tandem, as well as the more general apparatus surrounding the third and fourth chapters.

* * *

My thanks for assistance and information are legion:
to the parishioners of Myddle, Lord and Lady Saye and Sele, David Fiennes, John Marshall, Roger Finlay, the Birkett families, the National Trust, Lancashire Record Office, Karla Oosterveen, Tony Wrigley, the ESRC Cambridge Group for the History of Population and Social Structure;

to the East Sussex Record Office, the Revd John Bickersteth, the National Library of Wales, Hoare's Bank, Westminster School, Patric Dickinson, Michael Maclagan and the College of Arms, Donald Coleman, Tony Rudd, Howard Newby, John Nicholson, Michael Percival, the people of the Ashburnham estates new and old, Lieutenant-Colonel Richard Carwardine-Probert and Hon. Thomas Lindsay;

to Ann Kussmaul, for whom especial thanks;

to Hugh Hanley and the Buckinghamshire Record Office, the people of Quainton, Richard Luckett (Pepys Librarian) and the Master and Fellows of Magdalene College, Cambridge, Frank Stubbings and the Master and Fellows of Emmanuel College, Cambridge;

to Margaret Statham and the Suffolk Record Office, Bury St Edmunds branch, John Vaughan and the St Edmundsbury Borough Council, the townspeople of Bury, Greene King, the Metropolitan Museum of Art, the Arts Council of Great Britain, the British Library (Department of Manuscripts), the British Museum (Department of Prints and Drawings), the Tate Gallery, the Science Museum, Derek Keene, Vanessa Harding, Sutton's Hospital in Charterhouse, Greater London Record Office, and the Guildhall Library.

I have always benefited from discussions with Tony Wrigley, Richard Smith, Roger Schofield, Peter Laslett, Richard Wall, Chris Wilson, Ann Kussmaul, Peter Clark, Margaret Sampson, John Walter, David Weir, Peter Burke, Julian Hoppitt, Margaret Spufford, Keith Wrightson, Alan Macfarlane, Sarah Harrison, Tim Wales, Rab Houston, Susan Amussen, Jordan Goodman, Sheila Cooper, Lorna Weatherill, Marguerite Dupree and so many others.

Andrée Jenni typed the manuscript with demon speed and accuracy, especially once she had persuaded me to write in something other than pencil, while the personnel of Mirageland, Reality and PosNeg kept my spirits up. It was always a pleasure accompanying Peter Anderson on his photographic expeditions, with the fine results that are reproduced here. Many people and institutions have given permission to reproduce pictures in their possession: they are acknowledged and thanked separately. Anthony Blond, Antony White and Hal Robinson have nurtured this book, as Eric Drewery and Richard Johnson so expertly designed it.

Without Channel 4 and the confidence of Carol Haslam this entire project would not have been undertaken. The volume's dedication speaks for itself. Without David Starkey, whose fruitful mind and turn of phase found ways through, and whose persuasion got me into all this, the project could not have begun.

David Souden

INTRODUCTION

This Land of England is a voyage through time and place in search of the England that existed before the Industrial Revolution. It is an England that was rural and lightly populated. In one sense it is gone forever; in another it lingers in astonishing detail in the countryside of today. To find it, we journey in time from the sixteenth century to the nineteenth, with glimpses forward and backward. And in place we go from Sussex to the Lake District, and from East Anglia to the Welsh marshes. This Land of England is also a dialogue. One speaker is the past of our imaginings, of poetry, romance and the fiction that too often passes for history. The other is the past as it really was, in the plain clothes of facts, figures and the lives of men. "Telling it as it really was" perhaps sounds dull, but as usual the fact is much stranger, more surprising than the fiction.

The search for the past has often been attempted. Here we hope we do it well, and we certainly do it in a novel way, with new material and illustrations. But the dialogue with the past is the more important and original. Always the relationship between past and present is the hub of the historical enterprise. It is so above all when that relationship is changing, as it is now.

It is changing because the present is changing. I started work on the companion Channel 4 television series, This Land of England, in 1983. In the course of that year official figures revealed two major developments. The first was that Britain had, for the first time since trade figures began, imported more manufactured goods than she had exported; and the second, that, for the first time since the Corn Laws of 1846, she was on the point of exporting more grain than she imported. The two statistics proclaimed, in effect, the end of the Industrial Revolution. And in so doing they overturned more-or-less every received assumption about our past, our present and our future. To have this happen in the middle of production was more than we could have hoped for. It turned what we were doing from a worthy, pedagogic exercise into something relevant: a political, as well as an historical enterprise.

This will seem a strange remark. Isn't history fixed, dead fixed? It is. But our perspective on it (which is the only history that matters) is moving constantly with the present. So long as we were confident of our urban, industrial present, we knew also where we had our rural, agricultural past. But take away that confidence about the present, and the past dissolves into uncertainty and flux too.

First though, the certain past that we viewed from a certain present. Always we held up a mirror to the past and found our opposite there. The present (let us cheat just a little with time) is the way of the town: mobile, rootless and competitive. The past was the way of the country: stable, ordered and imbued with a profound sense of community, of cooperation and of caring and sharing. There was a place for everyone and everyone had a place. Horizons were limited and opportunities (and therefore worries) few. Sons followed the ways of their fathers and daughters their mothers. And as those parents aged, so they were cared for in the warmth of the family circle.

There was a dark side of course. Stability bred stagnation. It is modern enterprise, vigour and freedom that have created modern prosperity. Their absence produced the divided society of the past. A handful enjoyed lives of idle ease; the vast majority, downtrodden and impoverished if not actually starving, were condemned to an existence of toil and deprivation. And not only were their lives nasty and brutish, they were also short. If a violent neighbour did not get you, the plague would. The consequences showed with children in particular. Here it was a case of easy come and easy go: as infants were more likely to die than to live, there was little point in wasting affection on them, at least until they had won through. Anyway, you were probably too busy beating your wife or being beaten by your husband.

So it is, in a minor key as it were, with our parallel images of the modern countryside. This is felt to be a relic of the essential rural society of the past and to reproduce its virtues and vices. On the one hand, therefore, the countryside is a haven of thatched cottages and horse brasses, vicarage tea parties, Harvest Homes, and cricket on the green; the time is always half past three and the weather is always fine. The people are fine too: solid, rustic, caring. Alternatively, the countryside represents a survival of the feudal values of deference and obligation, and a perpetuation of the divided society they propped up: the landlord is a useless *rentier*; the farmer a tight-fisted exploiter, and the farm labourer too passive or too stupid to propel himself into better-paid and less physically demanding work in industry.

"It is. . ." no, "It was. . ." Remember I have been cheating with time, and though I have been writing in the present tense it is already an historic present. That confident present came to an abrupt end in the 1970s, and the statistics of 1982 were only the final echoes. Around us now, industry is collapsing; inner cities decaying; and services, suburbs, quasi-villages and even agriculture itself are booming. Fashion, that most sensitive barometer, has registered the change first.

For years the countryside was very nice but not – well – fashionable. Oscar Wilde's *The Importance of Being Earnest*, first performed in 1895, is a touchstone. "I am glad to say," remarks Gwendolen to the country girl Cecily, "I have never seen a spade. It is obvious that our social spheres have been very different." Lady Bracknell backs up her daughter with solid economics: "Land, Mr. Worthing, gives one position and prevents one from keeping it up". The same attitude survived much lower down the social scale and much nearer to the present. In smart 1950s council-house society, I remember, it was chic to have coffee come out of jars, veg. out of tins. Beans to grind and carrots to wash were strictly not "contemporary". Nor was cotton or wool to wear. Artificial, "man-made" fibres were popular just because they were that (no other reason could have led anybody to wear a nylon shirt).

As with the natural, so with the old. I, young fogey that I was before my (and their) time, did my best to collect antiques. My mother did her best to stop me; and any piece that was allowed through the door was scrubbed thoroughly in vinegar and warm water. I still apologize for the lack of patina but my mother thought only of "dirt". The same hygienic attitude shaped town-planning. My own town of Kendal was gutted by a benevolent conspiracy between the Borough Surveyor and, of all people, the Medical Officer of Health: old buildings, like old furniture, were "dirty", and demolition was even more thorough than vinegar and water. And still, in the Third World, dried, tinned baby food enjoys a disastrous prestige of being both "modern" and "manufactured".

Back here in London in contrast, a university examiner breast-feeds her baby in front of bemused colleagues. Taught by industrial retreat we have unlearned fast, and in the 1980s conservation and countryside carry all before them. The past dominates the present, and, in a re-run of the great population movements of the nineteenth century, the countryside floods into the town. Garden centres bloom where grass scarcely grew; Barbours are flaunted on the Tube; fashion correspondents attend point-to-points; and despairing of the horrors of Westway and World's End, we take refuge in the notion that the "real" London is a city of "villages" anyway. In this atmosphere the new sin against the Holy Ghost is to introduce industrial values into the countryside, and the farmer, once condemned as backward, has replaced the property-developer as the man we love to hate. The one tore down buildings; the other uproots hedgerows (and restores the land to the open appearance it may have had before enclosure).

Cows, fields, hedges and hills: the classic English landscape.

Historians tend not to belong to the "life-style class" (with academic salaries at their present level they can scarcely afford to). But as a profession they change world views more quickly than dandies change Argyll socks. And there are historical trend-setters too. One of the most important of these has been Peter Laslett, whose *World We Have Lost* was published in 1966. Hitherto social historians, rather like Lady Bracknell and my mother, had been concerned essentially with cities, industry and the modern world. "Pre-industrial" society mattered only in so far as the origins of industrialization could be found there; while the historians' picture of this early world differed little in substance from the man-in-the-street's. Laslett's book changed all this. Its subject was pre-industrial society itself; and its conviction was that we had all got it wrong. Gone were the village community of uncompetitive, self-regulating equals; gone too was the extended multi-generational family, in which the young cared for the old and were cared for by their offspring in turn. Instead, it appeared, the village consisted of a hodge-podge of the prosperous, the destitute and everything in between; while the family was usually made up only of a husband and wife and their children; in other words, it was nuclear. An unequal society meant that law and regulation were needed to maintain social order; while the nuclear family required a network of public provision to cope with the many who fell outside its narrow pattern, like the widowed, the orphaned, the chronically sick or to some extent the unemployed.

All this is important enough in itself. But Laslett wrote with a powerful mixture of irony, hard facts and evangelical zeal. The result was an impact rather like that of the historian Marc Bloch and the journal *Annales* in France. A new sort of history was born. Some have pursued the "new" history with traditional documentary methods; other have used the new techniques of "econometric" statistics and historical demography.

Such work has deepened enormously our understanding of England before Victoria. It has also narrowed it. The time was ripe for synthesis and speculation. These came with Alan Macfarlane's *The Origins of English Individualism* (1978). On the dust-jacket appeared Daniel Defoe's Robinson Crusoe. Defoe was a great collector of information; he also

caught superbly the social and political flavour of Augustan England. Macfarlane set himself a similar double task: to connect the detailed conclusion of the new social history with a broad re-interpretation of England's economic and political development. The result is uneven (it could hardly be anything else) but it is challenging and provocative. Laslett and the rest had unearthed a pre-industrial England that was not only different from what we had thought; it was also different from other countries as well. Little of Western Europe, it is true, has proved to correspond fully to the orthodox model of vast peasant families rooted to the soil, but most areas came significantly nearer than England. Macfarlane boldly drew the conclusion no-one else dared. Whereas mobility, the nuclear family and the like were supposed to be the results of industrialization, in England at any rate they were its cause. In other words, England had not become different because it industrialized first; it had always been different, Macfarlane claimed. And the continuity between past and present, and long continuities within the past, ruled all. The consequence of that brand of argument was to stand our idea of causation on its head; to play ducks and drakes with the notion of historical progress; even to take rattling skeletons like "national characteristics" out of the historians' cupboard, flesh them and give them new life.

We have come a long way from Barbour jackets and young fogeys. But, to re-animate another skeleton, young fogeys and new historians breathe the same "spirit of the age". Both are reacting to the challenge and confusions of a de-industralizing society; they may even be the same person. The problem is that their response may make the confusion worse. After all, does not the new history rob us of our last confidence in the past just as we have despaired of the present?

This is only superficially true. Our old confidence about the past was really an arrogant rejection of it. Overweaningly confident of ourselves, and of the future, we found the past merely primitive and backward. Certain of progress we could learn nothing from experience. So sure, indeed, were we of our superiority and difference that it was difficult at times even to recognise a common humanity between ourselves and our ancestors. That barrier has now gone. Change in the present and change in our understanding of the past have brought us together: they are more like us; we are less different from them.

Which, thank God, makes the whole business of writing history less clinical. The "scientific" historians of the early and mid-twentieth century, in contrast, prided themselves on their detachment. Although they were professionally committed to the past they shared their age's distance from it. This showed itself above all in their elimination of the personal from history. History was about institutions, classes, factors, forces, ideas; anything but men, or still less women or children. Biography became fit only for popular writers, and popularity was something scholars shunned as resolutely as Coriolanus. This is a pity, for history remained popular despite the historian and others rushed in to fill the gap in the market that their high-mindedness had left.

But filling that gap opened another and wider one between popular and academic history. At first sight the "new" history seems ill-suited to bridge it. Its methods are technical and it lacks the obvious excitement of political narrative. On the other hand, it is a history of villages that still stand, sometimes nearly untouched; almost always reconstructible with a little imagination and research. And it is a history of ordinary events in ordinary lives – like ours. Just like us, our ancestors grew up and got a job; got married and had children; grew old and died. And their lives too are recoverable, thanks to the leases they signed or the wills they made, and the papers in which they bared their souls to God, or their finances to their banker. And what they failed to write about themselves, others – a gossipy neighbour or a legal adversary — might well write about them. But more, much more, survives than papers. There are the buildings in which they lived; the pictures they had painted; sometimes the furniture, clothes or tools they used. Written in the landscape in bold strokes are the parks they created or the forests they planted; or, more faintly, there is the line in a field that was a canal or the hole in the ground that was a mine. "Nothing that is human is alien to me," quoted Cicero approvingly. We can add that nothing that humans have made is alien either. T.S. Eliot, echoing the words of his namesake Thomas Elyot who had lived four hundred years earlier, put it thus:

> "Houses live and die. . .
> . . .in that open field
> On a summer midnight, you can hear the music
> Of the weak pipe and the little drum
> And see them dancing round the bonfire
> . . .
> Lifting heavy feet in clumsy shoes
> Earth feet, loam feet, lifted in country mirth
> Mirth of those long since under earth
> Nourishing the corn."

The printed page is not so resonant as a landscape, but through people and places, in words and pictures, we shall try to recreate *This Land of England*, which was theirs and is ours.

David Starkey

——1——
THIS LAND OF ENGLAND ANOTHER COUNTRY?

"The past is a foreign country: they do things differently there." With its long hot Edwardian summer in the Norfolk countryside, the innocence of the child and the awful discoveries of adolescence, and the snobberies both blatant and subtle of English society, L.P. Hartley's *The Go-Between* seems both a lament for and an indictment of the past. But in fact his famous opening line is deeply ironic. The novel's central character knows that he was shaped by the past, and that many differences between his past and his present are only surface. As with the go-between so it is with us. We feel that the past is a foreign country. But how foreign, how different?

Stripping away the layers of time, by moving backwards from the present, the land seems to get ever greener and pleasanter. England before the Industrial Revolution certainly was a rural world, and the further back we look the more rural and stable it seems to have been. England is now an urban nation. The threshold was passed in 1851 when over half the population of thirteen million officially lived in towns. Fifty years before, the population was smaller by four million, and two-thirds of them lived in the country. There were six million people in 1750, three-quarters of them country-dwellers, and five million people in 1700, four-fifths of whom lived in villages. Back in 1600, of the four million inhabitants eight-ninths were villagers, and in the mid-sixteenth century (when figures of any reliability run out) three million people lived in England, and nine-tenths of them lived in the country.

Not only do the urban elements diminish when we move backwards in time. Motorways, railways, canals and metalled roads disappear, giving three million people room to breathe. These three million people produced food enough to support themselves, but often only with difficulty. In the sixteenth century, every hundred families in agriculture could produce some surplus, enough to feed another handful of families (at least when the harvest was successful). By the end of the eighteenth century, the hundred agricultural families were able to produce enough to support another few dozen families. But this was far from the twentieth century world in which a hundred families on the land can support thousands of others.

This was therefore a foreign world in which most people lived in villages and most worked in the agricultural economy. Where towns did exist, they were small. The dearth of large and splendid cities was

apparent when compared with France, Italy or Germany. One commentator in the mid-sixteenth century, Thomas Starkey, who travelled widely on the Continent, drew attention to the lack of care and interest which the English gave to their towns.

"As touching the goodly building of cities and towns, I trow in the world there is not less regard than here in England. . . Methoughts when I came into Flanders and France that I was translated into another world – the cities and towns appeared so goodly, so well builded, and so clean kept. . . And contrary here with us the people seem to study to find means how they may quickliest let fall into ruin and decay all their cities, castles and towns. Every gentleman flieth into the country: few that inhabit the cities and towns, few that have any regard of them; by reason whereof in them you shall find no policy, no civil order almost, nor rule."

English towns may not have been splendid places, but they were larger than the places where most of the people spent most of their lives. The many thousands of English villages, very often consisting of only a few hundred people, represented a more intimate face-to-face society, where everyone knew everyone else. The portraits of itself that the English rural past composed seem to confirm that.

The Dixton harvesters, *painted at their collective task of bringing in the hay in c.1710.*

One of the most remarkable English paintings, by an anonymous and otherwise unknown artist, is the record of the haymaking in Dixton in Gloucestershire, painted around 1710. If anything confirms the caring and sharing way of village life, this is it.

Dixton lies between the Cotswolds and the Severn, just to the east of Tewkesbury. The landscape stretches out towards the hills; in the foreground hay is being mowed, staked and carted away while further away is the ridge and furrow of the ploughed fields. Everybody from Dixton – at least, everybody capable of work – seems to be in the picture. Over a hundred tiny figures are at work: men are mowing and carting, women raking and stacking. Leaving the field, at bottom right, are a group of morris dancers, without whom no village would be complete.

The morris men are not the only figures not hard at work. In the centre on horseback are the gentleman who owns the land, his wife and daughter. Here we have the other aspect of the past we all seem to recognize – the many who needed to work and the few who did not. The figures at work are almost all indistinguishable, for there are no marks of status to differentiate them one from another, but the gentry family sit high and proud.

The naïve charm of the early seventeenth century estate map of Ashburnham, Sussex, RIGHT, George Morland's village inn, ABOVE, and surviving buildings, OPPOSITE, convey the various faces of the past.

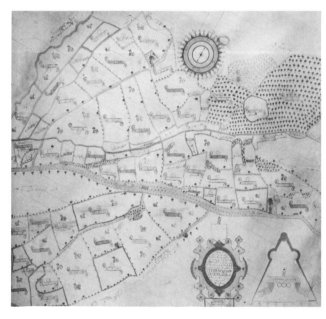

Cooperation is the key to this painting. These are not firm, individualistic farmers and their subservient labourers of the nineteenth or even the twentieth centuries. The painting is there also to show ownership: the man on the horse owned and controlled all that he (and we) could see.

Ownership was depicted in a different way on the estate map of Ashburnham near Battle, in Sussex. This was very much a record of possession: the sizes of the fields are included, as are the scattered farmsteads. The decoration is appropriate to the map: these are, however crudely depicted, the people who lived here and the animals who grazed on the land. This was all property of the Ashburnham family, who had owned most of the land for over five hundred years before this early seventeenth century map was drawn – and much of it is still owned by their descendants' legal trusts.

Clearly there are continuities with the past shown in these pictures: the landscape is still there at Dixton and Ashburnham, and some of the fields retain their ancient boundaries. But equally this is a world that has vanished, a world with a deep social divide but without class; a world of villages and agriculture rather than of towns, industry and commerce; a world of cooperation and mutual help.

George Morland painted another of the primary institutions of English village life in *The door of a village inn*. In the painting, as in Oliver Goldsmith's word picture, there is the bucolic essence of the village inn.

> ". . .where draughts inspired,
> Where greybeard mirth and smiling toil retired,
> Where village statesmen talked with looks profound,
> And news much older than their ale went round."

In the painting, a traveller on horseback, probably a well-off farmer, buys a drink at a wayside inn, a house in a state of picturesque decay. Each person in the picture is in his or her appropriate place – the farmer elevated, the landlady subservient, the child quiet. The centrepiece is the mug of ale, the "jolly good ale and old" in which true Englishmen were "so wrapped and thoroughly lapped".

More soberly, the Wiltshire village of Great Cheverell sounds a model of all the virtues from the description of it written by the rector, Revd John Hayes in 1713. He had three hundred souls in his care, living in harmony in the parish's sixty houses and enjoying the fruits of rich farming.

"Here are also several necessary tradesmen and artificers. But no alehouses are ever suffered here, which is too often of ill consequence in other parishes. The young men here at their leisure times divert themselves chiefly in these two innocent and masculine exercises, football and [bell]ringing. . . They seldom drink to excess or are guilty of other debaucheries. And one thing is here remarkable, that for the space of forty years past and upwards no illegitimate offspring have been in this parish.

"The poor here have many good privileges not usual in other places, they having

not only a full employment in husbandry or otherwise but have also liberty to cut what furzes they think fit in the common for the fuel. And as for those old men whose labour is done, they are either sent to the Hospital [alms house] at Heytesbury, where they have a competent maintenance for the rest of their lives, or else they and all such others as cannot maintain themselves are allowed a comfortable subsistence by the parish, besides an annual distribution of money to every poor family in the parish upon Good Friday at the church immediately after divine service. And it was scarce ever known that any one poor person of this place did ever go a-begging out of this parish."

Heaven on earth.

These pictures and descriptions provide a consistent view of just what English was like – rural and quiet, cooperative and simple. How far that all seems from the modern world of towns and highways, haste and class division. What survives from the past – country houses, farms, cottages and the landscape itself – seems to reinforce that contrast.

But was life really like that? Do these pictures and accounts tell the whole truth? Or can we understand the survivals from the past in quite other ways? Our purpose is to answer these questions, through a wide variety of places and different forms of historical discourse and enquiry. We shall see.

2
LAND AND STATUS

MYDDLE

Before the Reformation the walls of the Church would often have been painted with brightly-coloured scenes of the life of Christ and the Saints. These were whitewashed over in the sixteenth century, and instead the walls and floor were progressively filled with the tombs of the deceased aristocracy and gentry of the parish, who thus lorded it in death as in life. The succession of four Tollemaches, each called Lionel, is commemorated in the Suffolk parish of Helmingham. On the tomb of Lionel III the inscription reads:

> . . .*My many virtues, Moral and Divine,*
> *My Lib'ral hand, my loving Heart to mine,*
> *My Piety, my Pity, Pains and Care,*
> *My Neighbours, Tenants, Servants, yet declare;*
> *My Gentle Bride Sir Ambrose Jermyn bred,*
> *My Years lack Five of half my Grandsire's Thread*

while on the tomb of Lionel IV we are told:

> *Here with his Fathers sleeps Sir Lionel,*
> *Knight, Baronet all Honours worthy well,*
> *So well the Acts of all his Life expresst,*
> *His Elders Virtues, and excell's their best. . .*

The inscriptions speak with all the pride of Ozymandias, and with less irony since the monuments are unbroken and there is still a Tollemache in Helmingham Hall.

Less flamboyant than monuments and inscriptions, but at least as important in inculcating order and degree, were the pews. Now they seem dull enough; then they were a matter of moment and a whole book, and a very interesting one, was written about them.

"Almighty God hath created and appointed all things in heaven, earth and waters in a most excellent and perfect order. In heaven he hath appointed distinct orders and states of archangels and angels. In the earth he has assigned kings, princes, with other governors under them, all in good and necessary order,"

read the minister from the "Homily on Obedience".

> *"All things bright and beautiful,*
> *All creatures great and small,*
> *All things wise and wonderful,*
> *The Lord God made them all.*
>
> *"The rich man in his castle,*
> *The poor man at his gate:*
> *God made them, high or lowly,*
> *And ordered their estate,"*

sang the congregation (until twentieth century susceptibilities removed the last verse). From the sixteenth to the nineteenth century the parish church told as much of the relations of man to man as the relations of man to God.

God – or at least His altar – did not even occupy the prime position in the Church. The altar was of course that focus in the Middle Ages, and the Victorians, out of a mixture of piety and antiquarianism, put it back in position to create the interiors we are familiar with today. But in between the Church looked very different. The Reformation of the sixteenth century replaced a ritualistic religion centring on the sacrifice of the Mass with an evangelical religion centring on the "Word of God". The focus of the Church changed accordingly, from the East End and the altar (which was itself destroyed) to the pulpit from which lengthy sermons were preached. The Church in fact became a lecture theatre and the congregation sat in high-sided pews, not looking but listening. One seventeenth-century Essex clergyman described his congregation as his "sleepy hearers". The pews were enclosed, to keep out draughts, and seats faced in all directions rather than progressing eastwards in an orderly fashion. But *order* and *obedience* were the perennial themes of the sermons the congregation heard.

And secular order and hierarchy dominated the structural fabric too. *"A pew is a certain place in church encompassed with wainscot. . .for several persons to sit in together. . . A pew or seat does not belong to a person or to land, but to a house, therefore if a man remove from a house to dwell in another, he shall not retain the seat belonging to the first house."*

Quoting legal precedents, the Shropshire farmer and antiquarian Richard Gough began his "observations concerning the seats in Myddle and the families to which they belong". In writing a history of his parish, around 1701, Richard Gough recaptured the local social structure in a unique way. In his church, as in others, seating was hierarchically organized – like a modern theatre, the more you paid the closer you were to the front. The payment was, however, indirect: seats were allocated to the farms and houses on the basis of how much was paid for them in local rates. The church's seating plan is thus a map of the local hierarchy. Position in the social structure was governed by personal wealth, landholding and the place given to the individual by friends and neighbours. A prominent local landowner, whether a member of the aristocracy or not, would have the most important seat; but Richard Gough's parish had no resident major landowner, and the pews at the

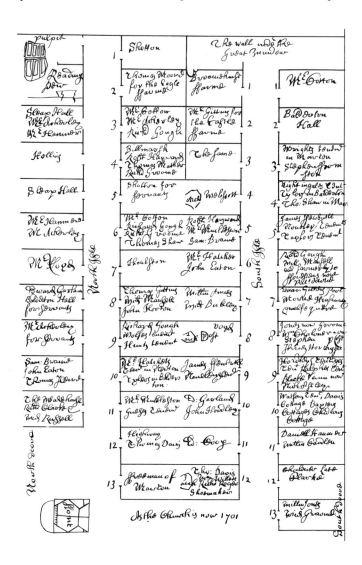

Myddle church, ABOVE, is a rebuilt version of that shown in Richard Gough's 1701 seating plan OVERLEAF.

front were occupied by the families of the leading gentlemen-farmers. Our word "gentleman" carries a sense of politeness. To Gough and his contemporaries that sense was accompanied by notions of the importance of birth, appropriate wealth and the recognition of those around. Our word "farmer" however would have been alien to Gough: descriptions based on status took the place of our generic term for an occupier and cultivator of land. The larger farmers were *yeomen*. They may have been freeholders, or may have been tenants, but their wealth and landholding were reasonably substantial. They usually farmed more than fifty acres. In Myddle, they occupied the middle pews.

Farmers with small acreages and with less personal wealth were usually termed *husbandmen*. Their economic position was not easy. A husbandman with thirty arable acres in the early seventeenth century might make a net profit of £14 to £15, which would give him a surplus of a few pounds. That would be in a normal year: in a year with a bad harvest that small surplus would have been wiped out.

Below that level and sitting at the rear of the church were the *cottagers* and farm *labourers*, with only a few acres if any on which to subsist. Their income came from wage work for other people, or from having a double occupation – spinning, weaving, woodworking, in addition to their main activity. *Craftsmen* were also an integral part of the village social structure: blacksmiths, carpenters and stonemasons. Their families too would occupy seats in the rear half of the church.

So these were the categories of people filling Myddle church on a Sunday. Social status was not cut and dried, for there were no official barriers between the groups. The wealthier husbandmen were usually better-off than the poorest yeomen, and the proverb "It is better to be the head of the yeomanry than the tail of the gentry" may well have tripped off the yeoman's tongue (if not the gentleman's).

When Gough wrote, he had about 450 fellow-parishioners, sitting in their appropriate stations all around him. Gough's scheme is a graphic description of the social structure: we can easily imagine the serried ranks of the inhabitants on a Sunday, the stately pews with well-dressed occupants at the front, the seats made from planks nailed together crammed in at the back with their equally tatterdemalion inhabitants.

Richard Gough's parish was Myddle, in Shropshire, a few miles north of Shrewsbury. Apart from the tower, built around the time of Gough's birth in 1635, nothing of the church he knew survives. The old church was rebuilt in the late eighteenth and mid-nineteenth centuries, but the rather curious layout, shown in his plan of the interior, with a double nave, is preserved.

The organization which Gough described was by no means unique. It was an accepted feature of parish churches that people sat in accordance with their status and plans similar to those which Richard Gough drew exist for a number of churches. Even in a few instances something of the old system survives as in the Sussex church of West Grinstead, where the pews have the names of the farms to which they were allotted painted on the back. Within the general scheme local practice varied: in some parishes servants sat with the families they worked for, in others all servants sat together. Sometimes, too, paupers, children, and in a few instances men and women, were segregated. The church in the mid-Devon parish of Cruwys Morchard has box pews with place names, and separate seating, well in the public gaze, for "boys under 16" and for "girls under 14". And in the church at Staunton Harrold, Leicestershire, standing beside the great house there, men and women to this day sit separately, on either side of the centre aisle.

If what Gough was describing in 1701 was neither unique nor surprising, the considerable detail he included in his history makes his work unlike any other. His stated aim was to write "concerning the descent and pedigree of all, or most part of the families . . . of the parish". And his descriptions of those families was to be warts and all.

"If any man shall blame me for that I have declared the vicious lives or actions of their ancestors, let him take care to avoid such evil courses, that he leaves not a blemish on his name when he is dead, and let him know that I have written nothing out of malice."

Richard Gough was a great collector of facts, gossip and folk memories. That personal detail he provided about the parish's inhabitants is otherwise unrecapturable. As his mind's eye and memory moved down the rows of pews, so skeletons were taken out of their cupboards, the dissolute were shown in their true colours and the good were commended. Behind each generalization which we advance about pre-Victorian rural society lies the great variety which Gough is able to show us.

Take Sleap Hall for example. This was one of the largest farms of the parish: the family who lived there occupied one of the most prominent pews in the church. The property had long been owned by a Cheshire family called Maynwaring, and they let the farm to tenants. The first group to run the property that Gough writes about were the Groomes, who held the property for many generations. But John, the last Groome (and Gough's grandmother's half-brother) proved to be a poor farmer, and left the property for something smaller and more manageable. One of the Maynwarings took over; after a while he moved back to Cheshire and Rowland Plungin became the tenant. Who he was and where he came from we do not know. Of his two sons, Arthur proved himself unworthy by marrying the young widow of Thomas Tyler, who already had a number of small children. The Tylers were notorious: Thomas Tyler's grandfather had been a well-known thief and troublemaker, and Thomas "did imitate his grandfather's morals . . . but he lived not half his days, for about the 27th year of his age he was killed with a cart". For marrying into the Tylers, Arthur Plungin was cut off by his father, and Arthur and his instant family went to live in a tiny house, part of the Tyler property.

John, the second Plungin son, did rather better for himself: he married Margaret Jukes, a local farmer's daughter who brought with her what was then a considerable dowry of £50. All went well until John inherited the tenancy on his father's death. John, having to stand on his own feet, was revealed as a poor farmer: he made consistent losses, fell into considerable arrears with his rent – and eventually the Maynwarings turned him out of his tenancy. John Plungin took over Balderton Hall – itself a substantial property – but failed just as badly. "He now lives in a cottage in Myddle where he maintains himself by day labour."

When Plungin had gone from Sleap Hall, a new tenant came from Cheshire – possibly from another of the Maynwaring properties – and he prospered.

Stability, continuity, order: the story of the Plungins contains none of these. As John Plungin fell from grace, so his fellow-parishioners would have seen him move from the most prominent seat in the church, across to a lesser position, and finally down to a lowly place at the rear. In his description of the sequence of events, Richard Gough treated it all in a matter of fact way: it was a shame but no great surprise that a family fortune could be entirely dissipated from one generation to the next by pigheadness and bad management.

If some fell in the local social structure, others rose. Balderton Hall still stands, with a wide frontage of mixed sixteenth, seventeenth and nineteenth century date. When Gough was writing, the Hall, the staging post in John Plungin's descent, was owned by Robert Heyward. That much is straightforward: the rest is complicated. Robert Heyward came from a family long-established in Myddle – but not one exclusively locked into the parish with no wider horizons. Robert Heyward's uncle had been cook to the Archbishop of Canterbury, and Robert was his uncle's heir. Both Robert and his brother had been apprenticed into the silver trade in London. After the Restoration Robert had been involved in the insurrection against Charles II, and was imprisoned with his master. After their release, they went to Wales, to work in lead mining. On his frequent visits to Shropshire, Robert courted an older woman from Shrewsbury, who had two basic attractions, land and money. Gough describes her as "short-sighted and not at all beautiful". The couple married, and eventually – having inherited the property in Myddle from his uncle – Robert Heyward returned to his native parish. He continued to prosper, and bought out some of his neighbours, including Thomas Hall, the then owner of Balderton Hall. Revenge was sweet, for Hall had bought up property from the impoverished Thomas Heyward, Robert's father. All had come full circle: Balderton Hall, and much of the land around, was in Robert Heyward's possession. After living in the Hall for a while, Heyward leased that property to a number of tenants. Unsurprisingly, he had no children and named a nephew from Shrewsbury as his heir.

So Thomas Hall was ousted. When he had sold out to Heyward, he had retained a life interest in part of the property, but by the time Gough wrote had left to live with his eldest son, by then vicar of Abingdon in Oxfordshire. Hall had originally come from outside Myddle. He was the successful man amongst the many suitors for the hand of Jane Lath, the only daughter of Matthew Lath, who then owned Balderton Hall. As Gough tells us,

"Thomas Hall lived at Balderton with his father-in-law, and during his life was a reasonably good husbandman, but after his decease he let loose the reins to many disorderly courses, as cocking, racing, drinking and lewdness. He had one bastard born to him in his own house, by a daughter of William Bickley."

And Thomas Hall's eight children tended to follow in his footsteps: apart from the eldest, the one who became the vicar of Abingdon, drink would seem to have got the better of most of them. At least Matthew Lath had not lived to see the decay of his family: he was a self-made man, "born to no estate", who had been a farm servant and then married the daughter of a tenant farmer (perhaps a man he had worked for), at a place called Wall Farm near Adeney, in eastern Shropshire. Somehow Matthew Lath made enough money to buy Balderton Hall, vacating Wall Farm which he had taken over on his marriage.

Balderton Hall had been sold to Lath by Robert Zankey: Zankey was then a Colonel in the Parliamentary army in the Civil War (and died soon afterwards); he had inherited the property from his father who had been Rector of Hodnet (a parish some ten miles from Myddle). Previous to that, Balderton Hall had been owned by a Mr Webbe and by John

Balderton Hall, ABOVE LEFT, and the Oaks cottage, ABOVE RIGHT, stand as survivors from Gough's day, their pews respectively at the front and back of Myddle church. The cottage was once surrounded by woods; Fenemere, OPPOSITE, is the last of the post-glacial lakes to be left undrained.

Nocke, both wealthy Shrewsbury drapers who each in turn failed in business – largely as a result of the bankruptcy of men with whom they did business at the London end of the wool cloth trade.

And still Gough's history can take us farther back. John Nocke had bought the estate from the Chambre family: Michael Chambre had failed to pay legacies to his sisters, and the family's use of the law against him had forced the sale. The money had gone elsewhere:

"This Michael Chambre was wholly addicted to idleness, and therefore no marvel that he was lascivious. . . But the worst of this Michael was that his lewd consorts were such ugly bawds, that they might almost resemble ugliness itself. . ."

Michael's father had bought the Hall from William Nicholas, who had built the main part of the building which still stands. William Nicholas "was addicted to projects". To recoup the expense of building the house, he tried charcoal-burning and glass-making. All came to nothing, and he was forced to sell up and leave.

"But some say there came an old man in beggar's habit (some years after his departure) to Balderton, late in the evening, and sat under the barn wall and was found dead in the morning, and was thought to be this William Nicholas."

William had been born in 1550, and with the Nicholas family, Gough could go no further back. The rapid rise and fall of the property's owners is astonishing. Without Richard Gough's history we would have no idea that this still-solid building would have had so many owners through the seventeenth century; that in so many cases what had been painstakingly built up in one generation was to be smashed apart in the next.

Whereas much of the history of the Plungin family was bound up within Myddle, most of the Balderton Hall contacts were from outside the parish. Sleap and Balderton, with their pews at the front of the church, were amongst the more substantial properties: what of the places of less significance, of the families packed into the rear part of the church?

The eleventh pew back, against the church's south wall, was claimed for two cottages, William Candlin's in Myddle and Daniel Hanmer's in the woods. The description of the latter is precise enough – "at the south side of Myddle Wood, between the end of the lane that goes from Myddle Wood to Fenemere, and the end of the Lynch lane" – to identify it as a still-standing structure, a cottage now called "The Oaks".

The cottage dates from the 1580s or so, but the Hanmers are first found in it in the 1630s – Abraham Hanmer acquired it from his wife's family. Abraham was not a good neighbour, "much given to the law" in constant disputes. Abraham's father had come from Flintshire. Of Abraham's two brothers, one eventually left Myddle and ended his days as overseer of a forge in Sandbach, Cheshire; the other, Thomas, proved to be poor at farmwork and, being able to read and write, kept a small school and then became parish clerk in the nearby parish of Shawbury. Thomas had two sons, one legitimate, the other a bastard. The legitimate son was educated well – so much so that he was sent to Oxford, and married into a good Cheshire family, becoming vicar of Marchwiel, near Wrexham. Ever ready with personal gossip, Richard Gough remarked that he also had the family habit of quarrelling and dispute. The vicar's bastard half-brother Daniel was made their uncle Abraham's heir, and this Daniel Hanmer and his family were living in the cottage in Gough's day.

Thus the Hanmers who moved away tended to prosper, those who remained in Myddle were only labourers and smallholders. But they were not amongst the poorest families, as is evident from their cottage which, although small, is sturdily and carefully constructed. Some of the people who Gough describes were rather poorer than this: Thomas Chidlow lived in "a poor pitiful hut, built up to an old oak"; and Evan Jones, a Welshman who "could speak neither good Welsh nor good English" built himself a little hut, again in Myddle Wood. When the hut burned down, the parishioners had a collection for him, and he built himself a decent cottage with the money.

Some were so poor that circumstance forced them to live in caves. Early in the seventeenth century a member of the Fardo family converted a cave in the large sandstone outcrop of Harmer Hill into a dwelling, and was succeeded in it by William Preece and his wife. William Preece was the son of a reasonably well-off tenant farmer in the parish. He had been apprenticed in London but had run away to become a mercenary and fight overseas, eventually returning to Shropshire. Closer to Gough's day, one of the caves was being lived in by Richard Bickley *alias* Hall – the bastard son of Thomas Hall, the dissolute owner of Balderton Hall. Richard Bickley had had his leg amputated, at the parish's expense, when a young man; thereafter he went to London. "And from thence brought a wife, as he calls her."

These stories from Gough can be multiplied many times: there are few families about whom his book is silent, few without some telling anecdote or pithy phrase. In some ways, the detail he provides is almost overwhelming, as the vagaries of chance and human nature make generalization difficult. Nevertheless, certain features emerge very clearly. Myddle was remote – but it was by no means isolated. Many families seem to have had some link with London, and everybody would have had regular contact with Shrewsbury; the through-put of people was considerable, and the number of families which remained in the same place over the period through which Gough's memory and information ranged was tiny. Writing about the labouring Davies family, Gough clearly found their experience remarkable:

"Of these two persons Thomas Davies and his wife have proceeded such a numerous offspring in this parish, that I have heard some reckon up, taking in wives and husbands, no less than sixty of them and the greater part of them have been chargeable to the parish. Many great families in this parish have been extinct, but this has got so many branches that it is more likely to overspread it."

Most contacts were within northern Shropshire – marriage partners, trading, places for servants – but Myddle people had many links with Cheshire and across the border into Wales.

Is this one parish able to stand as typical, as representative of English villages of its day, in terms of the turnover of people, the range of its families' experience, the distance of its economic and personal contacts? In most regards, Myddle does not appear to be at all unusual. In almost any village of the seventeenth and eighteenth centuries, those who were born, lived and died in the same place were in a distinct, often tiny minority. Families died out, names disappeared with what seems to us astonishing rapidity. There is perhaps some evidence that those in the middle, the families of the husbandmen and poorer yeomen, were more likely to remain in the same place than were those above or below them in the social scale: they had more cause to try to hang on to what they had, relatively more to lose if they lost their grip.

However, Myddle does not fit the stereotype portrait of the 'classic' English village: houses and cottages nestling round spire and squire in the nucleated settlement characteristic of much of midland and eastern England. Myddle was a parish whose cultivable land had been won, often with considerable labour, from a landscape of wood and water. Almost nothing now remains of the woodland which had covered much of the parish, and only one of the lakes survives. The change had taken place in the 250 years before Gough wrote, and perhaps most of all in the later sixteenth century, when woods had been felled and lakes drained, adding many valuable acres to the cultivable area. Myddle village was only the central settlement in the parish; other hamlets had grown up, usually in clearings in the woods. Some of those places have already appeared in this chapter: Balderton, Myddlewood, Harmer Hill, Sleap, or Newton-on-the-Hill where Richard Gough himself farmed. When he described Myddle Wood, for example, Gough wrote:

"It was formerly a famous wood of timber; there is a great part of it enclosed, some into tenements, as Chaloner's, Cooper's, Watsons', Davies', Jones' and Parker's tenements. Several persons have cottages on this common, and one or two pieces [of land] enclosed to every cottage, as Endley, Jones, Higginson, Rogers the glover, Blanthorne, Rogers the tailor, Reeves, Hanmer and Groome."

So the extension of the available land meant that many more people could come into Myddle, especially poor labourers and squatters; many came from Wales.

The topography of Myddle parish presents some riddles which are only explicable when this history of drainage and clearance is known.

From the top of the main sandstone outcrop at Harmer Hill, where in the seventeenth century paupers lived in caves, ABOVE RIGHT, the view of the parish stretches out. The fields in front of the hill were once a great lake, drained in the late sixteenth century. On the far side of the parish lies the Hollins, ABOVE LEFT.

Take, for instance, The Hollins. This was another of the more important farms – its owners sat in the pew behind that of Sleap Hall. The property is much closer to other villages than it is to Myddle; access was always, and remains, difficult along water-logged lanes. Yet it was colonized from Myddle at an early date, and Myddle was the parish and church to which the farm's owners claimed allegiance.

The parishioners of Myddle were (and are) principally engaged in pastoral agriculture, raising cattle and sheep: although they grew crops, theirs was not the arable farming more characteristic of the south and east. Historians and contemporaries have often drawn attention to the differing nature of local societies between areas of "field" and "forest", "champion" and "woodland", "lowland" and "upland". Myddle is representative of the second of each of those pairs: but that is not to deny that it has very many representative qualities for the range of English villages of the seventeenth and eighteenth centuries.

High levels of movement characterized all villages. The villager who never moved was so rare as to be an oddity. Some places, like Myddle, experienced high rates of immigration, especially in periods of rapid population growth such as that which England experienced between

1560 and 1640. Rapid expansion of numbers meant that many had to leave villages unable to absorb a rising population, while hitherto underpopulated villages like Myddle could take in more people. Population growth meant an increase in poverty: Gough commented bitterly on the increased cost experienced in his lifetime of caring for the poor but, if anything, Myddle with its greater scope for housing people in the woods and elsewhere was less hard hit than many places.

Movement of people was an integral part of village life. Leases and tenancies of land and houses encouraged turnover of people. Marriage partners were commonly sought, and found, outside the confines of the parish. The towns attracted some of the village's inhabitants, especially those in their teens: Shrewsbury was the great local centre of attraction, London the national magnet. In early modern England, movement was the rule and long-term stability the exception.

If the church seating recaptured the local social structure, it could only do so imperfectly. In this mobile society, the most mobile were servants – teenagers and young adults who had left home, were as yet unmarried, and worked in a variety of places, in the household or on the farm, commonly on a series of annual contracts. Some of the pews in Myddle church were reserved for the servants of the larger farms, and those pews were quite prominently located. Service was not unusual: it was, if anything, the norm. And it was a stage in the life-cycle of people from most social groups: it was very rare to remain a servant for life. Richard Gough only tells us about farm or household servants when they come into the particular anecdote he recounts: they were too mobile to be able to be incorporated in his scheme and – not yet being settled and married – did not figure properly in his image of the local social structure.

Richard Gough's plan of the seating in Myddle church is titled "As the church is now 1701". The plan was different ten years before and ten years after that date: social and geographical mobility, marriage and demographic accident saw to that. So, rather than being a picture of a static social structure, the seating plan in Myddle church was the crystallization of a particular period. As the anomalies increased, so the time would come for a wholesale revision.

That had last happened in Myddle in 1655: claims had been staked to seats and, as the population of the parish increased, new seats were built in hitherto empty parts of the church. Matters eventually came to a head.

"There happened a difference between John Downton of Alderton and William Formeston, about the right of kneeling in the sixth pew on the south side of the north aisle, and John Downton put a lock on the pew door, but William Formeston, at Marton, who claimed a share in that seat, came on the Lord's Day following and giving the pew door a sudden pluck, broke off the lock."

A parish meeting decided on a new order of seating in the church and on a general tidying up.

"For it was held a thing unseemly and indecent that a company of young boys, and of persons that paid no parish rates, should sit above those of the best of the parish."

The loss of face involved in being prevented from sitting in the appropriate place in church could be considerable. This outburst of temper may have been an occasion still remembered in Myddle a generation later, but it was by no means unique in England. There are numerous other examples of disputes, and sometimes brawls, in church over seating and precedence. Large court cases could ensue. The social structure, as measured by seating arrangements, could be fluid. But if reality and plan came too far adrift, then angry measures were taken to redress the balance.

Myddle was – and still is – something of a backwater, but it was by no means stagnant. Movement characterized this place as it did every English village: there is no self-enclosed stability to be found here. Individuals and families came and went, some rapidly, some slowly:

"The family of the Downtons is so ancient in this town. . . there was three families of Downtons at one time. . . but now all these families are extinct, so that there is not one of that name now in this parish, except one widow. So that it appears that families have their fate and periods as well as particular persons – and no marvel, since families are made up of particulars."

BROUGHTON

The Dauntons were an "ancient" family of an insignificant Shropshire parish; what of the ancient families of England; the nobility? Did they have their "fate and periods" too?

The English nobility was peculiar, both in England and in comparison with the rest of Europe as well. To begin with, it was not a class: instead it was a tiny status group consisting of a handful of individuals and their families. There were between forty and sixty nobles in the sixteenth century; 120 in the early seventeenth, and 160 in the later. But since population had also increased from 2.5 million in 1500 to 5 million in 1700 the expansion of the nobility had little more than kept pace. And in any case as a proportion of the population the nobility remained minute. The head of each house sat in the House of Lords and had a title, ranging from Baron at the bottom, through Viscount, Earl and Marquess to Duke at the top. Barons were comparatively numerous; while the Earls and above, who made up the "magnates", were rather thin on the ground. Indeed between 1572 and the reign of James I there were no Dukes at all.

The different grades of the peerage represented a hierarchy of honour and status, which was marked by visible signs, not by access to pews but by different coronets and different robes: a baron's were trimmed with two bands of plain white fur, a duke's with four bands of ermine, with all other ranks arranged accordingly in between. The peerage was also a hierarchy of wealth as well. In the early sixteenth century a Baron might have £500 a year; while the Duke of Norfolk had over £3000 and Edward, Duke of Buckingham, a gigantic £6000. The income was derived largely from land and Buckingham's vast estates, for example, stretched through eighteen English counties and the Welsh Marches. He had two great houses in the south: Bletchingley in Surrey and Penshurst in Kent; at the same time he was rebuilding Thornbury Castle in Gloucestershire. The scale of rebuilding was gigantic; the style a characteristic mixture of late-medieval castle and renaissance palace and the whole designed to express his status as the King's first subject. Others lived less grandiosely, though even an up-and-coming (and upstart) baron like William, Lord Sandys (1470–1540) had a couple of substantial houses: The Vyne, Hampshire, an aggressively "modern" building with an unusually handsome gallery; Mottisfont Abbey, also in Hampshire, a straightforward monastic conversion.

The gradations of rank within the peerage were important: requests for promotion formed a staple of the post bag of any Prime Minister to the end of Victoria's reign and some families, in particular the Grosvenors, devoted their whole energies and vast wealth to a laborious climb from Baron Grosvenor of Eaton in 1761 to Duke of Westminster just over 100 years later in 1874. But more visible of course is the gap between the peerage and the rest. A baron was addressed as "My Lord"; the King himself called an earl "cousin"; while a Duke had an almost royal dignity: he was a "Right High and Mighty Prince", and his style was "Your Grace". This form of address he shared only with the Archbishops of Canterbury and York; indeed, it had been the King's own until the Tudors had inflated themselves first to "Highness" and finally to "Majesty".

Status, however, was not the same as stability. The most unusual thing about the English peerage was its smallness. This was ensured by the peculiar rule of succession. Whereas in Continental nobilities all the offspring of a noble were noble, in England only the eldest son was. In default of a son, the title (and usually the estates as well) would pass to the nearest male heir, and in default of such an heir the title would become extinct. This happened frequently, for straightforwardly demographic reasons: infant mortality was appallingly high and fertility, when rich widows were desirable as brides, often low. The result was that in the fifteenth century, for example, one-third of noble families died out in the male line each generation.

Nor was the failure of heirs the only problem that broke the continuity of noble families. The nobility were expected to be politically active: certainly in their localities, and usually in central politics too. They were the King's "born counsellors" and, as the "great estates of the realm", thought of themselves as collectively empowered to take charge of the kingdom if the King were incapable or incompetent. Nowadays political participation has only rewards: even the failures can look forward to the benches of the House of Lords or the even thicker upholstery of an EEC Commissioner's chair. Until the seventeenth century at least the rules were stricter: the rewards of success were almost infinite; the penalties of failure terrible. Being on the wrong side in a civil war or a Court faction struggle was construed as treason. And that involved death by hanging, drawing and quartering as well as the forfeiture of all property. Peers were spared the full grisliness of execution, and were only beheaded; but their titles were not exempt. They might be restored to a subsequent heir, but there was no guarantee of that. The Howards, for example, survived three forfeitures for treason in 1485, 1546–7 and 1572 (though after the last one it took nearly a century to recover the Dukedom of Norfolk); but the Staffords, Dukes of Buckingham, were destroyed utterly by Duke Edward's execution in 1521.

Political participation was one risky obligation of nobility: another was magnificence or ostentation. A noble was expected to have fine houses and large numbers of servants, to dress splendidly, and in later

THE NORTH-EAST VIEW OF BROUGHTON-CASTLE, IN THE COUNTY OF OXFORD.

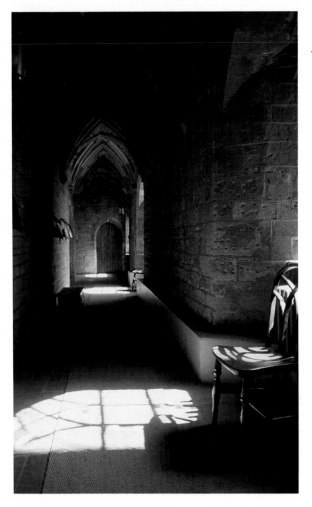

The engraving by Nathaniel and Samuel Buck, ABOVE, shows Broughton Castle in its eighteenth century decay, the fourteenth century corridor, LEFT, preserved and restored, the house's lucky survival.

centuries to be a discerning and lavish patron of the arts. The nobility had of course vast resources as well. But keeping income and expenditure in balance involved treading a fine line. Even a Buckingham found himself stretched at times and others could go right under. If they did they would certainly lose status; they might even lose their peerage title as well. We think of nobility as ancient blood; they thought of it equally as "ancient riches" and a poor peer was more-or-less a contradiction in terms. Sir Thomas Smith in the late sixteenth century laid down the rule that if a noble's wealth was diminished "by excess. . .so sometimes they are not admitted to the Upper House in the Parliament, though they keep the name of Lord still". Even that could go, however, and in 1493 Henry VII demoted Edmund de la Pole from Duke to Earl of Suffolk because his fortune was insufficient to maintain higher honour.

The English nobility, Henry James considered, appeared "to have everything. . . [and] to *be* everything". He was almost right. But to keep what they had – and to keep it from generation to generation – took both good luck and good management. How one family steered its course we shall find out through the castle whose history reflects its own.

Just a few years before Richard Gough wrote his history, the seemingly indefatigable late seventeenth century gentlewoman traveller Celia Fiennes passed by Myddle on her way to Shrewsbury:

". . .it's 14 mile to Shrewsbury and pretty level way, the miles were long and the wind blew very cold"

she wrote. The record of Celia Fiennes' journeys shows her to have travelled far and wide, seeing the country and visiting friends and relations. Her home was in Wiltshire, and later near London, but on a number of occasions she visited Broughton Castle in Oxfordshire, the home of her half-brother William, 3rd Viscount Saye and Sele. On her first recorded visit there she noted:

"Broughton is an ancient seat of the Lord Saye and Sele; it's an old house moated round, and a park and gardens, but are much left to decay and ruin when my brother came to it. . ."

Almost exactly a century later, another tireless traveller, the Hon. John Byng (later Viscount Torrington) wrote of his visit to the same house:

"Being fond of seeing old houses, I fancied that Broughton Castle might be worth viewing; and accordingly I prevailed upon the phaeton to go that way round. . .
"Broughton Castle, two miles from Banbury, is a noble old place, with a bridge and gateway of approach, and a moat around it, clean and transparent; the two distant gateways with the old wall are gone, but much of the turreted wall remains. The bed rooms are clean and convenient, with good old chimney pieces, and nice oaken floors: the chimney piece in the king's bedchamber, where King Charles lay, in several of his marches, is of the superb style. But the ornament of the house are the dining and

drawing rooms, which are noble apartments of complete proportion with lofty
chimney pieces. The entrance into the dining room I much admired, and the ceiling of
the drawing room is one of the most beautiful I ever saw; a model for such work.
"The whole house is well fire-grated, and looks comfortable; in short, it is a place
worthy of inspection; and we congratulated each other in having come to view it."

By then, Broughton was owned by Thomas, 13th Baron Saye and Sele.
Today, the description would be just as applicable, and the house is
owned by Nathaniel, the 21st Baron – a striking instance of family
continuity.

But Viscounts are higher in the league of peers than are Barons – what
had happened between the 1680s and 1780s? The answer is just one of
the many instances in which the seemingly effortless continuity of family
and place disguises the full range of fame and obscurity, wealth and
penury, luck and planning, success and failure.

"Old Subtlety" was the apt nickname given to William Fiennes, the 1st
Viscount Saye and Sele. He died in 1662, an old man who had helped
lead the opposition to the policies of Charles I in the build-up to the
English Civil War. In religion he was something of a radical, in his deep
attachment to the notion of peerage a conservative. He was the last
Fiennes to walk boldly on the national political stage.

William's existing barony was raised to a viscountcy by James I in
1624, through his temporary attachment at court to George Villiers,
Duke of Buckingham. The royal hand fed – and in return was bitten.
The Viscount held deeply puritan religious sympathies. In itself there
was little unusual in that: the Church of England in the early
seventeenth century was very much of that tendency. But that was
important because, under Charles I and William Laud, Archbishop of
Canterbury, considerable efforts were made to arrest those trends, to
reintroduce liturgy and full reverence and to eliminate Calvinist
tendencies.

Banbury itself was renowned for deeply-held puritan views – and was
satirized for it, so much so that 'Banbury-man' came to be a synonym for
Puritan. The odious character Zeal-of-the-Land Busy in Ben Jonson's
"Bartholomew Fair" came from Banbury, whilst in 1638 Richard
Brathwaite published the rhyme:

> *"To Banbury came I, O profane one!*
> *Where I saw a Puritane-one*
> *Hanging of his cat on Monday*
> *For killing a mouse on Sunday."*

The familiar "cockhorse" nursery rhyme immortalizes Banbury Cross –
and the lady may have been Fiennes rather than fine – but the original
cross was destroyed in a great iconoclastic outburst amongst the
townspeople. The political and religious influence of the Lord Saye and
Sele there was great, fostering and ripening deep religious sympathies.

The vicar of Banbury in the 1630s, for instance, was William Whateley, who was there under the Viscount's patronage, and who wrote a celebrated Puritan advice book on marriage and deference, *A Bride-Bush*.

Saye and Sele was part of a much wider like-minded group of gentlemen and nobles, their combined names cropping up time and again in the 1620s, '30s and '40s – the Earls of Warwick, Lincoln, Pembroke and Bedford, Lord Brooke, John Pym, John Hampden, Sir Richard Knightly.

Some amongst them were part of the set who followed the radical preaching of John Preston at Lincoln's Inn, and boys including sons of Lord Saye and Sele went to the Puritan stronghold of Emmanuel College, Cambridge after Preston's election there as Master. Most of this group were involved in overseas ventures, as projectors in the Providence Company. Providence, a small Caribbean island off Jamaica, had been discovered by one of the Earl of Warwick's ships in 1629. A company was formed for its colonization and exploitation and colonists were found – with a significant contingent from Banbury. Eventually this seemingly fool-hardy venture came to an end with the island's capture by Spain in 1641, in spite of the island's fourteen forts (including Fort Saye, Fort Sele, Fort Warwick and Fort Brooke). This was not the only colonial venture: in Connecticut, Saybrook is named after Lords Saye and Sele and Brooke. In the 1630s, Viscount Saye and Sele toyed with the idea of emigrating to New England, but he was deterred by colonial refusal to maintain an hereditary peerage.

The colonizers figured largely amongst those in growing opposition to the Crown during the "Personal Rule" of Charles I, when the King attempted through the 1630s to rule without Parliament. Meetings of the Providence Company often took place in isolated rooms at Broughton Castle, and it is assumed that much more was discussed besides. Antony Wood later wrote:

"For so it was, that several years before the Civil War began, he [Saye and Sele] being looked upon at that time as the godfather of that party, had meetings of them in his house at Broughton, where was a room and passage thereunto, which his servants were prohibited to come near. . ."

Certainly, Warwick and Saye and Sele attempted to have test cases brought against them for non-payment of the controversial Ship Money. Their attempts were successfully resisted, and John Hampden was prosecuted instead. The verdict went against "Stout Hampden", but his was the moral victory.

Viscount Saye and Sele was in the thick of the agitation which eventually led to Civil War. Even as Broughton Castle was being attacked in the aftermath of the Battle of Edgehill he rallied the city of London:

"Let every man therefore shut up his shop, let him take his musket, let him offer himself readily and willingly, let him not think with himself who shall pay me, but

rather think this, I'll come forth to save the kingdom, to serve my God, to maintain his true religion, to save the Parliament, to save this noble city."

Saye and Sele remained true to his principles, that King, Lords and Commons ruled together. Thus at the end of the war he attempted to secure a treaty with the King, by then on the Isle of Wight; he refused to sit "alongside brewers and draymen" when the House of Lords was abolished, and a new Upper House instituted; and he was disgusted by the King's execution. He exiled himself to his private island of Lundy in the Bristol Channel for the remainder of the Commonwealth period, coming back at the Restoration. Although he would not attend Charles II's coronation, he is supposed to have accepted the office of Lord Privy Seal. (Was the pun intended?)

Posterity has not been kind to the 1st Viscount. Clarendon, in his *History of the Great Rebellion*, described him with great malice:

"He was of a proud, morose, and sullen nature. . . and he had with his milk sucked in an implacable malice against the government of the Church. . . When he thought there was mischief enough done, he would have stopped the current – but he then found he had only authority and credit to do hurt, none to heal the wounds he had given."

Many alleged that he was an impoverished peer, and acted in order to improve his position, and hence his fortune. In fact his income was fair – the result above all of careful estate-management and reorganization – and was enough to make provision for all his many children (whose marriages provided alliances with other leading Puritan families) and to cover his overseas ventures. His house was badly damaged, and his reputation was to suffer posthumously, but he left an elevated title and many sons to carry his name.

'Godfather' is a term equally appropriate for William's great-great-great-great-great grandfather James, 1st Baron Saye and Sele. James had no Oxfordshire connection: instead, he was a Mafia-type boss in Kent during the second quarter of the fifteenth century. James had fought at Agincourt and was rewarded with positions; in 1430 he acquired Hever and its castle, the beginnings of his Kentish empire – which was to include the subsequently great house at Knole, the mansions of Seal (from which his unique title was partly to come) and Kemsing. Extortion, appropriation and election-rigging were to be his hallmark: for James was the protégé of the equally disreputable Duke of Suffolk, and supporter of his peaceable policies towards France. Together they secured ascendancy over Humphrey Duke of Gloucester and the young Henry VI. Recognition of Fiennes' position came with his creation as Baron Saye and Sele, at the 1447 Parliament held in Bury St Edmunds, and his appointment as Lord High Treasurer.

But the truce with France could not hold, and most of the French territory the English had conquered was to be regained by a revitalized France: disaster came in 1449 with the recapture of Rouen. Suffolk's political support disappeared and moves were made for his impeachment. Banished by Henry VI, Suffolk's ship was ambushed and the royal favourite was murdered. As defeated Englishmen returned from France, so men of Kent rose in rebellion under the leadership of 'Jack Cade'. They marched on London, with Lord Saye and Sele as one of their main objectives. The King deserted London; Fiennes was surrendered to the rebels and suffered summary justice at their hands.

"The Kentishmen would not suffer for him to abide the law, but led him into the Standard in Cheap[side], and there his head was smit off, and his body was drawn naked at a horse's tail upon the pavement so that the flesh cleaved to the stone. . ."

At Southwark he was drawn and quartered: the political ascendancy of the evil Baron was over.

1st Baron, 1st Viscount: after each of these powerful and manipulative men, who reached prominence in periods of increasing and bloody political division, came much gentler and less effectual men.

With William, 2nd Baron, came the move to Broughton Castle. The property had been inherited by his wife Margaret Wykeham: she was great-great-niece of William of Wykeham, the ecclesiastical grandee (and founder of Winchester School and New College, Oxford) who had acquired Broughton by 1392, and had engaged on substantial building operations. And Baron William also built on a grand scale, turning a substantial manor house into a semi-fortified tower house, building upwards for strength. William repudiated his father: the offices of Warden of the Cinque Ports and Constable of Dover Castle were surrendered; Hever was sold to Geoffrey Boleyn, and Knole to Thomas Bouchier, Archbishop of Canterbury. His father had supported the House of Lancaster; William transferred allegiance to Edward IV and the House of York. And he died fighting for his king at the Battle of Barnet in 1471.

His tomb effigy now lies in Broughton parish church, his face carved with haughty aristocratic features. Around his neck is a Yorkist collar of suns and roses; next to him lies the effigy of his wife's grandmother – they were placed side by side by bemused Victorian restorers – and around her neck is the Lancastrian collar, linked Ss. Here the two warring dynasties are united.

And with William's death the barony was allowed to lapse: for whatever reason, William's heir was never summoned to Parliament. Of the next three Fiennes, Henry, Richard, and Edward, each died before his thirtieth birthday. So when Edward's son Richard Fiennes inherited in 1528 he was only nine years old. He remained a ward until his majority, but when he could run his own affairs, he revived the family's local position – he became a JP, was knighted and was sheriff of Oxfordshire – and by the mid-1550s had transformed Broughton into a great and stylistically avant-garde house.

The pictures tell their own story: of a house ornamented with grandiose fireplaces of a self-consciously Renaissance classical style, of great rooms with elaborate ceilings in plaster, of vast new windows and, upon the jumbled north entrance front, a new symmetrical façade. To the medieval house was added a sequence of state rooms – great reception rooms, staircases, long gallery and state bedchamber – fit for the reception of a monarch.

Of the many surprises in the Fiennes' family history, perhaps this is the greatest: how was it that a relatively obscure Oxfordshire gentleman came to build in a style decades ahead of its time, rivalling the best of its kind elsewhere in England? The reign of Edward VI saw a remarkable flowering of Renaissance-influenced building in England, based in the circle around the Dukes of Somerset and Northumberland, political guardians of the young King, and including Sir William Sharington and Sir John Thynne, who built on a grand scale in Wiltshire at Lacock and Longleat respectively. There are only family connections and circumstantial links to place Richard Fiennes within this circle, but the physical evidence could place him nowhere else.

Richard Fiennes' work was largely completed by 1554, but there is no evidence of a great visit to warrant the construction of these great (and unusable) state rooms. After his death, his heir Richard continued a redecoration programme. The mid-sixteenth century work was financed out of income; although the second Richard Fiennes sold lands in Hampshire and Somerset this was part of a vigorous and hard-headed programme of rationalization of his landed revenue as much as it was to pay for the work on the house. His aim was to achieve a more compact, manageable and efficient estate, in Oxfordshire and in Gloucestershire. He petitioned Queen Elizabeth, in vain, to have the barony revived; in 1603, under the newly-arrived James I, he succeeded, and became the 7th Baron Saye and Sele, ennobling in arrears his forefathers. In the next generation, of course, William Fiennes was raised to a viscountcy.

In between the two great political (and aristocratic) operators in the family there was this curious period of seeming hibernation, a concentration upon the Broughton property and an astounding re-edification of that house. After an unsettled sixteenth century, of young deaths and lengthy periods of wardship, "Old Subtlety", the 1st Viscount, left a large and extensive dynasty. He had five sons, and in the next generation fifteen grandsons in the direct male line, to carry the family and its honour on.

But all those lines were to fail in little more than a century: William's great-grandson Richard died in 1781, the 6th and last Viscount Saye and Sele. His cousin once removed, Lawrence, 5th Viscount, and second cousin Nathaniel, 4th Viscount, had both died unmarried, and all were childless.

That would seem to be wilfully going against the grain. Why should these men seem to have chosen not to perpetuate their family line, to preserve their title and fortune? First, the Fiennes were no longer wealthy: inventories of the contents of Broughton Castle up to 1731 show the valuations to have fallen sharply from the first half of the seventeenth

Behind the new façade of the 1550s, NEAR RIGHT, Richard Fiennes built a sequence of state rooms, gallery, bedchambers and parlours, their decoration and fireplaces, OPPOSITE, making grandiloquent and avant garde gestures.

century. After the house's siege and capture by the Royalists there was, as Celia Fiennes noted, much repair work to be done. The 5th and 6th Viscounts (who no longer owned Broughton anyway) were poor backwoods peers receiving government doles or inducements. The 6th Viscount explained to the Duke of Newcastle that he would wish to attend the House of Lords but could not afford to do so. Newcastle took the hint and a pension of £600 a year guaranteed his attendance and his acquiescence.

But the Fiennes were not alone in their inability to renew their line: in England as a whole in the later seventeenth and early eighteenth centuries fertility was low and the proportion of the population which remained unmarried was comparatively high – and the aristocracy do not seem to have been excepted from those trends. In the eighteenth century about one-sixth of all peers did not marry at all. There was always a high rate of extinction amongst peerage lines: in 1700 there were 163 male peers, of whom sixty-three held peerages created since 1680, and 130 since 1600. By 1800 there were 267 peers, of whom four-fifths held peerages less than a century old. Extinction and new creation were the rule rather than the exception.

The Viscountcy had gone, but the house and the barony remained. The 1603 recreation had provided for inheritance through the female as well as the male line – with genealogically chaotic results. Old Subtlety's granddaughter Cecil Twistleton eloped with her cousin George Twistleton in 1668. Disinherited by her father, Cecil's son was to be reinstated in the order of inheritance by his second cousin, the next heir. Seven lines of descent had to fail before Cecil's line would succeed – and seven male lines failed. Through the workings of the 1st Viscount's will Cecil's son had inherited Broughton in 1710, and in 1757 her grandson inherited all the Twistleton estates. And Cecil's great-grandson Thomas Twistleton successfully claimed the lapsed barony in 1781, taking the title 13th Baron Saye and Sele a few months before the death of his distant cousin the 6th Viscount.

It was the 13th Baron who again took Broughton in hand, engaging his relation Sanderson Miller to repair and refurbish parts of the house in the fashionable Gothick. But the 14th Baron was to abandon Broughton: he married Maria Gideon, the wealthy heiress of the 1st Lord Eardley, and they lived in great style in Kent at Belvedere, near Erith. His son William was as raffish and rakish as only the Regency period could produce – a womanizer, a man "who could drink absinthe and curaçao in quantities perfectly awful to behold" and a spendthrift. To pay his son's debts the 14th Baron auctioned the contents of Broughton Castle in a great three-day sale in 1837. First to go were the Titians and Rembrandts, last were the swans from the moat. William was to hold the title for just three years, dying in 1847 unmarried (but with an illegitimate daughter).

A similar financial disaster was to occur later in the nineteenth century. William's clergyman cousin Frederick inherited: Frederick was

to become Archdeacon of Hereford, but Broughton Castle was his great love. He it was who took the mammoth surname Twistleton-Wykeham-Fiennes, he who undertook major restoration work at Broughton. His inherited share of the Eardley fortune meant that he was far from poor: he owned nearly 7000 acres of land in Oxfordshire, Lincolnshire and Huntingdonshire, upon which he took out mortgages to pay for the restoration work at Broughton. The disaster came because of the agricultural depression, which halved the value of his lands in the 1870s and 1880s, and the vast expenditure by his son and heir, John, on horses, women and drink. Whereas the "Regency rake" had been an engaging character, John was not. John had borrowed heavily on the expectation of his inheritance – an expectation which failed miserably. Frederick, 16th Baron, died in 1887 shortly after he had been forced to let the Castle, and the impecunious 17th Baron lived inexpensively near Reading. In 1912 the Twistleton-Wykeham-Fiennes returned to Broughton, fighting to retain and repair the house, with considerable restoration work in the present and previous generations, financed by land sales and government grants. House and family have survived – just.

The history of Broughton and its owners suggested at the outset an unruffled passage through time, with a few political high-fliers dominating the movement through many generations, for very few peerage titles now have their twenty-first holder. And yet the family fortune, title and name have swung back and forth wildly in 500 years. Political manoeuvring and the provision for inheritance of the title through the female line has kept that alive. Almost as soon as a fortune or political position was made it was dissipated. As often as the house

A house as metaphor for a family. ABOVE, the near-symmetrical, ordered façade; OVERLEAF, the more realistically disordered view of hindsight.

A scene, ABOVE RIGHT, which would have been familiar to the young Wordsworth, and symptomatic of the "discovery" of the Lake District: a view of Hawkshead and the hills and lakes around c.1809.

has been rebuilt or repaired it has been neglected or abandoned. The ravages of Capital Transfer Tax are just the latest among the many threats to the continued survival and family ownership of the house.

Compare the front and rear elevations of Broughton Castle. Driving through the park, crossing the drawbridge and emerging in front of the house, the visitor is faced with a great near-symmetrical Tudor building. This is the front which proclaims twenty-one generations of a peerage title. But at the back nearly every architectural style of the fourteenth, fifteenth, sixteenth and eighteenth centuries is there, happily jumbled together – the reality of genealogical fortune and the financial switchback.

HAWKSHEAD

It is with William Wordsworth above all others that we identify the Lake District. Daffodils conjure up the vision of the poet wandering "lonely as a cloud"; Dove Cottage can only vie with Anne Hathaway's for the crush of visitors in high summer; the mountains he taught the world to revere tower over the "primeval" farms inhabited by the sturdy, upright "statesmen", the independent freeholding yeomen he eulogized in poems such as *Michael*. Late in his life he was hostile to mass tourism – he fought long and hard against the coming of the railways – but his hostility was directed against those whom his *Guide to the Lakes* had helped to encourage.

In his *Guide*, as in the childhood sections of his great autobiographical poem *The Prelude*, he described a society close to the soil, hitherto unpolluted by outside influences. In one of the *Guide's* most celebrated passages he wrote of

"a perfect Republic of Shepherds and Agriculturists, among whom the plough of each man was confined to the maintenance of his own family. . . Neither high-born nobleman, knight, nor esquire was here; but many of these humble sons of the hills had a consciousness that the land which they walked over and tilled had for more than five hundred years been possessed by men of their name and blood."

Wordsworth's descriptions were by no means unique. In 1800 John Housman wrote in his *Topographical Description* of the cottager and statesman:

"Humble and unaspiring, they afford few instances of a rapid increase of fortune; and losses and disappointments are equally rare. Whatever patrimonial estates they inherit, they are generally transmitted to the eldest son without much in addition, or any considerable diminution."

These, and other informed observers at the time the Lake District was being opened up more to the outside world, describe just the stable, ordered society we have failed to uncover amongst the families in Myddle or even at Broughton Castle.

For these observers, the way in which land was held in what we now call the Lake District was the great distinguishing feature. Before the 1530s, and the Dissolution of the Monasteries under Henry VIII, a large part of the Lake District was owned by and controlled from Furness Abbey, the great Cistercian monastery just outside modern Barrow. The

Furness Fells were for centuries the main food and wool producing area for the monks and their lay workers.

By the early sixteenth century, the small farmers who provided for the abbey were sufficiently independent to be able to gain recognition of the tenure of their lands. At the Dissolution families like the Sandys – who had been Receivers-General of the abbey revenues – claimed considerable territory for themselves; the many smaller farmers acquired the land they had long held. Their names are often enshrined in existing farm names. The parish of Hawkshead, lying between Windemere and Coniston Water, for example, contains Atkinson Ground, Holme Ground, Borwick Ground, Sand Ground, Sawrey Ground.

These were the peasant proprietors eulogized by the commentators. On a pattern more reminiscent of Scotland than most of England, there were few surnames, suggestive of a 'clan' system with a high degree of inter-relationship. The landscape of the Lake District contains very many traditional farm houses and buildings – rough and plastered stone walls, slate roofs, all as much *part* of the landscape as imposed upon it.

That so much survives today is largely the result of strenuous efforts at preservation. The Lake District is a National Park, and much of it is owned by the National Trust, in part through the determined efforts of Mrs Heelis, better known to us as Beatrix Potter. She tried to conserve the way of life, the properties, the local Herdwick sheep.

Two of the properties she bequeathed to the Trust were Yew Tree and High Yewdale Farms, lying up the valley from the head of Coniston Water. Between the two properties runs the boundary of the parishes of Hawkshead and Coniston. The farms' present tenants are brothers; their properties proclaim the glories of the Lake District. Yew Tree Farm, with the fells behind and complete with its half-timbered 'spinning gallery', as seen from above at Tarn Hows (in itself one of Britain's most visited beauty spots), is for many *the* expression of Lakeland farming.

These farms – which we know from documentary evidence to be much the same size as they had been 300 years ago – and the wider parish of Hawkshead will be our means of testing the apparent stability of the Lakeland 'statesman'.

Or rather, yeoman and husbandman. The term 'statesman' which is commonly used to describe the farmers, to imbue them with sturdy and honest qualities, is but an early nineteenth century importation, part of the rustic romance of Wordsworth and his contemporaries. (If it originated anywhere, the term came from East Anglia and Lincolnshire.) Once established, the word took vigorous hold – the combination of simple uncomplicated virtue, rustic characters and the ownership of property was irresistible – and still survives in the guidebooks and textbooks. So are modern myths made.

First, the idea of family succession. By piecing together various types of information we can arrive at a sequence of ownership for the properties we are looking at. Entries of baptism, marriages and burials in the parish registers, information given on wills (and the

accompanying inventories of the goods and chattels of the deceased), lists of taxpayers and ratepayers often gave an individual's residence. All the information put together adds up to a very different picture of Lakeland life from that of received wisdom.

Take Yew Tree Farm. Nicholas Penny lived there in the 1680s, Richard Penny, a yeoman, died there in 1708, George Penny was living there in 1716. George Walker had died at Yew Tree in 1695, John Walker in 1703. William Walker was living there in 1709, George Walker in 1728, another George Walker in 1758, John Walker in 1768, William Walker in 1798. Members of the Walker family had lived at High Yewdale before that – Richard Walker, who died in 1640, and William Walker, died 1672. Apart from the Pennys, Walkers would seem to have followed one from another. But Robert Jackson was living at Yew Tree in 1712, Arthur Dixon in 1716, John Ashburner in 1737, and James Ashburner in 1768.

Some of the intrusive names in the Walker sequence come from the likelihood that there were *two* houses sharing the property – behind the present farmhouse at Yew Tree is the ruin of a second dwelling, labelled still as 'Penny House' on early Ordnance Survey maps. But the sequence of succession was – just as with the Fiennes at Broughton – not as smooth as it looks at first sight.

Yew Tree Farm and, OVERLEAF, High Yewdale – classic Lakeland farms, whitewashed and slate-roofed, as solid as the "statesmen" of the poets' imaginings.

39

When Richard Penny made his will in 1708, he described himself as a slater, although he clearly had reasonable farming interests. His estate, "All my customary messuage and tenement with the appurtenances and all the houses, closes, parcels of ground, wood, moss and turbary thereto belonging", he placed in trust for his son, George. If his son did not reach the age of twenty-one, then the estate was to pass to Richard's wife Deborah, while she remained a widow, and was then to pass to his friend Arthur Dixon. At the time Arthur Dixon, a waller, was living at Dixon Ground; when Dixon himself died, in 1716, he was a bachelor lodging with the widow Penny.

In his will, dated 1695, George Walker bequeathed his land and farm to his "dear and loving brother" John. Eight years later John made his will, leaving the bulk of his estate to George his son. He insisted that the sheep be kept with the farm, George having to pay five shillings for each to his widowed mother. The first George Walker described himself as a husbandman, whilst his brother John had the socially more elevated status of yeoman.

Over at High Yewdale, Richard Walker divided his land between his two sons: High Yewdale to Roger, the Craghouse and the woodlands to Robert. When William Walker, husbandman, died in 1672, he gave High Yewdale, which he had purchased from Michael Holme, who then went to live up at Tarn Hows, plus the meadows he had bought from his neighbour, William Penny over at Yew Tree, to his widow.

These complications can be replicated for other farms in the parish, and for other parishes. Farmland was bought and sold, united and split, and inheritance patterns were hardly straightforward. Probably only in half the transfers of land did property descend in the simple way from father to son. And the long continuation of the Walkers at Yew Tree turns out to be quite *un*usual in the area.

Filed away in the archives with the wills of these men are often the inventories of their possessions, lists made by their neighbours in the days after their death. John Walker's inventory of Yew Tree in 1703 valued his worth at £40.15s.3d, a fairly average sum for the area. More than half of the value of his estate was in his animals. The sheep up on the fells were worth £10.7s.6d – but of greater value, at £13.14s.6d, were his cattle. In comparison, the crops were worth only £6. We associate the Lake District with sheep, the hardy Herdwicks on the fellsides: but this marked emphasis on cattle, "black cattle", is a common feature of the inventories of the later seventeenth and eighteenth centuries. The sheep were for meat and especially for wool: Yew Tree Farm retains its spinning gallery fronting the barn, and woollen cloths were produced throughout the region. The industry was centred upon Kendal, the nearest town of any size, and families throughout the region supplemented their meagre incomes with clothmaking and, later, stocking making. But cattle represented a wider and more lucrative market. The cattle were usually imported from Scotland, raised and fattened on these farms, and then driven down to the great markets of the south and east, especially the London market.

By the middle of the eighteenth century these farmers' incomes had increased by a considerable margin – the result of access to wider and more lucrative markets both agricultural and industrial. For wool was by no means the sole industrial commodity; metal, principally iron and copper, was an important part of the local economy. The parishes of Hawkshead and Coniston are littered with the remains of the metal industries: 'bloomeries' and furnaces for smelting marked by piles of slag, forges by place names – Force Forge, Cunsey Forge, Stony Hazel. Charcoal was the fuel used in smelting and so charcoal-burning was a further source of employment and income. The burners in Arthur Ransome's *Swallows and Amazons* novels were amongst the last of that tradition.

These then were not just self-absorbed peasant farmers in an enclosed world. Their wealth was being increased by involvement in the marketing of their agricultural and industrial production. The crops that John Walker grew in his small fields were of much less value: harsh conditions and a short growing season made grain production difficult, and oats long remained the basic food crop, when they had become fodder for animals in other parts of England.

So things were hard for the Lakeland farmers: their conditions may have been improving, but in comparison with other English regions they had puny incomes. But they were riches in comparison with prevailing conditions before the mid-seventeenth century. With less industrial involvement and no cattle trade, farmers then lived on an even finer edge, many in considerable poverty. When adverse weather conditions caused the failure of the grain crops – and especially when a series of harvests failed – people could starve. The appalling conditions of 1588, 1597 and 1623 resulted in greatly increased numbers of deaths: the result of eating contaminated food, of diseases accompanying the famine, and of outright starvation. Areas such as Cumbria, with no political strength, relatively isolated and unknown, suffered badly in those years.

"One year there hath been hunger; the second year there was a dearth, and a third which is this year [1596], there is great cleanness of teeth. . . We may say that the course of nature is very much inverted; our years are turned upside down; our summers are no summers, our harvests are no harvests, our feed-times are no feed-times, and the nights are like the days: we know not which are better."

Conditions of that severity were never to return. The north west would never be so isolated again, attached as it now was to a wider market through trade and industry, and possessed of greater wherewithal to import grain should shortages occur.

And that greater wealth and security was translated into the physical environment. We should re-examine our two farms, Yew Tree and High Yewdale. Rather than being built in ancient traditional materials with centuries-old techniques and designs, both date from the late seventeenth and eighteenth centuries. They almost certainly replaced flimsier and considerably more primitive structures, of draughty stone, or wood and plaster, with thatched roofs. Those earlier buildings have failed to survive (although some have been encased in the newer buildings). However ancient and unchanging the houses may appear, they represent the increase in personal wealth and changing styles evident throughout England from the 1660s.

At High Yewdale the earlier house, built towards the end of the seventeenth century, now stands empty in front of the larger newer house of the following two centuries. The older house probably remained in occupation until earlier this century – as a dwelling for a second household and subsequently as accommodation for farm servants. At Yew Tree the older seventeenth century house was extended in the eighteenth century with a new wing added at right angles, built in a more refined style, panelled and with a staircase (rather than a ladder) to bedrooms.

Lake District houses are noted for their use of datestones, the owners' initials and dates placed in often prominent positions. The house at Townend in Troutbeck, through many generations the home of the Browne family, is but the most baroque version of the trend. At Yew Tree, a carved chest dates from the 1660s, and the front door latch bears the initials:

W

G A

– identifiable from other sources as those of George and Agnes Walker, to whom twelve children were born in this house between 1758 and 1776. All this self-proclamation must be an index of the changes in wealth and the ability to build, which also produced the growth in the number and range of possessions: beds and bedding, chairs and cupboards, clocks and crockery.

Rather than the enclosed and unchanging world that those outside had imagined, Lakeland society can be seen to have been just as subject to change and movement as areas we have already looked at. The people of the north west frequently moved out of the poor region they were living in, and they were highly mobile at a local level within the parishes of the Lake District. But few moved in before the important economic changes of the later seventeenth century, and very few before the nineteenth century. The large numbers with the same surname are some index of that. There were 2000 registrations under the name of Braithwaite in seventeenth century Hawkshead parish: during the eighteenth century their overwhelming primacy was diminished rapidly as Braithwaites moved away and other families moved in. Today a single Braithwaite family remains in the parish. As another measure of the same phenomenon, population increase in the eighteenth century was slow despite a healthy surplus of births, the inference being that many moved away. The local economy was almost certainly unable to cope with ever-greater numbers: the long survival of the farming units (in spite of the sales, splitting and reunification we have seen in the case of Yew Tree Farm) is due above all to the need to 'export' surplus children. Surnames which were once distinctive as belonging to Hawkshead and the parishes around it are now found over all north Lancashire, and especially along the northern edge of Morecambe Bay; and many went considerably further than that.

Hawkshead poses particular problems of historical interpretation. We saw at the beginning how the world outside began to regard the Lake District. When Celia Fiennes travelled through, the picturesque beauty of the mountains received no mention from her (although she did admire the great lakes). What she saw was barren countryside and poverty:

"Here I came to villages of sad little huts made up of dry walls, only stones piled together and the roofs of same slate; there seemed to be little or no tunnels for their chimneys and have no mortar or plaster within or without; for the most part I took them at first sight for a sort of houses or barns to fodder cattle in, not thinking them to be dwelling houses."

On this evidence she thought the people lazy, unwilling to make their conditions more comfortable, although she did note, "Indeed here and there there was a house plastered – but there is sad entertainment." Her economic judgements may have been insecure – but this would seem to

have closer observation behind it than the "peace, rusticity and happy poverty", the "mountain virtue and pastoral hospitality found at every farm" eulogized in Thomas West's 1780 *Guide to the Lakes*, or Wordsworth's "perfect Republic of Shepherds and Agriculturists".

The arrival of popular artistic attention in the later eighteenth century, and the tourist hordes in the nineteenth, predispose us to believe that the area was hitherto isolated and backward. Poor they may have been: but Lakelanders knew much more of the world outside than that world outside knew of them. The growing economic interdependence of English regions produced demand for their metals, textiles and beasts, which in turn meant they could purchase goods from outside. When Leonard Keen, a yeoman of Lower Keen Ground in Hawkshead, died in 1746 he was clearly running a shop or was peddling: he had a stock of "Manchester goods", linen, laces, handkerchiefs, paper, Barbados treacle and Virginia tobacco. A range of consumer goods was available.

At the centre of Hawkshead parish is Hawkshead town itself. A market charter was secured in 1608. By the years after 1700 the poor and struggling fledgeling town had developed sufficiently to possess not only many new houses, inns and shops, but also two wigmakers and a hatter, a musician and a dancing master.

Economic, trading links were by no means the only way to learn of and benefit from a wider world. Hawkshead Grammar School had been founded in the town in 1585 by Edwin Sandys, Archbishop of York, a member of the Sandys family who had been so successful locally under and after the rule of the abbey at Furness (and whose descendants remain important local landowners). The school was one of a remarkable set of such foundations in northern counties during the reign of Elizabeth I, and it became famous, attracting boys from a wide area. The nine-year-old Wordsworth came to the school in 1779 (from Cockermouth, on the Cumbrian coast), and went on to Cambridge. The school, with its books and succession of outstanding Masters, was one of the escape routes from Hawkshead – to the Universities, to London and beyond.

Broughton Castle, Myddle parish, Hawkshead and its wider Lakeland setting; the owners of Balderton Hall, the Walkers at Yew Tree Farm, the Fiennes and their stately home: everywhere, the social and geographical movement of people has been considerable. Other people in all these places moved in terms of their social standing, moved from house to house, village to village, village to town. Although Hawkshead seems to have been slower to join in with other parts of England in terms of wealth and movement and seems to have been more enclosed, change was rapid long before the area was discovered from outside — long before Thomas de Quincey and others marvelled at picturesque echoes (engineered at five shillings per explosion) or the watercolourists and engravers produced their images.

These three examples are here not because they were wayward but

Hawkshead town, a tourist paradise of alleys, OPPOSITE, streets and Wordsworthiana.

45

because they were in the mainstream. Local society in England was not composed of individual "closed corporate communities", with all their inhabitants' thoughts, actions and movements focused in upon themselves. We have chosen the three, very different places we have been looking at not for their unusual characteristics but for their survivals: the *documentary* evidence, of parish registers and family genealogies, of Gough's *History* and lists of farmers' meagre possessions, and the *physical* evidence of houses and landscapes.

It is usually extraordinarily difficult to discover the sort of information presented here about people and their houses in the past: records do not survive – or, more often, were never kept in the first place – and documents which do survive may be scattered, torn and stained, indecipherable, or fail to provide enough detail. Anyone who has tried constructing a proper family tree will appreciate that.

We know as much as we do about Hawkshead parish because of the efforts over the years of a number of historians, both amateur and professional. Parish registers are a prime source for local history of this sort. From 1537 the Anglican church was supposed to keep registers of baptisms, marriages and burials in each parish; until civil registration of births, marriages and deaths began three hundred years later, the parish registers were *the* place for recording. On the basis of evidence from parish registers historians can, for example, build up running totals of burials year by year as a way of measuring mortality: that is the statistical basis for knowing the extent of the great subsistence crises in English regions in 1597–98, or of major outbreaks of disease across the country in 1603–4 or 1741–2. Comparing series of baptism figures with death figures will provide insights into the growth of the local population. In Hawkshead, usually more children were baptized than adults and children were buried; this might suggest that topsy-like, the parish population grew. But since we know from other sources that the population of Hawkshead expanded very little then we have to conclude that emigration from the parish was high.

With Hawkshead (and also with Banbury) we can take the parish register information one step further by linking all the names in the parish register together into their families. Wherever it is possible – and given high rates of migration it is impossible to get all the information – we can then discover not only when a husband and wife were married but also when both partners were baptized and buried, and their children's baptism, subsequent marriage and death. Other information such as the wills and inventories, if they were made, can amplify the picture of the family situation. This labour of love – for it takes many thousands of man-hours to do – is not merely of antiquarian interest, for these *family reconstitutions* provide us with information about the population which we could never otherwise know.

The task is so complicated and time consuming, and demands such good quality parish register material, that it has been done thoroughly for fewer than twenty English parishes of varying types and sizes, of

A form used in family reconstitution details, OPPOSITE ABOVE, the recoverable vital information on one of the families to occupy Yew Tree Farm, OPPOSITE BELOW – the view and the statistical reality.

MARRIAGE

	no.	place	date	date of end		date of next		LITERACY	husband	wife
M	2385	Hawkshead	9-11-1768	-		-		L	5	5

HUSBAND

	surname	name(s)	date of baptism(birth)	date of burial(death)	order of marr.	earlier FRF no.	later FRF no.	residence at baptism
H	Walker	John	31-5-1730	25-5-1807	71			

residence (occupation) at marriage	residence (occupation) at burial	date	residence (occupation)	date	residence (occupation)
Hawkshead	Yew Tree (tanner)	1769	Cunsey		

Husband's father

	surname	name(s)	residence (occupation)	FRF no.	Husband's mother	surname	name(s)
HF	Walker	George	Yew Tree	11516	HM	Agnes	-

WIFE

	surname	name(s)	date of baptism(birth)	date of burial (death)	order of marr.	earlier FRF no.	later FRF no.	residence at baptism
W	Wilson	Elizabeth	13-7-1746	-				

residence (occupation) at marriage	residence (occupation) at burial	date	residence (occupation)	date	residence (occupation)

Wife's father

	surname	name(s)	residence (occupation)	FRF no.	Wife's mother	surname	name(s)
WF	Wilson	James	Wray	11601	WM		

CHILDREN

	sex	date of baptism(birth)	date of burial (death)	status	name(s)	date of marriage	FRF no. of first marr	surname of spouse	age at bur.	age at marr.	birth interval	age of mother
1	C F	13-8-1769			Nancy	19-9-1790	2093		-	21	-	23
2	C M	14-10-1770			Edward	30-7-1797			-	26	14m	24
3	C											
4	C											
5	C											
6	C											
7	C											
8	C											
9	C											
10	C											
11	C											
12	C											
13	C											
14	C											
15	C											
16	C											

H/WALKER/WILLIAM/-/-/>=1/-/-/-/-/-/1699/ARNSIDE
W/TOMPSON/JANE/-/23-10-1738/>=1/-/-/-/ARNSIDE
C/F/22-10-1699/-/-/ELIZABETH

M/2427/H/26-7-1709
H/WALKER/WILLIAM/30-1-1681/5-8-1744/>=1/-/-/-/H/YEW TREE(HOUSE-HOLDER)/1709/EWE TREE
HF/WALKER/WILLIAM/DALE PARK/11548
HM/-/RACHEL
W/WALKER/ELIZABETH/-/-/>=1/-/-/-/YEW TREE
C/M/14-12-1709/26-4-1731/S/JOHN
$
M/2428/H/23-3-1730
H/WALKER/WILLIAM/-/14-3-1746/>=1
W/SCALES/MARTHA/12-7-1630/-/>=1
WF/SCALES/RICHARD/WHITE STOCK HALL/11260
WM/-/ANNE
$
M/2429/H/26-8-1746
H/WALKER/WILLIAM/-/14-10-1748/>=1/-/-/-/EASTHEAD(HOUSE-HOLDER)
W/PIEL/SARAH/-/-/>=1
F/M/L
$
M/2430/H/15-11-1791
L/S/L
H/WALKER/WILLIAM/27-11-1744/-/>=1/-/-/-/H(TAYLOR)/-/1792/TOWN(TAYLOR)
HF/WALKER/EDWARD/GRAYTHWAIT FIELDHEAD(COLLIER)/11515
HM/-/AGNES
W/NICHOLSON/MARY/-/-/1/-/-/-/H
C/M/21-10-1792(20-6-1792)/-/-/-/JOHN/-/11534

which Hawkshead is one. Together, they include many hundreds of thousands of English men, women and children from the middle of the sixteenth century to the middle of the nineteenth.

That requires high computer technology to analyse. But in the magnetic tapes and discs, print-outs and VDUs are the intimate details of real people's lives, details which are otherwise often irrecoverable. Both sexes married relatively late, on average in their mid- to late-twenties. In comparison with, say, modern Third World countries, fertility was quite low, largely because of late marriage: completed family size was a little over five children. Usually between 120 and 200 babies in every thousand died before their first birthday, and another hundred or more before their fifth. Compared with the present day, that is very high – but compared with other European countries of the time those conditions were quite favourable. Expectations of life at birth were low by our standards, around 40 years in 1600, 36 years in 1700 and 37 years in 1800, but once people had survived the hurdles of infant and childhood mortality then they could legitimately expect to live at least into their 50s or 60s. Once past the age of fifteen, life might have been "nasty and brutish" but it was not necessarily "short".

These statistical operations can give us details of things we might think could never be recaptured – for instance, estimates of how long women breast-fed their children (usually over a year) or whether families were consciously attempting to restrict their fertility in marriage by contraception (usually they were not).

All these details build into a picture far removed from the conventional assumptions. Couples in England in the sixteenth, seventeenth and eighteenth centuries were not having as many children as they could from as early as they could. The population was not constantly building itself up to be knocked back by plague or famine. Mortality and fertility were not at a constant level but changed over time in a cyclical way – and changes in fertility were engineered by changes in how many people married and how late they did so. Illegitimacy was not especially high – and was particularly *low* when marriage ages were highest rather than the opposite as we would expect. Families were nuclear, with parents and children, not extended with grandparents, brothers, cousins, and other relations. And people moved: they moved from place to place, especially in their teens and twenties, and there were not rigid barriers to social mobility (whether it be up or down). If only a few moved far, geographically or socially, movement was an integral part of society all the same.

All these confident statements about "England and its population" are possible because England was an astonishingly homogeneous country. Unlike continental countries – France, Italy, or even smaller areas like the Netherlands – regional population differences were slight, and trends moved in the same direction. If marriage ages were rising in seventeenth century Devon, they were also rising in Essex, Warwickshire, Lancashire, Shropshire or Lincolnshire; and so it tended to be with illegitimacy, infant and adult mortality, family sizes and fertility rates. Different regions changed in very similar ways.

Many features of this past society seem familiar rather than alien. The Industrial Revolution and modern economic growth from the nineteenth century did not smash apart an old order but grew out of it. For it was so much easier for England in particular, and Western Europe in general, to achieve industrial and economic growth on the basis of what had gone before. A population which has very high birth rates and very high death rates will have to put most of its economic resources into feeding and caring for children – many of whom will die before they can become economically useful. England on the other hand did not have to spend all it produced on filling hungry mouths: there was room for saving and consumer spending.

We began in Hawkshead with the Wordsworthian sense of isolation, and with the plaster and slate of the farmhouses. We end with computers, and the knowledge that the basic population characteristics of the place were little different from other areas of England. That differences do exist is evident from the variety of people and especially of places in this book. To understand the English past we have to recognize diversity *and* similarity, change over time *and* the existence of basic, little-changing structures. We are not "the same" as the Englishmen and women of the past – but in many ways they feel astonishingly close.

Country parish, country house, countryside and country town: in the chapters which follow we explore all these themes further. The messages may appear contradictory – that early modern England was an ordered society, but was mobile; that underlying apparent stability and continuity was the switchback of fortune; that there was an enduring population and economic structure, which was subject to cycles of behaviour; that the past was both very different from and strikingly similar to our own experience. They only appear contradictory because we are tempted to view the past from a fixed perspective; instead we should recognize that all our perceptions of the past are relative. The only unambiguous fact is that there never was a Golden Age.

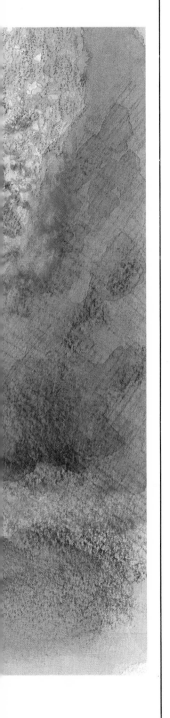

—3—
LORDS OF THE LAND

The model English aristocratic family came over in 1066 – in any event, the only date in history we all know – and now probably languishes in fading style in its country house, fitting in a little huntin', shootin' and fishin' between opening the doors to the rubber-necking hordes.

The model families we look at here do not quite fit that caricature: both came over with the Conqueror, soared to the heights – and spluttered out. For one family the "stately home" was a great fortress castle, for the other something more standard. Land, money and political power equalled success – and loss of tight control produced failure. Their histories are separated in time, but the pattern remains the same.

DE VERE

The Fiennes, Lords Saye and Sele, are an ancient family and a distinguished one. But never were they magnates: they rose no further in the peerage than a Viscountcy – its next to the lowest rank – and, despite two brushes with power, one in the service of Henry VI and the other in the destruction of Charles I, they were never one of the great ruling clans. Were they, dare it be said, *real* aristocrats?

None of these doubts can apply to the de Veres, Earls of Oxford. Aubrey de Vere, descendant of the de Vere who came over in 1066, was created an Earl in 1142, and his last descendant in the male line died in 1703, the 20th Earl. By then they had outlived every other medieval magnate family and their name had become a by-word for antique aristocracy. Moreover the fortress from which they ruled their domain, Castle Hedingham on the Essex-Suffolk border, still stands: four-square and bleak without, exquisitely chevroned arches within, it is the model Norman castle for the model Norman Lord.

In terms of land-holding, admittedly, the de Veres were not in the first division, and they held virtually no territory at all in the county from which they took their title. What made them important was office. The first Aubrey was already the King's Master Chamberlain when he was made Earl, and the position developed into the hereditary post of Lord Great Chamberlain of England. Its formal duties were minimal and consisted of such things as holding the bowl of water in which the King washed his hands before and after the Coronation banquet. But it had enormous prestige and repeatedly carried the de Veres into the mainstream of politics, with its opportunities and perils.

Both were experienced by the two most prominent members of the family, the ninth and thirteenth Earls. Robert, ninth Earl of Oxford, was the closest friend of Richard II: in 1385 he headed the invasion of Scotland, and for his achievements was made successively Knight of the Garter, Marquess of Dublin and Duke of Ireland – the first non-royal Duke. But, accused of treason, he fled to the Continent and his great wealth was forfeited. His cousin Richard, eleventh Earl, was son-in-law of the great John of Gaunt. And John, 13th Earl of Oxford, was greatest of them all.

He succeeded to his title in 1462 at the age of 20, and was closely involved in the dynastic struggles of the Wars of the Roses as one of the leading supporters of the House of Lancaster. His father was executed in

The de Vere flag flies out over Castle Hedingham, LEFT and TOP RIGHT, their Essex power centre. Their star, ABOVE, shines out from the churches across their territory, especially at the super-rich wool town of Lavenham, OVERLEAF.

1462 for plotting against Edward IV of York, and in 1469, when the mighty Earl of Warwick quarrelled with Edward, John joined the Kingmaker to dethrone Edward and restore Henry VI. Two years later in 1471, Edward defeated the strange allies at the Battle of Barnet (where the 2nd Lord Saye and Sele died fighting for him). Warwick was killed and Oxford fled into exile where he was to remain for the next fourteen years. Then in 1485 he returned with the last faint hope of Lancaster, Henry Tudor, Earl of Richmond, and led the vanguard of the Tudor army to victory at Bosworth. Apart from Henry's uncle Jasper, de Vere was the only great noble to support the new King, and he was heaped with wealth and honours. His estates, forfeited by his rebellion and exile under the Yorkists, were restored, and the offices of Lord High Admiral of England, Ireland and Aquitaine, High Steward of the Duchy of Lancaster south of Trent and Constable of the Tower of London (as well as the Knighthood of the Garter) were added to his hereditary Lord Great Chamberlainship.

From de Vere's restoration flows one of the most extraordinary assertions of lordship in later medieval England. For, to the greater glory of God and of de Vere, the Earl placed his thumb-print all over his lands – the de Vere five-pointed star from his coat of arms shines out from church and church tower across the Suffolk-Essex border: at Castle Hedingham, Sible Hedingham, Earls Colne, Colne Engaine, Bures and above all at Lavenham. The star *was* de Vere: the Earl's tenants fought

in battle behind it, paid their dues to officers wearing it, entered church beneath it.

The great late Perpendicular church of Lavenham and the torrent of half-timbered houses are one of the great English showpieces, visited by coach-loads of tourists who cram the streets every summer. The tourists "see" what England "was really like" – compact, half-timbered and picturesquely crooked. What in fact they see is the local power of the Earls of Oxford, the might of industrial wealth, and a fossil. The Earl of Oxford twisted arms to raise the large sums of money needed to build the new church encrusted with his stars. But people could well afford it, for this tiny town was one of the wealthiest places in early sixteenth-century England.

Lavenham's wealth was based upon wool, on the blue cloth produced in the region. Wool was spun in the surrounding villages, woven in the villages and small towns, fulled, sheared and finished by specialists in the towns. Exported *via* London, Lavenham cloth was sold all over Europe, the marks of its great clothiers a guarantee of quality. Lavenham's inhabitants included some of the great cloth merchants, the Spring and Branch families; it is to them that the town owed its great wealth, to the industry they controlled its overall prosperity. Thomas Spring III was in 1525 the wealthiest commoner in England, and his merchant mark, the de Vere star, and the Tudor rose stand side by side along the base of the church tower.

The wool merchant, ABOVE, produced the wealth which made Lavenham, TOP, a beautiful town; the death of his industry preserved the town.

After the boom came slump. Within a few years Lavenham's prosperity collapsed and the markets for their cloth dried up as European demand shifted towards lighter, brighter textiles. Lavenham was amongst the first to be affected by the change: other English cloth-producing areas, for example in the West Country, were eventually able to switch production to the new cloth. But for Lavenham and its region the expertise was not available, and their wealth evaporated. The Springs moved up and out, into the landed gentry, and other wealthy families followed them. So the Lavenham of today is a great beached whale: wealth built fine houses, the loss of wealth meant that those houses were not replaced in later centuries. Parts of England were like Lavenham: but it can hardly be described as typical.

The Earls of Oxford had encouraged the industry on their land, securing rights and privileges for their tenants – and benefiting from a share of its wealth. Now, as Lavenham declined, so did the Earls. The 14th Earl was John de Vere's nephew, the 15th Earl a second cousin. Edward, 16th Earl of Oxford, was one of the great spendthrifts of the Elizabethan age. Some have always believed him to be the true author of Shakespeare's works, most believe him to be a minor poet. His father-in-law was the great Lord Burghley, whose ward he had been: after the suspicious death of the cruelly abused Countess, Burghley pursued a vendetta against the wasteful aesthete. The Earl secured money from the Crown, and tried a variety of money-making projects (mostly unsuccessful) to recoup his losses from being a courtier, a lavish patron of the arts and of overseas expeditions. Castle Hedingham itself was sold to Burghley.

Thereafter, the downhill slide continued. The direct line could not perpetuate itself easily, and the 19th Earl succeeded his second cousin only after his right to the title had been contested by another distant cousin. Aubrey, 20th Earl, held Court positions after the Restoration: but when Samuel Pepys visited him in 1665 he found him in bed

"at half past 10 o'clock, and Lord help us! so rude a dirty family I never saw."

The Earl was buried in Westminster Abbey in 1703: but he left only daughters, and the line stretching back to the Conquest ended.

The Earls had gone, but their survival was to be a metaphor for longevity. In the Court action in 1625 over the hereditary Great Chamberlainship, which the Earls had previously held, Sir Ranulph Crewe was moved to make his great pronouncement:

"And yet time hath his revolution: there must be a period and an end to all temporal things. Finis rerum, an end of names and dignities, and whatsoever is terrene. And why not of de Vere? Where is Bohun, where's Mowbray, where's Mortimer? Nay, which is more and most of all, where is Plantagenet? They are entombed in the urns and sepulchres of mortality.
"And yet let the name and dignity of de Vere stand so long as it pleaseth God."

The name stood only for the remainder of the century: today the urns

St Stephen's Chapel, Bures, curious and isolated last resting-place of many of the de Veres.

and sepulchres of de Vere mortality stand in the restored chapel to which they were moved for preservation earlier this century, isolated above Bures and the Stour valley. Their tombs, their buildings, their marks alone survive; and in the late eighteenth century two Lavenham girls composed the lines

> *"Twinkle, twinkle, little star,*
> *How I wonder what you are."*

In one sense, therefore, the story of the de Veres simply confirms what we know already. A magnate family follows the same cycle as the baronial family of Fiennes: sometimes great; often down and finally, unlike the Fiennes, going under completely. But it also adds a new dimension in John de Vere's management of the family at its moment of supreme power and wealth. "Management" indeed seems the right word: the de Vere star is used like a trade mark, while the Earl's association with Lavenham and its woollen industry has an almost entrepreneurial quality. What is a Lord Great Chamberlain doing when he hobnobs with the likes of Thomas Spring?

Karl Marx wrote that "the ruling ideas of each age have ever been the ideas of its ruling class". That the nobility was the English ruling class, or better the predominant elite at the head of the landed ruling class, is not in doubt. But what were its ideas? The de Vere episode raises one sort of doubt; Lord Macaulay, Marx's elder contemporary, another when he remarked "thus our democracy was, from an early period, the most aristocratic, and our aristocracy the most democratic in the world". By aristocratic values we mean continuity, attachment to land, defence of property, the sacrifice of quick immediate profit for slow long-term gain, and above all restraint and decorum as a model for behaviour.

How far does this fit? Let us turn to another, much less well-known case.

ASHBURNHAM

A simple mark, prominently displayed, like the de Vere star, is a powerful badge of ownership and overlordship. The badge of the Pelham family in East Sussex was a buckle, granted them after the 1369 Battle of Poitiers. They were not a medieval peerage family, although in the eighteenth century Pelhams were to be created Barons and then to become Dukes of Newcastle, and the great Duke was one of the leading politicians of the age. But three hundred years before, the Pelhams had marked their position as dominant gentry by placing their buckle on buildings throughout East Sussex. The badge appears on their houses at Halland and Laughton, the font at Burwash, in the stained glass at Penhurst and above all on a group of fifteenth-century towers they paid for. Just as with the de Veres, church towers were a potent symbol of the might of God and of men, and the Pelham buckle is fastened onto the churches at Wartling, Ripe, Laughton, East Hoathly, Dallington, Crowhurst (where the tracery of the west window takes the same form), Chiddingly, and Ashburnham.

But Ashburnham church, standing beside the remnants of its great house, Ashburnham Place, speaks of a locally more powerful family. Apart from the Pelham tower, the rest of the building is in a restrained Gothic style dating from the mid-1660s. In the chapel above the vault which he built is the monument of 1671 to John Ashburnham, lying between his first and second wives. The inscription records him to be

"son of the unfortunate person Sir John Ashburnham whose good nature and frank disposition towards his friends in being deeply engaged for them necessitated him to sell this place (in his family long before the Conquest) and all the estates he had elsewhere not leaving his wife and six children the least subsistence"

although the inscription hastens to add

"which is not intended to the least disadvantage of his memory (God forbid it should be understood to be a charge of disrespect upon him)."

But next to the monument is a plaque to the memory of Lady Catherine Ashburnham, "last of that name and line" – dated 1953. The earlier monument's boast was incorrect – the Ashburnhams had arrived *at the* Conquest – but there was no mistaking the family's continuity and resilience. The monumental inscription goes on to inform us:

The Pelham buckle, LEFT, on the tower of Ashburnham church ABOVE, guards access to the family monuments of the Ashburnhams – of Cavalier, Cofferer, collector and Lady Catherine.

"but to give God the praise who so suddenly provided for his wife and children, so that within less than two years after the death of Sir John there was not any of them but was in condition rather to be helpful to others than to want support themselves."

We have seen economic vicissitudes before – at Broughton Castle, and with the Earls of Oxford. With the latter we have seen the extinction of a line. Who today knows of the Ashburnhams? Few beyond those who were connected with the estate; or historians for whom some aspect of the family's history or interests is important; or families into which the Ashburnhams married. And yet the Ashburnhams were for some centuries in the select and tiny group of wealthy families dominating English social and political life. Their story is filled with interest, their history an example of much wider relevance.

THE EARLIER ASHBURNHAMS

Thomas Fuller, writing in the middle of the seventeenth century of England's worthies, concluded of the Ashburnhams:

"My poor and plain pen is willing, though unable, to add any lustre to this family of stupendous antiquity."

Rather more indicative of the family's condition is the declaration of the 3rd Earl of Ashburnham in 1830. He

"can attest the uniform tenor of a life, throughout which he has as sedulously avoided, as others, at any period of theirs, have sought, to attract public notice."

This self-examination came as part of the preface (what he termed the 'Introductory Apology') to his publication of the *Narrative* of his ancestor John Ashburnham – the man whose tomb stands in Ashburnham church. He was a close friend of Charles I and one of his attendants in the Civil War, indeed the only Ashburnham who is at all well known to the world at large, and the man who set his family on their subsequent course of success.

Ashburnham is only a few miles from Battle in East Sussex, where William the Conqueror gained victory in 1066 and where the Ashburnhams' ancestor fought with his fellow Normans. The estate is on the edge of the Sussex Weald, the heavily wooded clay lands in Kent, Surrey and Sussex. Even today Ashburnham, as elsewhere in the Weald, has extensive woodland, with narrow lanes taking circuitous and often hilly routes between settlements which had once been woodland clearings. Occasionally there are remnants of the early iron industry which flourished throughout the Weald (just as it did in Hawkshead), using local raw materials, wood for charcoal and iron-bearing stone.

The Ashburnhams took their family name from the place they acquired after the Norman Conquest: their original name was the more ominous-sounding de Cruel (or Criol). Their early history is obscure, and much of what has been written was the product of the imaginative zeal of an Elizabethan herald. By the thirteenth century they were a largely respectable family of knights and small feudal lords. Bartholomew Ashburnham, captured at the battle of Boroughbridge in 1322, was hanged for homicide and robbery, and drawn and quartered for acts of treason. He was perhaps the most adventurous and least respectable member of his family. And by the early fifteenth century, the Ashburnham family had established itself as a county family, acquiring more land and holding office as knights of the shire and sheriff. By the later fifteenth century the Ashburnhams were usually marrying into other local leading families – John Ashburnham who died in 1491 married a Pelham. And if they could, they married heiresses, who contributed to the consolidation of the estate.

William Ashburnham died in 1532; his son's wife was a Hampshire heiress and he was able to leave to his grandson and heir John the manors of Ashburnham, Broomham, Peryland, Petowes and Penhurst. John was to inherit immediately "if John Sackville Esquire cause the said John Ashburnham mine heir to be married unto his daughter now being about the age of five years, according to such communications and agreement." The two were married (eventually), and with this particular John Ashburnham, who died in 1562, the family's true prosperity began. His will made sufficient large-scale bequests for him to be considered wealthy, and in it he referred to his ironworks in Ashburnham, Penhurst and Dallington. Owning the land and possessed of the rather limited amounts of working capital needed, men like John Ashburnham could foster the use of available raw materials for the production of iron and casting, most notably for cannon and shot.

In the next generation (perhaps with the additional expertise of Protestant refugees from the Low Countries) the iron trade prospered further. But this prosperity was insufficient to maintain the family's local strength, for the next John Ashburnham who succeeded his father in 1562, was continually being fined for his adherence to Catholicism. After fourteen years of harassment and many unpaid fines, his estate was sequestrated by the Crown in 1588 and later farmed out to Elizabeth I's master cook, William Cordell. John's children had widely varying starts in life therefore: Thomas, his second son, was sponsored at baptism by great figures at Elizabeth's Court, by the Lord Treasurer William Cecil and by Henry Hastings, 3rd Earl of Huntingdon; George, his fourth son, was born in London's notorious Fleet prison and died in infancy.

John the next heir was either less religiously motivated or less principled: when he succeeded his father in 1592 he recovered the Ashburnham estates. But this was the "unfortunate person whose good nature and frank disposition towards his friends" nearly ruined the family. Perhaps he attempted to spend his way into the royal circles at Court – his wife (when a widow to be created Baroness Cramond in her own right) was a cousin of Lady Villiers, mother of the Duke of Buckingham, and later through Buckingham's patronage their son John Ashburnham made his way into royal favour.

The English peerage is a relatively small body: yet only here, in the second quarter of the seventeenth century, did the paths of the Fiennes and Ashburnham families cross – and both through Buckingham.

Whatever the cause of the financial diaster, John Ashburnham had had to sell his estate for £8000 in 1611 to Edward Bromfield, later a Lord Mayor of London. In 1634 the estate was resold, to William Relfe of nearby Mayfield. Only in 1640 was John Ashburnham given leave to regain the estate from the trustees of the Relfe estate. Frances Holland, the first wife of this, the famous John Ashburnham, was an heiress, and her money rescued the family's estates and well-being.

John Ashburnham and his daredevil brother William were almost as important in the Royalist cause as the Fiennes were in the Parliamentarian. To Charles I John Ashburnham was "dearest Jack" and a favoured Groom of the Bedchamber. In 1642, in the build-up to Civil War, the King refused to permit Ashburnham and Endymion Porter to be summoned before the House of Commons on the grounds that they were needed at Court for personal attendance on the King and the Prince of Wales. By the time hostilities had broken out and the Royalists were in Oxford, Ashburnham was acting as an unofficial war treasurer: the State Papers of 1644 and 1645 record payments out of the Exchequer, the payment of troops, and loans to the King passing through the hands of John Ashburnham. Royal letters to Nathaniel Williams and Thomas Dixon of Loughborough, for example, requested the loan of £40, to be delivered to John Ashburnham, "the which we promise to repay as soon as God shall enable us." Between April 1642 and October 1643, Ashburnham received £162,047.3s.3d for the King. Some had their doubts about him: Edward Walsingham wrote to George, Lord Digby, in 1645, "I had almost forgot to tell you that the men here have resolved lately to get into Mr John Ashburnham's bosom by one means or other, for the junto hold him a very necessary person for their ends and therefore he must be laid hold of; but one of them affirms him to be a slippery piece and dangerous to build upon."

Even the King may have harboured his doubts: in a letter written in code to Queen Henrietta Maria the following year he wrote of the plans to increase dissension between the religious sects on the Parliamentary side. "Upon my word I neither have nor intend to acquaint any with this business but Ashburnham. . . that if anything come out we may know whom to blame." Charles already owed Ashburnham personally nearly £10,000. During the Interregnum Ashburnham was harried by the victors: he was sued for the dead King's debts; he was forced to compound for half of his already depleted estate, and was persecuted by committees trying to discover who had lent money to the King during the wars. Meanwhile his brother William, who had held the town of Weymouth for the King for some months in 1644 before it finally fell to Parliament's forces, was implicated in a plot to kill Cromwell in 1654.

At the Restoration the brothers gained money and distinction. John was given back the office of Groom of the Bedchamber and was appointed a guardian of the Duke of Monmouth; and loans to Charles were repaid by grants of Crown leases and of land at Ampthill in Bedfordshire. William meanwhile was made Cofferer of the Household by Charles II, a very lucrative and prestigious financial position.

Together, the two brothers devoted their energies to their family fortune and their Sussex inheritance. John married twice, first the Frances Holland who helped rescue the family lands, and then Elizabeth, widow of Lord Poulett and again a woman with money. William the Cofferer married Jane, Countess of Marlborough. With restored personal fortunes and wealthy new connections, the two brothers set about the task of renewal. They rebuilt Ashburnham Place. William built almshouses at Ashburnham, and John rebuilt the church there, complete with the vault to house his own remains and those of his descendants.

In the chapel over the vault John Ashburnham's monument of 1671 is, like his church, deliberately old-fashioned. But the monument of eight years later to William and his beloved wife, with its free-standing sculptures and studied attitudes of public grief, heralds a Baroque new age.

THE FIRST LORD ASHBURNHAM

The heir to both the Cavalier and the Cofferer was John, respectively their grandson and great-nephew. His father had predeceased his grandfather. Born in 1656, the new head of the Ashburnham family was to be raised to the peerage by William III in 1689. With him the family's fortune and honour hit a new peak.

John Ashburnham had a considerable inheritance – the enlarged Sussex estates, and land in Bedfordshire; his great-uncle's Westminster house and estates in Wiltshire, Dorset and Hampshire. In 1677 John married Bridget, daughter and heir of Walter Vaughan of Breconshire, in King Henry VII's chapel, Westminster Abbey: through her he acquired 7000 acres of Welsh estates, at Talgarth and Porthamel in Breconshire, and at Pembrey in Carmarthenshire.

Despite their prominence, local or national, John Ashburnham's forebears cannot quite come alive for us: we have many records of their actions but few of their thoughts, statements of their wealth but no analysis as to how they created it. But John Ashburnham can come alive: for this "little brown man", as an observer called him, was active, even hyperactive, in pursuit of revenue and status. And we may follow him through his diaries and subsequently his voluminous correspondence. He demonstrates not only what it was like to be an aristocratic landowner but also what it was like to be a new boy within the peerage, needing to consolidate his position.

John Ashburnham was only in his mid-teens when he inherited from his grandfather, and in his early twenties when his great-uncle died: in each case he had to wait whilst the inheritance was administered by trustees.

Only in 1687 was the Cofferer's will finally settled. In what we shall see was characteristic style, Ashburnham confided to his diary when he received at last everything, "Mr Trevor, Mr Jennings and Sergeant Phillips were counsel for the trustees, they are a parcel of blockheads. So ends this book with one of the happiest actions of my life." Happy indeed: he had just taken full control of his Sussex estates, and nearly £30,000 was paid over to him.

John Ashburnham fulfilled the roles appropriate to his position: he was M.P. for Hastings from 1679–81, 1685–87 and in 1689. As Hastings' M.P., and so one of the barons of the Cinque Ports, he helped hold the canopy over James II in 1685 – and did so again at the coronation of William and Mary in 1689. Clearly he welcomed the new monarchs: in May 1689 he was created Baron Ashburnham and thereafter took occasional part in the activity of the Lords, as a staunch Tory. In 1701 Ashburnham's son was the candidate for the Hastings seat that the Baron had held before his elevation: Ashburnham was confident that his son should gain the seat on the basis of "his stake in our English hedge". And he affirmed his principles: "Whenever England comes to be settled and made happy it must be done by councils of such who love their country and value their estates beyond anything else."

Lord Ashburnham could never have been accused of being otherwise. He had both the rolling acres and grand houses that are the mark of the English landed aristocracy, and did his utmost to bring about change and improvement. Before 1640 the revenues of the Sussex estates – at least according to the evidence presented by John Ashburnham the Cavalier when threatened with sequestration – were valued at £70 per annum. An undated document of the post-Restoration years (when the Ashburnham brothers were reviving their Sussex wealth and position) put the annual value at £490. Thereafter, there was clearly major change, for an account drawn up in 1690 for the newly ennobled Baron showed his Sussex revenues to be just under £3000. The properties itemized included not only Ashburnham and the surrounding area, but also large areas of valuable grazing land in the coastal marshes around Pevensey, and some town properties in Battle and Hastings.

Similar accounts do not seem to exist for his other properties, but it seems likely that financial improvements on the same scale were evident in Bedfordshire and Wales. Lord Ashburnham promoted improvement not through wholesale change but through close supervision and an unerring eye for detail. In January 1696 he added a note to a letter to his steward in London, "P.S. I would have you get me a table book for memorandums that will last twenty years every day writing and washing out" and then, "I would have a chagreen cover, armed on the corners with silver, and a silver pen." He might have to get his hands dirty, but he would do it in style. And later, when he wanted another such book, he unwittingly gave us another glimpse of himself: "pray let the vellum be very good and serviceable, for it will be in a continual daily use turning over and pawing almost every hour."

Lord Ashburnham used his books. Through the medium of paper he exercised organizational control, and often a particularly close control – through the reams of letters to his various stewards and agents, account and memorandum books, leases and covenants. He wanted improvement: that was to be achieved by more efficient farming, more effective methods, more incentive for his tenants. In 1696, for instance, he instituted an annual survey of the farmers' management and methods – what crops they grew or how much pasture they had in each field, and therefore whether they were making the most efficient use of their landholding. He was adamant that this was as much for their own good as for his. And those who failed to see things Lord Ashburnham's way could go: like one tenant who had been given notice to quit for spoiling the woods to the detriment of his farm, contrary to the covenants in his lease. Should he be arrested for breaking the covenant? The question vexed Lord Ashburnham early in 1697; the following year he decided to sue, to set an example to his other tenants.

Impatience with tenants who could not or would not move as fast as their lord required brought out some typical outbursts.

"I am not surprised at John Duke's behaviour, for before the estate can become well settled and very easy, Duke and one or two more must turn out, and have nothing to do in it. I think upon this occasion you [Ashburnham's steward] will do well to drive his stock and enter also upon his corn and hay for rent due. For if now my back is turned, even though my wife is there upon the place, what will they do when you are single and alone? Some examples must be made with knaves, and I think you cannot pick out a much greater to make an example of."

Conscious of the political niceties of that course, he added:

"This will be a great deal more proper to do in my absence than if I were upon the spot."

On occasion Ashburnham considered the amalgamation of farms to be the most efficient course to follow – and tenants who were unwilling to take the added burden could also go. William Walkings, for instance, could "not be brought to serve both himself and me" in that regard – Ashburnham always stressed the mutual benefit – so

"I shall be obliged immediately to dispossess him of those farms and lands he now holds, and let them out to such as shall be better inclined for my interest and service than I take him to be."

We hear no more in the letters about William Walkings: either he paid up and shut up, or he went.

Throughout the dealings of Lord Ashburnham there runs a firm sense of the efficacy of self-help, and of the necessity of ensuring prompt payment without abatement or arrears. The level of arrears of rent payments, at least on the Sussex estates, certainly seems less than upon other more or less contemporary large estates. John Palmer, his steward in Sussex, was congratulated after the Michaelmas (ie. 29 September)

1698 rent instalments were due for his successes in getting tenants to pay.

"I have for some time been persuaded that no other methods but pecuniary ones will be a check upon them for their habitual knavish proceedings, in that as well as in several other matters relating to the improvement and well managing their farms – all of which I hope to live to see rectified. . ."

Clearly when times were difficult for farmers the lord could not afford to press too hard for payment: but he would **never** allow matters to run on for too long. When the tenants on his small Wiltshire estate applied for reductions in their rent in advance of the Michaelmas of 1697, Lord Ashburnham was adamant that they would have to pay in full. He had already abated the rents by £100 per annum; he had had new buildings put up which were worth £200, and in any event grain prices were high and so his tenants could better afford to pay.

It must have seemed to the Baron – or, at least, so his correspondence would suggest – that everyone he employed was lazy or incompetent, and every tenant out for the easiest return: the Welsh estates, being furthest away and least frequently visited, were especially recalcitrant. Torrents of rage and abuse fell upon the luckless Dalton brothers, his agents there:

"Now, in the name of God, what are all these words of yours but mere amusements fit for no honest man to use nor for any but women and children to give any credit to. . . Why, Mr. Dalton, the way to remove my displeasure is to pay me up all you owe me, no other way can ever do it."

The money arrived.

What Lord Ashburnham could provide, which none of his stewards or agents could do, was a sense of overall strategy, and of political manoeuvre. Many of the Sussex farms had land in the main portion of the estate and rights to grazing in the coastal marshes of Pevensey levels. Clearly the land drainage had to be maintained. However in 1699 another landowner was allowing flooding to take place, and so Ashburnham needed to intervene. But he could do so only covertly: so he instructed his agent to "stand behind the curtain, and set on two or three bold forward fellows that are sufferers in land and pocket" to send round a petition.

By juggling his resources, and knowing when to delegate, Lord Ashburnham proved an enterprising landowner. Having estates in different, and widely differing, areas provided continuous points of reference and comparison. On one of his (infrequent) visits to the Welsh estates, for instance, Ashburnham had seen water meadows in operation – the controlled flooding of grassland to promote lusher growth. With his keen eye for profit, he was captivated – land values were said to have been increased from 2s. an acre to 18 or 20s. an acre. So, instructions on the floating of watermeadows were despatched to Sussex: with them, he was "hopeful to make of one acre the profit of two acres." Although he reminded his Sussex men of his wishes, the subject was soon dropped: whether the experiment failed – or his instructions were never acted upon – we cannot tell. For clearly Lord Ashburnham believed himself to be the cat, his employees and tenants to be the mice who play:

". . .I shall remember the husbandry of the counties through which I am to pass now in my journey. And if they exceed us in good husbandry I shall lay the fruit at your doors and reproach you all with it when I come home."

The strategy for administering the estate included being able to take advantage of the inter-connectedness of the various parts. As ideas could move, so could people: the Baron wrote to Wales and to Devon (from his Bedfordshire home) requiring good farmers to be sent to Sussex. A Bedfordshire huntsman and hounds went to Sussex, as did another farmer:

"This man is a farmer's son of the Duke of Bedford's [estate] and has been bred to it from the cradle; his skill in laying land finely in tillage to the best advantage, and seeding them, is what is much commended."

Timber from the Wealden woodland of Sussex was despatched (by sea and river navigation) to woodless Bedfordshire, while cattle raised in Wales were driven across to his other properties.

So Lord Ashburnham was interested in *movement*: he moved himself from one part of his estates to another, he moved paper, personnel and ideas. His was the strategic influence, his the eye for wider trends and yet he still felt able to involve himself in the small details of, say, haymaking or calving. In 1697 he demanded an account of the grain stock on the Breconshire land, since grain was dear in England: he thought it best to capitalize on the position by selling. Two years later he was issuing instructions to Sussex that tenants should continue the improvement of their fields, with mud and lime, so as to get good early crops.

"in which they have all the encouragement imaginable by the probability, or rather certainty, that corn [prices] will hold up for some years, the scarcity being such in some parts of England and chiefly in Scotland that hundreds die daily there for want of food."

Famine did haunt Scotland, but Ashburnham saw profit in the predicament. This was a short-term consideration, but elsewhere he affirmed that he took "pasture lands to be the highest and best improvement for landlords at long run."

We should note how often Lord Ashburnham seems to have read the signs properly. The Lake District, which we looked at in the previous chapter, was not the only English region to prosper from greater demand for meat. The long period between the mid-seventeenth century and the mid-eighteenth witnessed a marked slowing in the rate of population growth, improvements in wages and general living standards, and a switch of emphasis in agriculture from grain-growing to pasture. Despite short-term fluctuations with the state of the harvest, most grain prices were astonishingly stable over a long period; on the other hand, pressure of demand for meat and dairy produce kept those prices up – and persuaded more farmers to convert most or part of their output. What we see is a greater interconnectedness of regions: Lord Ashburnham sought advice, for example, on fairs within a fifty mile radius of London that dealt in Scotch cattle – beasts driven from Scotland, the north west and the north east of England – which could be purchased on his behalf and sent to Sussex to be fattened on the coastal marshes. The beasts' principal ultimate destination would then have been the London meat markets. And there are records of cattle being brought for Ashburnham at the great annual St Faith's Fair near Norwich as well as at fairs in south eastern counties.

What gains did Lord Ashburnham make from his agricultural estates? Unfortunately there are no final profit and loss accounts, but it seems undeniable that considerable improvement was made. Clearly he felt that there was a great deal of catching up to be done, and the extent of his success was visible to his neighbours – he was dismayed at his tax revaluation in Sussex in 1697 because he felt that since the estate had previously been so mismanaged by his trustees, it was now, with improvement, being unfairly compared with its neighbouring estates. Improvement was not to be found in technological innovation on any grand scale but through efficient and well-supervised husbandry. If Ashburnham felt his motives were not entirely selfish, that all was to his tenants' advantage as well as his own, he also had a mission to increase his income and maintain a lifestyle appropriate to his family's newly acquired peerage status. As he once wrote to his attorney, he was "busied in the dirty acres, but good rents I hope".

That lifestyle was maintained in his properties. Lord Ashburnham had his ancestral home at Ashburnham, rebuilt by his grandfather and great-uncle, and his wife's ancestral home at Talgarth (which he only visited on a few occasions, and which was clearly not of the same standard of comfort). Charles II had given John Ashburnham the Cavalier land in Bedfordshire, at Ampthill, and here the Baron decided he would make his new family seat. A grand new house was built – using some materials brought in from Sussex, as we have seen – and attention was lavished on the grounds with formal avenues of trees, gravelled walks, terraces and a symmetrical garden layout. The trees in his new park were an abiding passion – he instructed his keeper at Ampthill that his

"chief and greatest application be in the well looking-after my trees both in park and gardens and well ordering the gravel walks, which I prefer infinitely before turnips or cabbage."

His architect was John Lumley from Northampton, building onto a new house of the 1680s which had been put up for his then tenant, the Dowager Countess of Ailesbury.

Only two of the Ashburnham
homes remain more or less
intact: Ampthill Great Park in
Bedfordshire, ABOVE, and the
Westminster town house in
Little Dean's Yard, LEFT.

69

Sir Christopher Wren designed the Ashburnham pew in Ampthill parish church. Over that pew the Baron fought long and hard.

For the existing local magnate was the Earl of Ailesbury; and, seeing Ashburnham's arrival and intention to construct a grandiloquent Baroque pew in church as an affront to his own dignity, he persuaded the Bishop of Lincoln to refuse permission for the pew to be built. Ashburnham tried gentle bribery, and later gained the Archbishop of Canterbury's support; eventually he won, and Ailesbury withdrew in disgust, threatening never to employ an Ampthill tradesman or workman again! Ashburnham could lord it over Ampthill without a rival.

Every substantial nobleman needed a town house, a London base for the enjoyment of metropolitan society and for his political and financial affairs. The only such seventeenth century grand house which survives more or less intact today is Ashburnham House, in the precincts of Westminster Abbey. The house was built soon after the Restoration by William Ashburnham the Cofferer: here his great-nephew and heir lived when in town. For us it is a little-known but magnificent architectural gem – but Lord Ashburnham, incensed at the amount he had to pay in Land Tax for it, stormed that he "thanked God he had better houses and places to live in!" Later, Ashburnham followed fashion, forsaking the Westminster house in 1707 and moving into the recently-constructed magnificence of Southampton Street, between Covent Garden and the Strand, as his son was to move westward with the *beau monde* into St James's Square.

Land, farms and great houses make Lord Ashburnham a representative member of his class. What singles him out for attention is the keen eye and entrepreneurial drive he brought to his other money-making activities. The increased wealth of his Sussex gentry ancestors had come largely through their involvement in the Wealden iron industry, and the Ashburnham Sussex estates remained a prime location for that industry.

Ironstone was quarried on Ashburnham land; charcoal made from Ashburnham trees; the iron smelted at Ashburnham furnace and castings especially of cannon, balls, and guns made there. Iron-working was a lucrative source of income, for landlord, ironworkers and farmers alike. When engaged upon one of his attempts at amalgamating farms into more effective working units, Ashburnham was sure that "Soame's own little farm joined with Woodruff's would make a pretty employment and livelihood for a farmer, lying among the woods and *so near the furnaces*." For the most part, the ironworks were let to specialist ironmasters: but for a period they were run directly by Lord Ashburnham, with the attendant management problems but with greater profits.

Maximilian Western, a London ironmonger, was his principal tenant: strict covenants existed covering which woods could be used for charcoaling, which equipment belonged to the furnace, and over which routes cast items, especially the heavy cannon, could be transported. After some protracted negotiations with a group of ironmasters in 1705 and 1706, including Ambrose Crowley, the leading and wealthiest ironmaster of the day, much was brought under direct Ashburnham control.

That day was not unprepared for: even as a younger man, with his estate only newly-acquired, Ashburnham had been storing up information about the activity. In the autumn of 1686 Ashburnham was seeking advice and asking pertinent questions. Some of his neighbours advised him to run his own iron works, because ironmasters took only the best and left things unfinished: the likely profit was £1000 a year. We can easily imagine the eager young landowner watching and wondering on one of his rides around the woodlands.

"Coming home by the furnace, I stayed to see them cast a gun of about 16 cwt. Diamond told me he had £5 per ton for casting some sort of ware, but for guns he had but 20 crowns. He said the furnace was to go upon guns for the King till Midsummer. Skinner. . . told me they made 1 cwt. of iron every hour. Diamond told me Western sold his guns for £16 or £18 per ton."

Fifteen years later all this came in useful, as he decided whether or not to take over the iron works himself and began drawing up lists of costs and likely returns. It was apparent to him that the Sussex iron industry was restricting itself to the less lucrative end of the iron market, to casting – guns, cannon balls, rollers and the like. If a forge were built, producing hammered and forged metal objects, then considerable improvements could be made. Indeed, a forge was constructed on the Ashburnham estate, a mile downstream from the furnace, with a water-driven wheel for the bellows or the hammer. And the Ashburnham iron works closed in the 1820s, the last Wealden iron working to remain operative and only making a loss in its last few years of operation.

For the Baron's new venture, a little covertly-obtained information from the neighbouring large-scale iron works such as those of the Fullers at Brightling would not come amiss. So he instructed his steward,

". . . if upon your own account you met with [those] skilled in the affairs of iron works you might so order your discourse as to draw from them such lights as might be useful to me in this business, without giving them a handle or leading them into anything that might seal up their mouths by discovering our design."

And at the same time that he was deciding how far to become an iron entrepreneur in Sussex, he was discovering whether he could become a coal entrepreneur in Carmarthenshire, at his Pembrey estate. His first interest in finding coal there was expressed in 1701, and in 1706 he was convinced that he was about to succeed. Agents in London were set to enquire the likely market for Welsh coal in the capital and freight costs – or to see whether the Newcastle trade was so dominant that no other coal would be able to break into the market. On 5 June 1707 he wrote to Pembrey with obvious impatience – what about the coal mines? Did they

need more iron tools to help with the search? – he could have them shipped from Sussex. Five days later he wrote again: "What of the coal mines?" Within four days he had news of success, and he was busy making calculations of new profits – 4s. per day profit from one worker and, if he could get a quick sale of coal through the coasting trade, then a hundred men could be put to work on coal mining. So, sample bags were to be sent out to smiths, throughout the south west of England and perhaps to Ireland.

In the woods at Ashburnham stand forlorn relics of the iron industry, parts of the water system coming down from the hammer ponds and, OPPOSITE, remains of the furnaces.

Accounts for the years 1714–21 show how far that had paid off: coal was shipped to Devon and Cornwall, Somerset, Ireland and occasionally to France. The profits were tidy rather than spectacular, but these were early days for the Ashburnham coal workings.

The profits from coal and iron as well as those from farming swelled the revenue of Lord Ashburnham: but this was by no means the end to his enterprise.

"I must own to you", Ashburnham wrote to his attorney in 1698, *"that of late a country life has made me so thoughtless and lazy that I can hardly bring myself to an opinion of anything above the ordinary low methods of* little but certain, *which. . . makes me the less solicitous in matters of* greater profit and more danger."

73

Scenes from W.H. Pyne's **Microcosm** *illustrate the charcoaling of wood, for the furnaces, and the founding and forging, ABOVE LEFT and RIGHT, to produce the Ashburnham finished product.*

Profit and danger: the note of relish in Lord Ashburnham's words reflects his obvious excitement in financial dealings, following in the footsteps of his great-uncle the Cofferer. And a combination of circumstances in the late seventeenth century offered plenty of opportunity for the instinct to manifest itself.

First, there was the mortgage market. During the seventeenth century mortgages on land became easier for the borrower: a borrower who could not repay on the specified day no longer stood to lose his land permanently, and whilst interest on the loan continued to be paid the lender would not foreclose. For the lender, a market in mortgages enabled him to realize money by selling the mortgage to a third party. Individuals could lend out spare money to earn a steady rate of interest; borrowers could use cash raised on mortgage for their short-term needs, for debts or building projects, and for the long-term to provide marriage portions for their daughters, or separate provision for their sons.

Second, the government's pressing need for finance, above all in William III's wars against Louis XIV, promoted substantial (and very expensive) government borrowing in the form of direct loans and in anticipation of taxation revenues. For the latter, investors purchased tallies (notched lengths of wood split in two to make a unique matching pair) issued by the Exchequer against a specific tax or revenue, and redeemed with interest when the revenue came in.

And finally, Lord Ashburnham could invest in company stocks, most notably the lucrative stock of the East India Company with its giant trading interests. Lord Ashburnham did not live to see the great boom and slump of the South Sea Bubble: on the evidence of his financial acumen, it seems doubtful that *he* would have been taken in!

Lord Ashburnham used his money in all three ways, playing the finance markets. His business was organized by Richard Hoare, one of the London goldsmiths whose activity in the later seventeenth century became increasingly that of banker. Hoare indeed founded the dynasty which still presides over what is today the country's sole remaining private bank, still bearing the family name. Although often advised by Hoare, Ashburnham issued his own instructions as to where money should be placed. Hoare's Bank still displays a letter written to Richard Hoare by the Lord Ashburnham, dated 12 May 1698:

"Sir,
For the present I am not disposed to lend more than the £1000 of Mr Barnwell's for which I pay a very high rate of interest, and therefore I would have it disposed of as soon as conveniently may be, either on the Poll Tax or Coal Act; the performing of which I leave absolutely and entirely to you, who upon all occasions have so eminently showed your affection, care and diligence in promoting the welfare of me and mine, in a due sense whereof I shall never be wanting, nor shall those that belong to me."

(The bank does not display the correspondence going on at exactly the same time, in which Hoare was the secret bidder for Ashburnham's

Devon estate at Staverton. Ashburnham drove too hard a bargain, so Hoare retired, hurt!)

The financial problems of the 1690s drove up interest rates – on government borrowings from 5 to 8 per cent, on mortgages from 4 or 5 per cent to 6. Given that price inflation was virtually non-existent (and there were still debates about the ethics of charging more than small rates of interest) these were in real terms high rates of return. Between 1688 and 1697 over £32 million was raised in short-term loans at the Exchequer, above all to finance war. This was expensive, for anticipating revenues involves considerable risk – would the revenue actually arrive? Not only were the tallies struck at the Exchequer bearing a substantial rate of interest, but also they were bought at a substantial discount, reflecting that uncertainty. For example, money was borrowed by the government in anticipation of the Malt Tax in August 1697, at 8 per cent interest but with a one-third discount, making the true rate 10 per cent. In the event, the fund was not deficient, and all was paid out. But in the preceding spring there had been a major crisis: the deficiency on short-term tax funds was more than £5 million, and a government lottery organized to raise £1,400,000 was almost entirely unsubscribed. Investors like Lord Ashburnham *could* get their fingers burned – but, equally, could reap handsome profits, and the correspondence gives no indication that the Baron did otherwise.

The government's salvation was the establishment of the Bank of England in 1694, to arrange the easier passage of money: by 1700 discounting had vanished and interest rates had stabilized. For a man like Ashburnham with considerable sums in spare cash to invest, and with a willingness to take a chance, the reigns of William III and of Anne could mean substantial gains. The high rates of the mid 1690s could not be allowed to last without financial disaster ensuing – government borrowing was around 14 per cent for long-term loans, and 8 per cent for shorter – and the creation of institutions to cope with the problems and a surer foundation of the National Debt ensured that by the middle of the eighteenth century governments were able to borrow much more money and at around 4 per cent interest.

So, for instance, in May 1697 (in the wake of the financial crisis) Ashburnham wrote to his banker that he wanted £3000 worth of tallies on the Land Tax. "I had much rather have tallies at this time and for this sum than a mortgage. Though if one may not be had I would not go away unprovided of the other." Lord Ashburnham's lending to his fellow-landowners was considerable: but in collecting interest payments there were many more social niceties to be observed than in dealing with the Exchequer. John Briscoe owed three years interest on his mortgaged lands:

"I take the liberty to make you acquainted with it and to put you in mind of the great arrear of interest, by which I am a considerable loser, and have also disappointed others who expected to have money of me."

Running arguments with Briscoe, Lord Sherard, the Earl of Radnor, John Austen and others appear in Lord Ashburnham's letters, over the non-payment of interest, increases in interest rates, and threats to foreclose. At the end of 1696 (in a period when Ashburnham was especially busy in rearranging his investment portfolios) his attorney wrote to Robert Austen that if payment was not forthcoming within three weeks then Lord Ashburnham would "deliver and declare in ejectment to your tenants". Against this stick, Ashburnham offered the carrot of extending the mortgage at a higher interest rate so as not "to frighten your tenants or expose your good reputation as to your debt on the estate." In such circumstances Ashburnham could not afford to be too harsh, especially in dealing with more senior peers, such as the Earl of Radnor who proved particularly recalcitrant but in the end had to sell land to pay the debts.

All this financial business was highly lucrative for Lord Ashburnham – "greater profit and more danger". An index of his degree of success was the amount of money which passed through his bank account at Hoare's. In the early 1690s about £4000 a year was going through the account: but in the heady years 1697–1702 almost £100,000 passed through Hoare's hands, and a further £50,000 between 1702 and 1707.

Even with all this activity, it would be unwise to see the Baron as a *businessman*. He was first and foremost a landowner, able and eager to exploit his assets. He may have had a business mentality, weighing risks and taking chances on money-making ventures, but he was loath to involve himself too directly in merchant or productive activity. It is revealing that Ashburnham seems to have kept no centralized accounts nor to have drawn up a set of profit-and-loss returns.

He was a peer and landowner above all else, but within those social constraints he was a mover – of people, ideas, money. He cannot stand in comparison with the great merchants and industrialists of his day, men like Ambrose Crowley who was at one time interested in taking over the Ashburnham iron works to add to his ventures in the West Midlands and north east. But in comparison with other peers and landowners of the time he does appear to have been particularly adventurous, exercising such a close supervisory control over his many areas of interest. Hundreds of letters a year flew from his secretary's pen, giving a particularly clear view of his dealings, motives and character. He was careful of his wealth and equally careful of his prestige: "but one wig" (which had been sent in a delivery from London)

"being a Spanish bob is too airy and sparkish for one of my gravity and circumstances, and therefore I believe I shall seldom appear in it."

THE EARLDOM

The 1st Baron's heir, who had been so keenly schooled in his father's ways and views, enjoyed his title for only a few months: for both he and his wife died of smallpox in the summer of 1710, and his brother became 3rd Baron. The new lord kicked the traces, refusing to follow his father's and brother's Tory principles. He would give no support to the new Tory ministry:

"May my estate sink under ground, my tenants be ruined, my family perish and myself damned if ever I give you a vote."

An eccentric and a tight Whig he may have been, but the 3rd Baron was closer to his family's traditions than this outburst suggests. The 1st Baron had married Bridget Vaughan, the 2nd Baron's wife was Catharine Taylor who was a Bedfordshire heiress thereby adding substantially to the Ashburnham estate in that county. The 3rd Baron was to outdo them all, marrying three wealthy women and heiresses in succession. Mary Butler was daughter of the 2nd Duke of Ormonde, grand-daughter of the 1st Duke of Beaufort. His second wife was the dowager Countess of Anglesey, co-heiress to the 9th Earl of Derby, his third the daughter and co-heir of the Duke of Kent. By 1731 he had outlived all three, with only a son and a daughter to provide for. His daughter's failure to marry prevented any leakage of the Ashburnham wealth into another family on the make.

Furthermore, the 3rd Baron revived the family tradition of close Royal service: between 1728 and 1731 he was Lord of the Bedchamber to the Prince of Wales and in 1730 in recognition of his services he was created Earl of Ashburnham. In 1737 his thirteen-year-old son John succeeded him, who was to preside over the Ashburnham empire for the next seventy-five years, the second major force in constructing the family's aristocratic greatness.

THE 2ND EARL OF ASHBURNHAM

We cannot get as close to the 2nd Earl as we could to his grandfather, for although isolated pieces of evidence survive there is nothing approaching the revelations of a diary and continuous correspondence. Nevertheless, the aggressive, money-making edge was there, together with much keener political ambition.

From a young man the 2nd Earl was a close personal servant of the monarch. Between 1748 and 1762 he was a Lord of the Bedchamber, between 1765 and 1775 Master of the Great Wardrobe and then from 1775 to 1782 was First Lord of the Bedchamber and Groom of the Stole. His political sympathies were Whig, and he tried to use his influence, for example in the crisis over John Wilkes' disqualification. The courtiers who danced attendance on the monarch *did* have influence: the dozen or so peers in the Bedchamber were seen as a political barometer and were amongst the closest men to the King. And George II and George III were both monarchs keen to intervene and mould politics.

The Earl of Ashburnham crops up in the various great collections of letters of the eighteenth century: and many stories about him record with delight what he saw as affronts to his dignity. The greatest affront came in 1782 when George III would not give him the Knighthood of the Garter that he felt rightly to be his after such a lengthy Court career, especially since he had been promised one. So he resigned from the Bedchamber; in 1800 he wrote to George III asking to be raised to the rank of Marquess, but again was not rewarded.

Horace Walpole's verdict on the Earl of Ashburnham was typically barbed: "A most decent, reserved and servile courtier. He did not want sense, but it all centred in self-interest." Self-interest and family interest were clearly seen by the Earl as synonymous, and his main achievement in that area was his marriage in 1756 (at the age of thirty-one) to the wealthiest heiress of the age.

In 1706 Ambrose Crowley III had negotiated with the 1st Baron Ashburnham to take over his Sussex ironworks: but, as we know, nothing came of it. Crowley and his proposed partner Major John Hanbury of Pontypool had driven too hard a bargain, and eventually for a while the Ashburnhams ran their own ironworkings. (Hanbury however leased the charcoal rights in the Ashburnham Welsh estate.) But this was not the end of a possible working relationship, for in the 1730s the executors of the estate of John Crowley (Ambrose's heir) leased the Ashburnham furnace, and held the lease until well into the 1740s. The Crowley dynasty were iron *manufacturers*, and this was one of their very few ventures into direct *production* of iron.

The Crowley enterprise was enormous, the largest industrial undertaking of the age: it probably employed more than a thousand people in its manufacturing bases, principally in the north-east, and at its shipping base in Greenwich. John Crowley moved the family into the landed gentry with his marriage to Theodosia Gascoigne of Barking in Suffolk. His sons both died young, and so the Crowley empire was to be split between Theodosia (who was to outlive all her family) and their three surviving daughters. Mary married the Earl of Chesterfield's younger son, but died within the year; Theodosia, the next daughter, married Charles Boone. In 1756 the dumpy Elizabeth was still unmarried, aged 28; but within the year she was married to the 2nd Earl of Ashburnham.

The match gave the courtly world great scope for hilarity. Horace Walpole called him "the noble lord upon the wool sack"; while Lord Chesterfield wrote from Bath, "Lord Ashburnham is very soon to be married to the youngest Miss Crowley. At an average of fat and lean they will make only *embonpoint* together." Through the particulars of the marriage settlement we are able to watch an eighteenth century mating dance of the wealthy. On each side, searching enquiries were made into the size of their respective fortunes. The annual value of the Ashburnham estates was almost £6000 per annum. The Crowley's business assets were valued (in a meticulously detailed inventory) at £200,000 yielding between £6000 and £7000 annually. The marriage agreement provided for the Earl £20,000 in stocks and bonds plus the

In the first of Hogarth's engraved series of Marriage à la Mode, *suitor and heiress take a side seat as* The Marriage Settlement *is worked out. House and fortune clearly depend on the outcome.*

one-third share (and eventually a one-half share) in the Crowley business, and at his mother-in-law's death the Suffolk and Greenwich estates. All told, the popular belief that the marriage brought a fortune of £200,000 to the Earl seems justified: and to translate that sum into our values we would have to add a couple of noughts at least.

The Ashburnhams never exercised direct control over the Crowley part of their augmented industrial iron enterprise: in 1782 the Earl formed a business partnership with the manager of the iron business and his Boone brother-in-law and until the business collapsed in 1863 the Ashburnhams simply collected their earnings. This is in contrast to their other exploitative enterprises. The Ashburnham iron works – furnace and forge – continued working into the nineteenth century; and in the late eighteenth century the Sussex estate capitalized on its many acres of woodland, doubling its receipts from forestry between the 1760s and 1790s, and trebling them again (to over £6000 a year) in the wars with France before 1815.

The greatest developments took place in Carmarthenshire, on the coal resources of the Ashburnham estate. In the first half of the eighteenth century coal was mined at Pembrey on a small scale; as with many industrial enterprises of that period, the miners were only part-time, spending the rest of their time in farming. Coal was taken from adit

mines – workings dug horizontally into the hillside directly into the coal seam. The seams were soon exhausted and so new adits were dug. The western side of Pembrey mountain is riddled with the sites of old adit workings, some still capable of being entered. Coal boats were beached on the wide sandy stretch of Cefn Sidan and the Gwendraeth estuary, and the coal was brought down from the hills on packhorses. Then at high tide the loaded ships floated off and away into the Bristol Channel or over to Ireland.

Coal mining – part of the landed Ashburnham wealth into which Elizabeth Crowley married, and which the 2nd Earl did so much to develop.

The *ad hoc* arrangements early in the eighteenth century were soon made more regular: the coal workings were leased to a tenant, and mining expertise was hired in. But the Earl maintained a close supervision. A small group of surviving letters for 1769–70 shows the extent of Ashburnham involvement and the Earl's strategic control. The steward at Pembrey and the mining agent had fallen out; the agent left – leaving flooded mine workings behind him. The problems of transporting the coal were becoming acute – the packhorse system was slow and expensive – and the men on the spot argued for coal working to be transferred to the eastern side of Pembrey mountain. But the Earl had wider vision – the solution was a canal system to take the coal out to the ships. The Welsh were unwilling because their livelihood from the horse trade would go, and only in 1796 was the Earl able to secure the consent of sufficient of his tenants to have a canal constructed.

The obvious model for the canal was nearby Kymer's Canal, constructed for coal traffic between 1766 and 1768 and rapidly showing a profit. The two-mile long Ashburnham Canal was dug between 1796 and 1801, with a branch canal dug in 1805. The life of the canal was short, for by 1818 the coal stocks on the western side of Pembrey mountain were exhausted. But the capital expenditure had been amply justified. By the late eighteenth century the estate's interest was turning towards the possibilities of extracting coal from the eastern side of the mountain, but the technical problems were greater and the degree of enterprise more considerable. The entrance to the 'slant' mine at Penllwyn still stands, with derelict cottages around, in the middle of what is now a small wood. The 'slant' disappears into the ground at a sharp angle; an underground tramway would have brought the coal to the surface, and at the mine's nineteenth-century height 150 men worked there. Further down the mountain, towards the coast, the shaft for the mine at Pwll Stanley was sunk in 1805 (and closed only in 1925). Connecting the mines on the eastern side was a tramway, to take coal down to the estuary and, from 1819, to a specially constructed harbour.

But by that time the Ashburnham estate had suffered a blow from which arguably they failed to recover. In 1795 a partnership had been established for the coal workings, between the 2nd Earl and Henry Child: the Earl's one-quarter partnership was soon taken over by his agent Anthony Tatlow. The Earl was ageing rapidly, but refused to delegate responsibility: and, betraying the trust he placed in Child and Tatlow, the two men took the Earl for a very expensive ride. The Earl took all the risks, Child and Tatlow all the profits (less the rent they paid the Earl). A later legal opinion rehearsed the facts of the case.

"By Tatlow's accounts it appears that the lessees did not advance any capital whatever for the working of the colliery, not even for machinery or stock of any kind, but that it paid for its own expenses among which is charged £30 p.a. to Mr Child for agency. And on enquiry it is found that the lessees incurred no risk whatever, as the practice of the county was and is, to employ undertakers to raise, carry, sell and ship the coal at certain rates per way. Levels had been found and a canal had been made by the Earl, and whatever repairs or additions were afterwards made thereto were paid for out of the produce of the sales."

In 1808 Child had sold his share to Tatlow: together they had been making handsome profits. By the beginning of 1809 the 85-year-old Earl realised he was too frail to continue, and handed over the estate and the business operations to his son and heir George. The 2nd and 3rd Earls were rather like Queen Victoria and Bertie – the already middle-aged heir had been given no access to the family business affairs, and had had none of the estate experience that previous Ashburnham generations had had.

So the new man at the helm only had Tatlow's advice to go on: without demur he authorized his father's money to be used to buy new boats – the profit from which would go to Tatlow; Tatlow meanwhile had been bribing footmen to witness the declining Earl's signature on fraudulent leases. Finally in April 1812 both the old Earl and Anthony Tatlow died within days of each other, and the truth emerged. The mine workings had been systematically undervalued, to the Earl's detriment: Tatlow had been offered £10,000 by competitors merely to close the mines. He was active in new canal ventures which would further enhance his coal assets – assets held, by the fraudulent leases, at long term and low rent.

Thereafter, the Ashburnhams never involved themselves directly in coal production again. That cannot entirely be attributed to this unfortunate incident, for other coal-owning aristocrats at much the same time were removing themselves from active involvement – partly because of the growing technical complexity of the operation, partly from changing social attitudes. But the Tatlow affair was an awful warning.

Accordingly a sixty year lease was drawn up in 1816 for Thomas Gaunt of Middlesex, Charles Bonner of Lincolnshire, and George Bowser of Carmarthenshire, to follow upon the construction of a harbour. The harbour, built in 1819, soon became incapable of coping with the quantities of coal being shipped out, and in 1832 a new harbour, at Burry Port, was constructed. The Gaunt-Bowser partnership had, however, over-extended itself: even by the mid-1820s about £150,000 had been spent on harbour works, opening collieries and building the tramroads, and within ten years the partnership was in financial peril. They raised new funds, at high interest, and by 1840 were bankrupt. Mining ceased for three years, causing considerable local hardship: but a survey of the mines in 1842 declared them still to be a sound concern, likely to bring profits of £3000 a year. The search for a new tenant proved painful; eventually production started again, with tin works being added to the existing coal mines and iron works of the previous company. But already the Ashburnhams were mortgaging these properties heavily. Their industrial empire was crumbling.

THE 3RD AND 4TH EARLS

It was the 3rd Earl of Ashburnham who proclaimed himself to be close and retiring: his energies, and wealth, went into art collecting on a grand scale. The Ashburnhams may have been quiet, but they were also very rich; perhaps because they felt secure enough, the wealth-creating edge of the previous four or five generations seems to have been diminished. That edge had not been lost – farming profits in the Napoleonic Wars were reinvested, and in the 1840s the land at Greenwich was developed for housing – but the Ashburnhams were cruising. Bertram, 4th Earl of Ashburnham, who succeeded to the title in 1830 in his early 30s, was to rule family and estate as the archetypal Victorian *paterfamilias*, stern and rarely-bending. He had two great passions: books and order. His was one of the great libraries of early books and manuscripts, including the fabulous Stowe collection bought at the sale of the Duke of Buckingham's effects in 1849. Ashburnham Place, which had been extensively altered by the 3rd Earl, was rebuilt again by the 4th Earl partly so as to contain his extensive and valuable collections. From the ordered and catalogued world of the book room he tried to maintain an

At the centre of Turner's celebrated watercolour of The Vale of Ashburnham *stands the Place, re-edified by the 2nd Earl. Any resemblance to a rural arcadia is entirely intentional.*

85

ordered world outside, ruling his estates with a heavy hand and a deep-grained conservatism.

He attempted, at Ashburnham and at Barking in Suffolk, to re-create an ordered, deferential rural past. Emphasis was placed upon tradition rather than innovation, upon keeping a changing modern world at bay rather than trying to keep ahead. Clearly he believed he was being true to the traditions of his family – and clearly he was deluded, for the past he was conserving had never really existed. His correspondence about tenants was a far cry from that of the 1st Baron Ashburnham.

"I wish to have a good farmer it is true" he wrote to his steward in 1837, *"but I also wish to have in every farm, and more especially to near by the house, a person to whom I need not feel afraid to show a disposition to oblige."*

Later the same year, on a new tenancy of another farm, he made his views on deference clearer.

"As it is, it seems to me that Jenner, not only as offering more rent but as being a tenant's son ought to have the preference. But I would willingly know something of the young man's age and character. . . It would also be well to make the same observations to him respecting politics *that you did to Wickham. Observing that tho' I do not interfere with the politics of tenants whom I have found in possession of their farms, that I do consider myself* more *than* at liberty *and hardly less than* forward, *to give a preference to those who are of my way of thinking in such matters, and therefore with whom I am more likely to live on such terms as are becoming to our respective conditions."*

Jenner was reported to be willing to assent.

Ashburnham and Penhurst were very much "closed" parishes: not only were prospective tenants vetted for their political views, but charities were provided for the inhabitants, with little being required therefore in terms of formal poor relief; while the churches were controlled from Ashburnham Place (and dissenting congregations could not be established). In order to retain a healthy supply of farm labourers – and to stem the drift from the land – farmers with grown-up sons working the land were discouraged in favour of farmers needing to hire labour, and special accommodation was built for unmarried labourers, with a resident housekeeper. The great majority of estate houses and cottages date from the 4th Earl's years.

With the 80-year-old Earl's death in 1878 the sands of Ashburnham time were running out. The 3rd and 4th Earls, as in previous generations, had married within the aristocracy; the Ashburnhams had usually produced enough males for the next generation – but not too many. But there were to be no more aristocratic brides, and the 4th Earl produced too many sons – who proved to be not enough! Between them, his six sons produced one daughter for the next generation, with whom the Ashburnham name and line was to end.

The sons of the 4th Earl stand outside the rebuilt Ashburnham Place, the 5th and 6th Earls-to-be among them, blinking at a new and changing world.

THE LAST ASHBURNHAMS

The 5th Earl of Ashburnham had converted to Roman Catholicism in 1872, and devoted many years to the attempts to restore Carlos VII to the Spanish throne – which cost him considerable sums and earned him little more than Papal thanks and decorations – and almost as many years to disastrous investment schemes in Colorado, South Dakota, Mexico, South Africa and New South Wales. Soon after the time of his inheritance the Earl was still one of the top 200 landowners in England, with 14,000 acres in Sussex, 3400 acres in Suffolk, 5700 in Carmarthenshire and 1400 in Breconshire. The gross annual value of the whole estate was estimated at over £24,000.

But rapidly the assets were to go. The Greenwich housing development had been sold almost immediately, and by 1897 the Welsh estates were burdened with a mortgage debt of £87,600. In 1883 the Government were offered the whole of the 4th Earl's magnificent library for £160,000. The Treasury declined the offer, but the Stowe collection was purchased for £45,000, and many other manuscripts were purchased by the Italian Government for £23,000. The rest of the collection was sold at auction in 1897–8 for almost £100,000.

In 1888 the 5th Earl married Emily Chaplin: within a few days their son and heir was born, but two days later he died. Their only other child was Lady Catherine Ashburnham, born in 1890 and who, after her mother's death in 1900, spent many of her early years in convent

surroundings. In 1913 her father died the classic Edwardian death, in a Paris hotel bedroom, to be succeeded by his only surviving brother who had married and settled in Canada. With the childless 6th Earl's death in 1924, the Earldom was extinguished. Lady Catherine Ashburnham emerged from seclusion to inherit the estates – estates which were of necessity dwindling rapidly with the advent of death duties, the decline in land values and the loss of enterprise. The Welsh estate was sold as was the Suffolk, and Barking Hall was demolished: but Sussex, the ancestral heartland, was to be preserved – nothing was permitted to change, and the prospect of commercial exploitation and rehabilitation of the estate was disregarded. As she became more reclusive with age, and was in any event separated from the people of the estate by her Catholicism, so the Ashburnham territory atrophied.

In January 1953 she died, the last of the Ashburnhams: she was buried in the vault created by the Cavalier John Ashburnham, with its forty-five spaces. Her coffin occupied the forty-fifth and final space and the vault was bricked up.

The end of Ashburnham is somewhat bizarre, and after Lady Catherine Ashburnham's death the estate changed further still. When her distant cousin, descended from the 4th Earl through the female line, inherited,

Features of a great estate: ABOVE, the manor house of Penhurst, an integral part of the Ashburnham heartland for over 500 years, and OPPOSITE, cottages for those who worked on or for the estate. These are in the woods, above the furnace.

he was faced with massive death duties and an equally massive house. And this was 1953, right at the bottom of the market for great houses and their contents, when so many country properties were being closed up, sold up and pulled down. Only a small part of the huge mid-Victorian pile of Ashburnham Place remains today – a section of the front, the orangery and the stables – although the park (by Capability Brown, of course) is intact. From the rubble has arisen a Christian Centre for conferences and prayer, while the ancient estate, stripped back to its core by land sales, is more efficiently managed than ever.

Pictures, furnishings and the trappings of aristocracy have been dispersed. Such has been the fate of many great aristocratic estates this century, as taxation and social change have taken their toll. Noël Coward's words sound hollow now.

The last days of the old Ashburnham Place, shortly before the death of Lady Catherine, Ashburnham ancestors lining the walls of the hall, OPPOSITE. And, ABOVE LEFT, the new Place, a fragment of the old building kept as a frontispiece to the new. The iron gates, ABOVE RIGHT, surmounted by coronet and ash tree, now stand as abandoned as do the iron workings.

> *"The Stately Homes of England,*
> *See how they stand.*
> *To show the upper classes*
> *Still have the upper hand."*

Painstakingly built up over the centuries, the end of the old Ashburnham estate came within only seventy-five years. If the fate of the landed wealth has been shared by others in recent years, the question still remains of how far the history of the little-known Ashburnhams corresponds to that of other, and perhaps better-known, great landowning families. Both de Vere, with whom we began, and Ashburnham experienced a lengthy and somewhat erratic growth, a period of stability with great wealth, then rapid (and, it must be said, somewhat eccentric) decline.

Perhaps it is dangerous to take these as a model, although we are dealing with a very small group. There were almost exactly 1000 holders of peerage titles in eighteenth century England: de Vere accounts for one, and Ashburnham for four of them. The 1st Baron was certainly not one in a million. The important thing to remember about aristocracy is that three things have kept them afloat or pushed them under: financial chance, political chance and demographic chance.

Wealth, in land and other forms of capital, had always been the mark of the aristocrat. The rise to prominence of the Ashburnhams from the ranks of the gentry into the upper echelons of the peerage has been repeated many times, often with even more spectacular results. The steady rise of the Grosvenors was matched almost step-by-step by the Leveson-Gower family. In 1631 the minor Yorkshire baronet Sir Thomas Gower married Frances Leveson of that landed and mercantile Staffordshire family. Their union paved the way for one of the great industrial estates of the eighteenth and nineteenth centuries, accompanied by a rise in aristocratic status. The Leveson-Gowers gained a barony in 1703, an earldom in 1746, a marquisate in 1786 and a dukedom in 1833. That series of elevations was propelled by even greater fortune than the Ashburnhams in marriage and inheritance – inheritance from the Earl of Bath in 1711 and from the Duke of Albemarle in 1736; the marriage of the Earl Gower to the Countess of Sutherland, with her million acres of Scotland, in 1785, and the inheritance in 1803 (as a result of a marriage contracted fifty-five years previously) of the enormous industrial Bridgewater fortune. They rose from Yorkshire baronets to the leading Scottish dukedom in 200 years.

The Spencers had been a considerable Northamptonshire family in the sixteenth century, famous (or notorious) for their aggressive policies of enclosure and depopulation to run cattle and sheep. Their status was matched by a number of other local families, for instance the Treshams. As the Treshams failed, partly because of their adherence to Catholicism and implication in the Guy Fawkes plot, so the Spencers prospered. A Viscountcy in 1761 and Earldom in 1765 was their reward – but more for their close family links with the Churchill and Cavendish families than their agricultural acumen.

The great family of Cavendish is more unusual than most in having been founded by a woman, the redoubtable Bess of Hardwick. That case also illustrates the role of infertility and multiple marriages in assembling a great estate. Born in 1518, daughter of a Derbyshire squire, Elizabeth Hardwick married four times, to Robert Barley, Sir William Cavendish, Sir William St Loe and the Earl of Shrewsbury. Although she only had children by Cavendish, she retained control of the Barley and St Loe estates, conferring the bulk of them on her son. When she married Shrewsbury she insisted on their families being united, and their respective children intermarried. The survivor of that generation, with all the combined family wealth, rose rapidly in the peerage, as Baron Cavendish from 1605 and Earl of Devonshire from 1618. The Dukedom was created in 1694. Even earlier a grandson of Bess had obtained the ducal coronet in 1665, when William was created Duke of Newcastle, having been made Earl and Marquess previously. The Dukedom of Kingston, created in 1715, also sprang from her, with her daughter's marriage to Sir Henry Pierrepont.

Hers was an astonishing record, strange yet utterly familiar. For Bess displayed all the talents of a modern City financier, as mistress of the merger, takeover and asset-stripping. Perpetually on the lookout for a deal, she struck with devastating speed when the moment was right. She had all the grand gestures of the modern magnate too, and she succeeded in building her monument, her italicized tower Hardwick Hall, "more glass than wall".

So there was little unusual in the rise of the Ashburnhams. They had the right connections and did the right things, while the English peerage needed a constant injection of new people to keep it going. As important landowners made the step up – although by no means all did so – the elevation of politicians into the peerage was, and is, of equal importance. The political control exercised by the aristocracy was enormous. The Ashburnhams usually controlled the election of the Hastings M.P. In the second half of the eighteenth century, the Leveson-Gowers usually controlled six or eight of Staffordshire's ten Parliamentary seats. That degree of control was to be found all over England.

The consolidation of a family's position came in political guise and in economic form. In agricultural terms, aristocratic landowners were usually more concerned with rentals and effective administration than with innovation. But they could and did promote aggressive new ways. In the late sixteenth century, the Fiennes and the Spencers had promoted enclosure as vigorously as did the great eighteenth century landowners. At Wentworth Woodhouse in the mid-eighteenth century the Marquess of Rockingham had two experimental farms testing crop rotations, and contemporary landowners such as the 3rd Earl of Egremont at Petworth or the famous Earl of Leicester, "Coke of Norfolk", at Holkham indulged in grand experiments, model farms and improved administration. The results may not have been as spectacular as the claims, but the example was there.

The net effect of agricultural improvement on aristocratic fortunes was considerably less than that of industrial development. The coalowners amongst the eighteenth century peers included not only Ashburnham and Gower, but also Durham, Northumberland, Fitzwilliam, Rutland, Dudley, Mansel, Kingston and Grosvenor. In Lancashire, the Earl of Derby had coal and lead interests, invested in canals and turnpike roads, and owned an early cotton factory. Their North Wales lead mines brought the Grosvenors profits of £3000 a year; their Derbyshire mines brought the Cavendishes even more, and until 1800 development in South Wales was almost entirely in the hands of great landowners, many of them English.

While there were many peers who failed to maintain levels of income and splendour, posterity has tended to record the successful. And the wealth of the successful could be enormous. In 1692 the Bedford estate rentals were £15,000, in 1739 they were £37,000, and in 1771 £51,000. The rise and consolidation of aristocratic estates provided capital for industry and agriculture, the basis for change if not the direct impetus.

"The most lasting families have only their seasons. . . . They have their spring and summer-sunshine glare, their wane, decline and death. . ." Near Ampthill, the ruins of Houghton House stand as a reminder of how Ashburnham ousted Ailesbury – and how the Ashburnhams were to go in their turn.

Ashburnham experience in the eighteenth century was widely reproduced, with more efficient and professional estate management, changes in land tenure, and an interest in "improvement"; with promotion of industrial development, and alliances both financial and marital with industrial wealth; with political and Court activity, and the social round.

And as they rose, so they fell. In the sixteenth and seventeenth centuries political disgrace was as active an agent as demographic or financial disaster in bringing down peers. The crazy investments of the 5th Earl of Ashburnham were a pale shadow of those of the great Duke of Chandos who, as James Brydges and Paymaster-General, had made a fortune at Government's expense. He invested in Baroque splendours, in worthless mining ventures, unprofitable housing developments and mineral explorations, and what he himself called "a most ridiculous undertaking", pearl fishing off Anglesey. The South Sea Bubble claimed him as one of its many victims.

The input of new names and lines into the peerage was constant. Just as medieval peerages failed to survive, with the honourable exception of de Vere, so in later periods new boys always outnumbered the old. The figures have already been given once, but they bear repeating. In 1700 more than a third of the peerage titles had been created within the previous twenty years, and more than four fifths within the previous hundred. There were then 173 peers; in 1800 there were 267, of whom nearly a half had titles created since 1780, and again about four fifths since 1700. Well below ten per cent of those peerages, at either 1700 or 1800, were of more than two hundred years' longevity.

The contribution of the landowning aristocracy to England's economic and political development can hardly be underestimated. Whereas few dirtied their hands directly in commerce and industry, most soiled their fingers in political intrigue and control. Their agricultural and commercial importance was in facilitating change and in operating larger units. As full-scale industrialization got under way, however, they took increasingly a back seat – creating for themselves a myth of non-involvement (at least until the advent of theme parks and lion reserves in the stately homes of England).

It was that myth in which, in the period of their decline, the Ashburnhams indulged themselves. Without that close attention to money and industry, they faltered. In creating for themselves an erroneous view of what had been and should be allowed to continue, they perished.

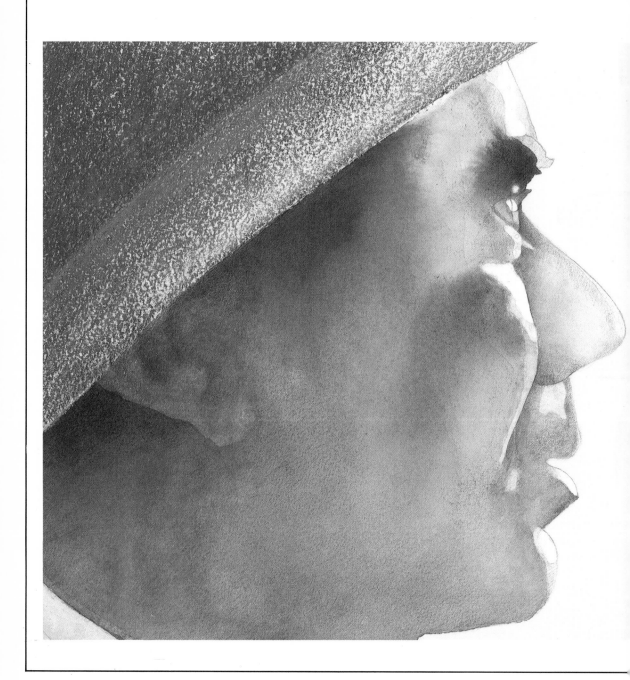

—4—
LAND AND LABOUR

"A time there was, ere England's griefs began,
When every rood of ground maintained its man;
For him light labour spread her wholesome store,
Just gave what life required, but gave no more:
His best companions, innocence and health;
And his best riches, ignorance of wealth."

That was the world which Goldsmith's *Deserted Village* had lost, his

"Sweet Auburn, loveliest village of the plain,
Where health and plenty cheered the labouring swain."

In England there had been a long process of smallholders being
squeezed out, as the holdings of larger farmers and landed estates grew.
But the "golden age" of a farming system of small, self-sufficient
producers had not properly existed in England's past. Wage labour in
agriculture had existed in medieval England, and grew until well into
the nineteenth century.

The problem for us is how to recapture the farm worker and his or her
world. Landowners, and often those who painted pictures for them,
tended to see the farm labourer as an element in the landscape. The late
Ashburnhams had tried to place a preservation order upon agricultural
labourers, without ever consulting the labourers themselves. Almost
every historical picture of farm labourers comes *from above* – whether it
be a picture of happy poverty or of ignorance and sloth, of the
forelock-tugging deferential worker or the slow and stupid yokel.
Richard Gough had much less to say about the poorer people who
crowded the rear portion of Myddle church, compared with those closer
in status to himself. Historians, for lack of more detailed information,
often view the labourer and pauper more as a statistic than a person. But
it is possible to see village life and labour from below, to see how all these
stereotypes and statistics matched up to reality.

QUAINTON

"There is a pleasure in recalling one's past years to recollection: in this I believe every bosom agrees and returns a ready echo of approbation, and I think a double gratification is witnessed as we turn to a repetition of our early days by writing them down on paper. . . . I was born July 13, 1793 at Helpstone, a gloomy village in Northamptonshire, on the brink of the Lincolnshire fens; my mother's maiden name was Stimson, a native of Caistor, a neighbouring village, whose father was a town shepherd as they are called, who has the care of all the flocks of the village. My father was one of fate's chancelings, who drop into the world without the honour of matrimony."

With these words the poet John Clare began his autobiography in 1821. Clare was to ascend from his farm labouring beginnings into public fame – and to descend into madness. His autobiography, even with its conscious literary air, is a rare phenomenon, the direct story of a man who came from and remained close to the lowest levels. Ten years before Clare's birth, in the neighbouring county of Buckinghamshire, another labourer's son came into the world.

"I, Joseph Mayett, was born in the parish of Quainton, in the Vale of Aylesbury in Buckinghamshire, of poor but I trust of honest and religious parents. My father had been the husband of one wife before my mother, and by both the father of ten children: but four was the most that ever was living at one time. I was the fourth child born – the second of mother – and was born on the twelfth day of March in the year 1783. . . My father was a labourer, and worked for six shillings per week in the winter, and nine in the summer, without any assistance from the parish till I was nine years of age."

The autobiography that Joseph Mayett left for posterity, written towards the end of his life, is a considerably less 'literary' work than Clare's (although not without its literary models). But as the record of a man who failed to escape from poverty and the labouring life, who received no acclaim and sought none, Joseph Mayett's life story is a rare direct view into the life of those who laboured on the land. Joseph Mayett will be a guide, his village of Quainton a setting, for investigating that world.

Mayett's Quainton was not much smaller than the present village, perched up on the side of the Vale of Aylesbury. In 1831 there were 1055 people besides Joseph Mayett in Quainton. The principal difference

between then and now is the hold of agriculture. 132 of the 207 families in the parish were engaged directly in agriculture – farming or labouring – and most of the rest were engaged in trades or services dependent upon the farming economy. Today, although Quainton is definitely not within Buckinghamshire's "gin and Jag" belt, some of the village inhabitants commute to London, and many work in Aylesbury, five miles away. Perhaps farming is less marginal an activity in village life in Quainton than in other villages, but the employment pattern has changed almost totally.

In 1831 there were 24 farmers in the parish who hired labour, and five who did not: to service those farms there were 117 agricultural labourers, about 5 workers for each farm. Today there are fewer than twenty full-time employees on Quainton's dozen or so farms. Mechanization, labour costs and higher wage rates elsewhere in the economy have produced the near eclipse of the employed farm worker. All told, hired farm workers in England numbered three-quarters of a million in 1831: Quainton's was about the average farm labour force size, although it and its surrounding villages were low in comparison with the rest of Buckinghamshire. But this hired agricultural labour force was further differentiated from that of today by its division into two kinds of worker – the labourer proper, married, living in his cottage, and the servant, single and living on the farm under a year's contract.

Farming past and present has moulded the appearance of Quainton, which has all the ingredients of a "real" village: church and chapel, village school and village hall, farmhouses and farmyards, manor house and almshouses, thatched cottage and a sprinkling of new dwellings, a windmill and a complement of pubs. (To complete the picture, there is even a steam railway, but that is outside our terms of reference.) The village is essentially linear, lying along the spring line with the hills

Quainton, (ABOVE, and pp. 100–105), has all the ingredients of a real village: church and almshouses, ABOVE, proud farmhouses, OVERLEAF, cottages and village green, FOLLOWING PAGES.

Denham Lodge Farm, LEFT, was the home of Sir Richard Winwood, who founded the almshouses of 1687, and a century or more later home of the Mr Cox who was a "friend of the Baptist cause" in Quainton.

Before and after: a dilapidated and poor row of cottages in 1906, RIGHT, has become a sparkling old farmhouse, OPPOSITE.

behind and the vale before it. Some of the farms are in the village itself – Cross Farm House at the head of the village green proclaims early eighteenth-century prosperity – while other farms stand in the surrounding countryside.

Animals – cows, sheep and also horses – are still the key to the local farming system, although they are perhaps losing the dominance that they have had in the past hundred years. In Joseph Mayett's time cows were important, but grain crops were also vital. Half of Quainton's farm land was still in open, common fields – part of the village had been enclosed early, in the sixteenth century, but the rest was enclosed very late, almost the latest in Buckinghamshire, and indeed in England.

So this was the village in which Joseph Mayett, labourer, was born, and in which in 1839 he died. With only this information to go on we might be tempted to see him as "Hodge", the archetypal village rustic rooted to the spot. It is true that Mayett spent most years of his life living and working in Quainton. But at certain times in his life – appropriate points in his *life-cycle* – Mayett was frequently mobile and for a while moved considerable distances. If it were not for his writings we would have had little idea of his existence except in 1831 as one of the 117 farm workers in Quainton, of the 16,743 in Buckinghamshire, of the 744,407 in England. He would be just another statistic: but here the statistic speaks.

He speaks for example of his childhood. As elsewhere through rural Bedfordshire, Buckinghamshire and Oxfordshire, Quainton families often supplemented their incomes through lace-making. Women and children worked long and hard at their bobbins in conditions which were later to be considered to be a national scandal. Joseph Mayett blamed his parents' need for the income he could provide from lace-making for the fact that he was put to work and "was deprived of a liberal

education". Using their children's labour was essential for these families: such was also John Clare's experience.

"Winter was generally my season of imprisonment in the dusty barn. Spring and summer my assistance was wanted elsewhere in tending sheep or horses in the fields or scaring birds from the grain or weeding it, which was a delightful employment, as the old women's memories never failed of tales to smoothen our labour, for as every day came new giants, hobgoblins and fairies was ready to pass it away."

Clare's father could read a little; but Clare was able for at least a part of each year until he was twelve to go to school, "first with an old woman in the village and latterly with a master at a distance from it". Both Mayett and Clare were able – as had generations of children before them – to learn to read, and Clare had gone a step up by learning to write.

For Joseph Mayett, as for others, learning to read could transport a child into a wider world of experience.

"My mother being able to read and write a little, though in some cases hardly legible, yet she taught me to read at a very early age. . . When I was four years of age or thereabouts my godmother presented me with a new book: it was the Reading Made Easy, *it had many pictures in it which I remember I was much delighted with. . . there was nothing so well suited so well as my book. . . My godmother soon*

The village green some sixty years ago, ABOVE, and today, OPPOSITE, is dominated by another of the great farmhouses, Cross Farm. The stump of the medieval wayside cross still stands, cottages in various states of repair ring the green, and the windmill is being restored, but the village pond has gone.

provided me a testament, but my mother not being able to read the first chapter of St Matthew's Gospel, I began at the second and read it through as well as she could teach me, and then I began it again and read through the four Gospels, and by this time I began to enquire into the meaning of that which I read..."

Young Joseph received some Sunday schooling – improving his reading but not learning to write – until the world of adult work beckoned.

SERVICE

To us, the word "servant" conjures up images of *Upstairs, Downstairs*, boot-boys and butlers, ladies' maids and tweenies. It was into service that Joseph Mayett went: but not to this kind. His fellow-servants were milkmaids and shepherds, ploughmen and carters, horsekeepers and cowkeepers: they were youths hired into employers' families. It was a very rare country child who stayed at home with his or her parents until marrying: children left home and lived with other families, frequently for ten years or so. They did not, however, stay with one family for all that time; instead they moved frequently, usually once a year, and they moved outside the immediate locality.

This service – "service in husbandry" – has been lost from our collective memory. But it is likely that almost two thirds of the English population in the age group 15 to 24 during the seventeenth and

eighteenth centuries were servants. Some of those were personal household servants, and quite a few were craft apprentices, but the great majority, men and women, worked on farms.

So in 1795, when he was barely twelve, Joseph Mayett left home for the first time. Two years later, in September 1797, he entered into a proper contract on his own account: before that he had probably gone to work and live where his parents could arrange for him to go – and probably his wages were sent home to them. They were near at hand, but he was out of their immediate control.

Why did service exist? Service had many functions, and it is impossible to rank clearly the importance of those functions. Evidently service could match surplus with deficit: families like the Mayetts had too many growing (and therefore expensive to keep) children to care for, and farms needed labour. However, the children of farmers – of yeomen and husbandmen – often went into service, taking over properties themselves when they left service, so this was not just an institution catering for the labouring poor. Service was training: as a child became older and stronger, so he or she could acquire and develop a variety of skills. Service was freedom: the young person was freed from parental control, and although living in somebody else's household was able – particularly on a property with a number of servants living together – to fraternize more easily with others of a similar age. The less savoury aspects of Mayett's character came out almost immediately with this freedom: he worked initially at the farm on which his father also worked.

"I was now out of the jurisdiction of my mother and not always with my father, and being in the company of those who practised swearing and all other ill habits. . . I soon learned to swear."

And the next year, on another farm,

"I was under no kind of restraint whatever, so that I gave up myself entirely to vice and folly, as far as my age and knowledge would admit."

Service could mean saving: servants were usually paid lump sums, which could be accumulated over the years to provide for a new household when they married. Service was a means of producing the quite high ages at marriage characteristic of pre-industrial England. Service allowed the young person to find out more, through moving from farm to farm, about the wider area in which he or she lived – and enlarged the pool of persons of the opposite sex amongst whom to choose and eventually to settle down with in marriage. Service might teach Joseph Mayett and his like to stand on their own two feet – and might, in times of economic hardship, protect them from insecurity of food and income.

Service was a social institution and a legal institution: lest it sound too good to be true, we should remember that it was administered by people who varied considerably in their kindness and patience – and who benefited from it as much as did those whom they employed. Should either side, and especially the farmers who employed servants, consistently lose advantage, then service could not be permitted to continue in existence. The contractual nature of servant hirings – undertaken, and often registered, in many parts of England at annual "hiring fairs" and "Statute Sessions" – could provide leverage for hirer and hired.

Take William Harvey, who was living in Quainton in 1757, twenty-five years before Joseph Mayett was born. He was a pauper, and was examined about his past. As an example of practice meeting theory, it is worth recounting at length.

". . . he hath lived as a hired servant at divers places, and that at Winslow Statute Fair which was on Thursday before Michaelmas [3½ years previously] he was hired to John Deverell of Swanbourne for a year. . . He entered on his said service a day or two after Michaelmas, and continued therein till within two or three days of the Michaelmas day following, when his master telling him he had not done his business as should be, asked him what he would abate of his wages. [Harvey] answered, One shilling, and thereupon his said master turned [him] out of his service, paying him his wages all but the said shilling."

This was significant, as we shall see, for his entitlements under the Poor Laws. But the story continues. William Harvey

"then lived for about half a year in service at Thornborough. On the Tuesday next

following Christmas week he was hired to Mr John Eeles of Quainton till the next Michaelmas, at £3.10s. wages, and served his said master all that time – except only one day, which was the fifth day after his hiring, when not liking his place, he absented himself from his master's service all that day. But at night his master received himself into his service again.

"*About a fortnight before the time of his hiring expired, he was hired to John Eeles again till the then next Michaelmas. He continued in his service till within about a fortnight of Christmas, when, being engaged in an* amour *he did not like, he quitted his master's service, without his master's knowledge and with intent never to return into it again. However, on the third day after, he returned to his master Eeles, and his master received him into his service again without any further agreement.*

"*He stayed with his master till 25 January, when his master's son having affronted him he went away a second time, and hired himself to James Tatham of Quainton, with whom he lived a fortnight only and then returned to Mr. Eeles again, offering to serve him the remnant of the year and agreeing to abate ten shillings of his wages for all the time he had been absent. . .*"

So William Harvey, who had been born in Addington, Buckinghamshire, was hired in various places as a servant: Addington is some six miles from Quainton, Winslow and Swanbourne about the same distance, and Thornborough a few miles further north. This was a fairly standard pattern of movement; it could be paralleled many times over in the course of two centuries, and is on only a slightly more restricted scale than the circuit within which Joseph Mayett moved as a servant.

William Harvey's testimony is unusually full: it is rare to learn of such details as an *amour* he did not like or the affront from his master's son. (The two may not have been unconnected, of course.) How much more revealing then is the detailed life story of Joseph Mayett, giving us information about himself, his moves and motives to set against the wider picture of service we can put together from less detailed sources.

Through his years as a servant, Joseph Mayett was hired twelve times. Almost all the hirings were for a year, made at Michaelmas (29 September). Service was an institution heavily guided by custom: most contracts ran from Michaelmas in the south and east, or from Martinmas (11 November) in the north, or in more pastoral economies from Mayday (1 May) or Lady Day (25 March). His first hiring was a short one, his first time away from home; the other non-Michaelmas hirings occurred because of some temporary problem, and they ran only to the following Michaelmas. Not only was the Michaelmas to Michaelmas pattern expected, but it was also likely to be difficult to find a farmer willing or needing to take on a servant at odd times of the year.

Except in the early years in Quainton, where hirings were made by word of mouth, Joseph Mayett usually went to a hiring fair to find a new position at Michaelmas. He does not describe these events to us: but in 1798 and 1799 he was hired at Aylesbury, in 1800 at Bicester, lining up with other potential servants to be hired, receiving their "earnest" sixpence or shilling from their new master to seal the bargain, and often taking the opportunity to break into the lump sum payment from the previous year's employment.

The process is described – albeit for Yorkshire and 150 years before – by the gentleman farmer Henry Best.

"In hiring of a servant, you are first to make sure that he be set at liberty, after that to inquire of him where he was born, in what services he hath been, with what labour he hath been most exercised, and whether he can do such and such things. And after that, to go to his master, or some neighbour of his that you are acquainted with, and tell them that you are about to hire such a servant and so know of them whether he have been true and trusty, if he be a gentle and quiet fellow, whether he be addicted to company-keeping or no, and lastly to know what wages he had the year before. . .
"When you are about to hire a servant, you are to call them aside and to talk privately with them concerning their wage. If the servants stand in a church yard, they usually call them aside and walk to the back side of the church, and there treat of their wage. . .
"When servants go to the sitting [Statute Sessions], they put on their best apparell, that their Masters may see them well clad. They get their breakfasts and so got to the sitting immediately, yet the towns are seldom called before 10 or 11 of the clock. Yet they will stay till it be almost dark afore they come home. . ."

And over 250 years later much the same Yorkshire scene is evoked in Fred Kitchen's autobiography *Brother to the Ox*:

"We would stand about in groups. . . until a farmer came along. After eyeing us over like so many oxen, he would say, 'Nah, my lads, any on yer seeking a place?' Being warmed up with good ale, we answered truculently, or offhandedly at least, that we 'didn't care a damn whether we got a place or not', and, 'What sort o' chap are yer wanting?'
"He would then say. . . and after singling out a man or boy that took his fancy would begin questioning him on his qualifications."

The hiring was a *real* labour market: master and man (or woman) were on a closer footing than they would be at any other time, sizing each other up, bargaining over a wage, making a mutually binding decision. In some regions these hiring fairs seem to have been rare or non-existent – servants found places by word of mouth or direct application – and often the hirings registered pre-existing agreements, but this does not detract from the wide and pervasive character of hiring.

Where was Joseph Mayett hired to work? His first three and a half years were spent close to hand in Quainton, but after that only short periods were spent as a servant in his home parish. He was hired to work in Wingrave, Ludgershall, Godington, Waddesdon Hill and Lenborough: Godington, the furthest of those places, over the border into Oxfordshire, was no more than nine miles from Quainton, and almost all these places are to the west and north of Quainton in an area defined by the ancient Akeman Street (now the more prosaic A41).

The nature of service was that it was upon an annual basis: but after the 16-year-old Mayett left Quainton to go to service elsewhere for the first time (*via* the Aylesbury hiring fair) he never served a full annual hiring again. On occasion that was his own fault: but also on occasion he was the innocent victim of circumstance, for Joseph Mayett was living through a period of great change in an institution which had probably always seemed immutable.

Throughout his life, he had an independent spirit: but that quickness of temper and an ability to fall out with those around him dogged Joseph Mayett. He tells, for example, of his fourth hiring. His master frequently came home drunk at night, and would beat Joseph when the boy was sent out to help him stagger home. After four such beatings in a week he resolved – egged on by his workmates – that this should stop.

"My mistress ordered me to go after him, but I told her I would not go unless she gave me sixpence – for I thought it was worth sixpence to have a hiding, and if he was determined to give it me I was determined she should pay for it. She called me a saucy fellow for this",

and told his master when he returned, who threatened to turn Mayett out on the spot.

"But I told him I would not go out naked, and laying hold of a working tool that was in the room, I swore if he touched me again I would beat his brains out – which I believe I should have done."

Joseph stormed off home: but his parents, who were both ill, and so possibly in need of the occasional money he could provide, persuaded him to return, and his master took him in again.

"But I lost my job of going after him, for my mistress never asked me to go anymore – nor never spoke to me no more for six weeks."

After a further uneventful year on a lonely farm in Quainton, Joseph was hired to live in at Wingrave – and lasted only three days.

"The master was like a madman. The first word in the morning was an oath, every morning while I was there – but that was not long, we all ran away together on Wednesday morn."

Immediately, Joseph found another, congenial place at Ludgershall: here, he was to experience the first of the religious dreams his autobiography recounts in such detail. The next year he must have believed the apocalypse was near: after only a month with Mr Thomas Tompkins of Godington, "a very odd man" (and a Roman Catholic), Mayett's master told him he

"should not suit him and paid me for my time and told me to take my clothes and go: but he never told me the reason nor he and I never disagreed."

Joseph had to go home, and get the only work he could which was organized by Quainton parish for 8d. a day.

"This was the first time that the cares of the world laid hold on me, and now I began to wonder what I should do: for bread was almost all that year – until near the next harvest – at 3s.8d. the ½-peck loaf and I worked for four shillings per week."

Food prices had never been so high as in the desperate winter of 1800–01, and poverty was acute. This was undoubtedly the reason Mayett had been asked to go – it was too expensive to feed a living-in servant, and much cheaper to employ casual labourers.

The farmer to whom the parish had sent Mayett took him on as a labourer: but Mayett wanted to live in, as a servant – that was his rightful expectation, even though times were hard.

"I was obliged to live chiefly on barley bread and hog peas. . . but it being winter, and provisions dear, and many servants out of place, I could not extricate myself from it. . . Now I began to be a little political."

Joseph's scheme was to go over to Oxfordshire on his free Sunday to enquire for a place – and back in Quainton the head cowman was to drop heavy hints. The master took the bait.

"He must hire me, or else he should lose me, for work was just coming at that time. So on Monday, when I was at plough, he came to me and said, 'Well, Joe, did you get hired yesterday?' I told him, 'No', to which he replied, 'If you wish to go to service, you may as well set yourself to me.' This was just what I wanted to hear."

That Michaelmas he moved away again. His temper in his "politically"-gained service had got the better of him on more than one occasion, and in one outburst he had broken the rib of the cow he was milking. (In remorse, he managed to repair the damage.)

In his next hiring, to a widowed woman farming at Waddesdon Hill, he was shamed when, for his liaison with a local girl, he was publicly denounced from the pulpit of the new Baptist chapel there; his mistress had reported him out of spite, but they were not to stay together much longer.

"The servant girl told [the mistress] that she heard me swear at one of the daughters, about eleven years of age, which I was not guilty of: for the words that I said to her, [were] 'Go to 'Enley upon Thames', but she stood me out of it to my face, that I bid her 'Go to hell and be damned'. Although the daughter came forward and declared what I did say, yet the mistress would not believe her. . .
"I only told them to provide themselves with another servant, for I would stay no longer, and away I came that very morning. . .She told me. . . she would blast my character so that I should not get a place within five miles, but this did not disturb me in the least for I knew better. But instead of my pitying her weakness, I was weak enough to laugh at it."

Standing defiantly with his back to the artist, the orderly in the Bucks. militia, OPPOSITE ABOVE, *might well have been the prickly Joseph Mayett himself, away during the Napoleonic Wars from a life of toil in a Buckinghamshire village economy, making lace as a child,* OPPOSITE BELOW LEFT, *and working in the fields thereafter,* BELOW RIGHT.

And the mistress *was* wrong: he got field work immediately, and a new hiring two months later.

Again, in the sultry heat of harvesting, his temper broke. A fellow servant picked a fight with him and, although it did not end in blows, *he would neither fight nor shake hands, at which I fell in a passion and said I would go for a soldier. But I did not think of going when I said so, but I set out up the hill and the rest of the people thought I had gone – but I only went to fetch my cows for milking."*

Joseph was hoist with his own petard: goaded by his master's thirteen-year-old son, he did go to enlist – but the recruiting party had already left. And in his next hiring, at Lenborough near Buckingham, his half-hearted resolve was made full-hearted.

Not for the first time a young man – Mayett was nearly twenty – was seduced by the uniforms and the music.

"Satan obtained his ends on the 12th of February. I enlisted for a soldier into the Royal Bucks. or King's Own Militia; and on the 4th of March 1803 I was sworn in at Wing, in the Hundred of Cottesloe."

His days as a servant were over. Still aggrieved at his past mistress interfering with his liaison with the girl at Waddesdon Hill, obstinate and obviously quick in temper, and bemused because service seemed to be crumbling under his feet, Joseph Mayett acted in haste – and repented at leisure. In 1815, when the Napoleonic Wars were finally over, Mayett was discharged, and came back to life on the land as a labourer.

Apart from its own intrinsic interest as a man's life story, this portion of Joseph Mayett's autobiography has an added dimension in that the institution of service, which seemed almost as natural a part of the farming economy as the annual harvest or the daily milking routine, was on the wane. Since the mid-eighteenth century England's population had begun to rise quite sharply: from just over five million in 1700 and 5¾ million by 1750, to over 8½ million by 1800 and, faster still, to 13¼ million by 1831.

A larger population placed greater pressure on wages, tending to force wage levels down. Whereas in 1700 there had been a relative shortage of farm labour, in 1800 there was a relative surplus, which grew even further as labour productivity gains were made in farming.

Consider the position of the farmer: he wanted to maximize labour use but minimize the cost. When wages were high and food prices low, as they were around 1700, then it made economic sense to keep farm servants. They lived in the farmer's house and ate cheaply at his table, in return for security on both sides and a lump sum payment. One commentator, in the very year 1700, concluded that "'tis better to have Work wanting for our Servants, than Servants for our Work". But a century later, the tables had been turned: high food prices and low wages were to make service relatively expensive, labourers who could be hired and fired at will that much cheaper. The seeds of destruction were being sown.

As many commentators noted – and as the rebuilding of farmhouses in many parts of the countryside testifies – the years of Mayett's life also witnessed changing attitudes of farmers towards their servants. Probably fewer farmers' children were going into service, and certainly there was a growing distaste for clodhopping farm servants eating at the farmer's table and sleeping in the farmer's house. Or, as a Suffolk correspondent to the Select Committee on the Poor Law put it in 1834, "Since farmers lived in parlours, labourers were no more found in kitchens."

It is the Poor Law which illustrates well the system of *mutual* rights and responsibilities of service. Under the terms of the 1697 Act of Settlement, the right to poor relief was governed by a pauper's place of settlement, the parish to which he or she legally "belonged", in terms of the Act. There were various ways in which such a settlement could be gained: and one of those was serving a year's contract as a servant. So a young person could leave home and serve for a full year in each of four places: until (and unless) a new settlement was obtained, the fourth parish was the place of legal settlement, the place to which the person would have recourse in times of necessity. In such circumstances, the pauper might have to return to his or her place of settlement, or money might be sent for relief. In return for providing labour, the servant acquired future rights: but only if the full letter of the law was obeyed. That was why William Harvey had been examined by the Quainton parish officers: where was he legally settled? Who would have to pay to maintain him? This system of settlement and relief would work well on a tit-for-tat basis. But as places within an area became more differentiated economically and so wanted servants in differing ways, and especially as the cost of poor relief rose dramatically in the latter years of the eighteenth century and first decades of the nineteenth, and rate-payers (as ever) resented the cost, that easy matching broke down.

Employers used a variety of expedients to refuse settlements to their servants: they hired for 51 weeks; they refused to pay the full amount owing; they terminated the contract before it expired. So they hoped to reduce the cost of poor relief – although often they were cutting off their nose to spite their face. At the same time that Joseph Mayett was being turned off without explanation in 1801, more explicit exclusion was taking place elsewhere. In Waddesdon, Quainton's neighbouring parish, the twenty "principal inhabitants" signed an agreement that "whoever shall hire any male servant so that he shall belong to Waddesdon and become chargeable to the said parish shall forfeit the sum of £20." And in the next county, Bedfordshire, farm tenants on Sir Gregory Page Turner's estates found that their renewed leases had a new clause forbidding them to hire servants by the year.

The relative cost of keeping servants, their diminishing social acceptability, and the perceived dangers to the working of the Poor Law produced an atmosphere of distrust which eventually – and in the south and east of England, rapidly – brought about the decline of service. Counties like Buckinghamshire were the first to witness the decline.

It is dangerous to assume that this experience was absolutely novel – that farm service was an institution which had always operated in much the same way and at much the same level, to be ripped apart by the changes of the early Victorian economy. The features may have persisted – but the level was by no means fixed. Over a long period the English population, and the prosperity of wage-earners, moved in long cycles of growth and retreat. There are many structural similarities between the early nineteenth century and the late sixteenth: high rates of population growth, rapidly falling real wages in agriculture, and low proportions of young adults in service. The late seventeenth century (and we might assume also, the fifteenth century) witnessed population stagnation, high real wages and a higher incidence of service. The difference is that between 1600 and 1700 the institution of service went through part of its cycle: but between 1800 and 1900 a new industrial economy broke that cycle for ever.

So it is that service has vanished from our collective consciousness. In pockets in the north and west of England it survived in some form into the 1950s, especially for specialist skills in dairying; but to all intents and his purposes it had long since gone.

MILITIA

The usual form of exit from service was to marry: but Joseph Mayett enlisted, as did many men in those years. After the frequent but short-distance mobility of his past ten years, the next twelve were to take him the length and breadth of England, and to Ireland. But in the end he came home again.

Mayett was in the militia – that is, he was not part of the "thin red line" in battle, but kept order at home and never fought in the Napoleonic Wars himself. That was not for lack of opportunity: but whenever the militia asked men to step forward to volunteer for the regular army, Joseph Mayett took a firm step back. He chafed under army discipline, for it was hard and he was rarely without a grievance – of a pay sergeant who was cheating him, or a surgeon who refused to come to treat him when he had smallpox, of the boredom of long periods guarding against an invasion threat which never materialized. Equally, he was proud of his little victories over authority – officers who abused him getting their come-uppance, acts of bravado when others were afraid, his ability to maintain a sober appearance and escape punishment even when drinking heavily. "This was done by policy for they knew not what I done in the dark."

The regiment was based in Kent, then Devon, and back to Sussex and Kent: his verdict on that time,

"We marched to Dover in Kent, where we stayed two years, six months and seven days"

was clearly heartfelt. At a time of civil unrest the militia was used to put down riots: Mayett did his job with no discernible interest or emotion. He was a soldier, obeying orders and quietly resenting authority.

"In the month of April we had an expeditious route to Chatham at the time that Sir Francis Burdett was sent to the Tower. . .
"In the beginning of February 1812 we got an expeditious route to Nottingham at the time of frame-breaking. . .
"On the first of May we got another expeditious route to Manchester, at the time they broke the Royal Exchange, and here we lay until the 27th of May; and then we marched to Kersel Moor camp, about three miles from Manchester. Here we lay under a very severe general. He was a tyrant if ever there was one. . . He ordered the regiment to go to Stockport to fire ball."

The militia went further north – to Newcastle and Northumberland, to Liverpool and to Ireland. In 1814 the regiment returned to England, but only a year later (and after much expectation) Mayett's militia days were over.

"I being the oldest soldier in the regiment, I was discharged on the 10th and arrived at Quainton at my father's house safe on the 13th of May 1815."

Joseph Mayett had just passed his thirty-second birthday. He was changed by his military experience. A friendly officer had helped him improve his writing. He had fought with his conscience – and usually lost: having found religion at one time, he lost it again with a vengeance. He had more money than he was ever to have again – and for one period became positively miserly. But,

"I lost my spirit of covetousness, and I'm sure I lost the worst torment I ever had in my life. For in all my straits in poverty I never was so miserable as I was in the love of money."

At one time, he had contemplated suicide; at another time he had contemplated marriage.

"We went to Cheshire, and there we lay sixteen days. Here I was on the point of marriage with a young woman that was with me at the captain's before he resigned. But the route came for us to march [north]. . . Having this long route nearly 200 miles prevented my marriage."

Perhaps if he had married this woman, he would have emerged from the militia to live somewhere completely different. But he had not married, and so gravitated back to Quainton.

MARRIAGE

"When thou art married, . . . live of thyself with thy wife, in a family of thine own", advised William Whateley, vicar of Banbury and author of *A Bride-Bush*. Like all good advice it was firmly based in experience. Marriage in seventeenth and eighteenth century England (and probably long before) had two abiding characteristics. Newly-married couples were expected to set up home on their own, not to live in extended families with their relations (by blood or by marriage); and those couples tended to marry late. On average individuals were in their mid to late twenties when they married, and few people married in their teens.

Independence was the key – an independent household, and an independent choice of marriage partner. These were ideals, ideals which varied according to the social group from which the partners came. For a labourer like Joseph Mayett, small savings and opportunity to rent a cottage could be the spur to marriage; for some whom we have seen in previous chapters, access to land and money may have weighed more heavily in the decision-making balance.

So Joseph Mayett and Sarah Slade, his bride of 18 December 1815, emerged from dependence – in his case the army, but in her case, as more commonly, service or apprenticeship – into the harsh light of independence. No clear picture emerges of Sarah Mayett from her husband's writings: she was sickly, and there were no children from the marriage. At a particularly disagreeable time, some of the people about him tried to persuade Mayett to run away, so it is quite possible that the marriage was not a happy one. Certainly, Joseph Mayett confided no particular thoughts about her, one way or another, to his autobiography. Sarah was doubtless part of the intended readership.

If the marriage did prove difficult, this should not be taken as an indication that couples in the past married for financial gain or without affection. In every source available, our common supposition that only modern marriages are made in heaven turns out to be false. (Even at the top of society, where dynastic and territorial considerations were often paramount, the assumption is false. The 2nd Earl of Ashburnham, courting Elizabeth Crowley and her £200,000, was nevertheless described in terms of love rather than avarice.)

Nor, on the other hand, was inclination given free play. Service was an institution which promoted a system of late marriage, keeping young people dependent for longer than otherwise might have been the case, providing a framework for controlled (if limited) saving, and holding the lid down on fertility. If a woman marries in her late twenties, about half of her child-bearing years have been lost. It is now clear that in the centuries before 1800 the course of English population change, and the boom and bust cycles the population went through, were particularly governed by changes in the age at which women married, and by how many remained spinsters, rather than by changes in patterns of death – whether it be the mortality of infants, the impact of disease or the lack of nutrition. After a period of population growth between the mid-sixteenth and the mid-seventeenth century, England experienced stagnation and slow population for another century. From the mid-eighteenth century population growth set in again, accelerated by such factors as the decline of the institution of service. If young people were no longer living-in on a dependent basis, what was to be gained by delaying marriage? By the early nineteenth century even in very rural areas teenage marriage was becoming quite common, whereas before it had been rare.

Rapid population growth had severe economic penalties – it helped produce the poverty and falling wages of men like Joseph Mayett, and had had very similar effects in the early seventeenth century. That cyclical pattern of English population growth was broken by sustained economic growth in the nineteenth century, and so demographic expansion did not force a return to the slow growth and stagnation of 150 years previously.

Marriage was a key element in pre-industrial life: not only did it usually mark the passage from dependence to independence, but variation in the timing and incidence of marriage were of the greatest importance in determining economic well-being (or not) on a wide scale.

LABOUR

Agriculture is a seasonal activity. Fields have to be ploughed, sown, weeded and harvested; cows have to calve and be milked, and sheep to lamb; fleeces have to be shorn, hay to be mown, grain to be threshed; the produce has to be sold. The different types of agriculture – arable, pastoral, mixed – have different work routines, rhythms and intensities, but all are governed by the seasons of the year. All these activities were part of the province of the farm labourer: and since he was at the mercy of the weather and, when labour was in over-supply, of the farmer's whim, the problem of seasonal unemployment could be acute.

It was to labour glut that Joseph Mayett returned in 1815: not only was there a rising population, but the end of the war brought returning soldiers back to the land, and brought an end to the prosperity for farmers from the abnormally high prices of the war years. Labourers were in a difficult position since their employers were able to depress their wages or increase their hours, or else lay them off, while the workers had little or no bargaining power. The fifteen years of labouring life that Joseph Mayett recorded for posterity show his health broken, but not his spirit.

Fresh from the militia,

"I was a strong man and in good health, and happened to get into a good place of work at the best price, so that everything went on very pleasant the whole of the summer."

But, at Michaelmas the farmer he was working for went out of business, and there was no work:

"So I set off to gather old rags and sell a few things, such as tapes, laces, thread and cotton etc., at which I done fairly well at first, and still enjoyed my liberty."

But the local peddling could not last: the high food prices of 1817 forced his custom to dry up and, in debt, Joseph was squeezed back into farm labour. Squeezed indeed: "I received seven shillings per week to maintain me and my wife, and bread was three shillings per loaf." The pattern of loss of work, depressed wages and high prices, then followed by relatively easier times – "After harvest, I met with a place of work at the squire's, at ten shillings per week, and the price of bread was sunk to two shillings per loaf" – was to recur many times.

In January 1818 the squire's bailiff reduced the wages of men like Mayett who had no children: so in March these men found work elsewhere. By October Mayett found himself a place at one of the large farms. By mid-1820 disagreements with the farmer over his wages came to a head, and Mayett moved on. He was employed through the winter, but was turned out with other men in March. After disputing with the parish, he found other work for a while, but was then forced into casual work. He was bringing home only six shillings a week, his wife was sick, rent and fuel cost 3s.2d., bread was priced at 2s.4d. a loaf. Moving to a cheaper house and finding new work saved them: he was lucky – and it is probably a mark of his worth as a worker – to find employment every time he was put out of work.

By 1823 he found himself with a Quainton farmer who had not employed him before: Joseph was expected to work on Sundays, and in summer to labour from 4 a.m. to 8 p.m., two hours longer than the other men on the farm, but for the same money. He stormed out – and found another place, for shorter hours and higher wages. Again, by January 1825 he was out of work and forced to take a poorly-paid job, milking on the squire's farm. In May he argued over wages and was sacked: for the next three years he held the inadequately-paid position of hayward of Quainton's remaining open field – so inadequate that by Spring 1828 he found that he would have been better off receiving assistance from the parish than continuing in work. Other work was available, but not always locally. That summer and the next he went over twenty miles away, into Hertfordshire, to work in the harvest. On each occasion he was taken ill: after the first illness he took to peddling again, selling yeast in the villages around Quainton until the following winter. Through the period until the next harvest he found casual labouring where he could: and, racked with pain from the severe chill he caught when away harvesting the second time, his health broke and he was off work for some months. His return to work brought on illness again, and his condition was declared incurable.

Joseph Mayett believed he was about to die, although a second medical opinion thought that with care he would survive. So Mayett's life story ends in 1830: he lived until 1839, and we do not know if he ever worked properly again.

In his most straitened circumstances, surviving on a few shillings a week, Joseph Mayett's army days – when shillings changed hands easily for drink, wagers or dares – must have seemed very remote. Were it not for his illnesses and his temper, Mayett's strength and skill should have given him a better chance in finding and keeping work than many others. In the early decades of the nineteenth century other workers were beginning to make gains in wages. Not so farm workers, whose absolute position changed little, and whose relative position sank. But if Joseph Mayett and his fellow-workers thought of moving to new jobs and new places, there is no sign. Some local people went over to America in the mid-1820s, and in 1834 Thomas, Joseph's surviving brother followed across the Atlantic, with financial assistance from the parish and "a firm promise that he will never return to England".

With Mayett we have the other side of rural labouring life from the forelock-tugging that the Ashburnhams tried to encourage on their estates. The farm worker is usually seen as a *deferential* worker, subscribing to the values of the farming society in which he lives and outwardly content with his lot. That view disguises considerable antagonism – on the Ashburnham estates as elsewhere in the early 1830s "Captain Swing" rode out, as labourers engaged in covert but sometimes violent action against their employers – burning hay ricks and occasionally barns and houses, sending anonymous letters and threats. The 4th Earl of Ashburnham, for instance, received an anonymous letter in 1840 that his tenants would be "happy to trample his face in the mire". Rarely did antagonism go as far as violence, but men like Mayett would instantly recognise the truth of the country saying overheard by Henry Best on his farms in the mid-seventeenth century:

> *"I can sow and I can mow and I can stack.*
> *And I can do my master too,*
> *When my master turns his back."*

Joseph Mayett did not always act behind his master's back – although his "political" schemes as a servant are a neat instance of that. Those dependent upon farmers and landlords might resent their treatment, but

Pyne.

London Pub. Feb.? 1, 1804 by Pyne & Nattes.

were often too cowed to remedy their situation. A pamphleteer of the 1650s criticised the labourer's lack of will –

"labouring poor men which in times of scarcity pine and murmur for want of bread, cursing the rich behind his back; and before his face, cap and knee and a whining countenance."

Given his straitened circumstances, Joseph Mayett was perhaps often too ready to make a fuss and stand upon his rights.

So it was in 1825.

"In the month of May the squire wanted to hire me for the summer, and bid 12s. per week. But I wanted thirteen. He said he would give me twelve, and that was the same he gave the rest of his men: but I said he had told me I was a good labourer and could get the best of wages – and then was my time to stick up for it, and if he would not give it I knew them that would. And if he had my labour he should pay for it, or else he should not have it. So he discharged me."

Deference, "cap and knee", and contentment with his lot, were not part of Mayett's character. He was a Nonconformist and in a dispute within the Baptist congregation to which he belonged, he displayed the anger of righteousness – "so I told him they did not mind offending God by punishing an innocent person so long as they did not offend a gentleman." And Mayett viewed with contempt the tracts which circulated in the early nineteenth century, often from the prolific pen of Hannah More, exhorting the poor to be content with their poverty and position in society.

Two views of those who worked on the land. Pyne, ABOVE, saw an upright and somewhat defiant figure locked into an explicit power relationship; Rowlandson's Dr Syntax OVERLEAF, saw happy poverty and rural sport.

In *The Shepherd of Salisbury Plain*, for example, the moral tone and didacticism come through loud and clear as the upright Mr Johnson meets the shepherd of the title.

"'You think then,' said the Gentleman, 'that a laborious life is a happy one?' 'I do, Sir, and more so especially as it exposes a man to fewer sins.'"

Joseph Mayett for one did not receive the message of happy poverty in the spirit with which it was intended, although he also extolled the virtues of the Sunday School.

"At this time there was a great many tracts come out, and their contents were chiefly to persuade poor people to be satisfied in their situation. . . and in fact there was little else to be heard from the pulpit or the press. And those kind of books were often put into my hands in a dictatorial way, in order to convince me of my errors. For instance, there was The Shepherd of Salisbury Plain, The Farmer's Fireside, *and* The Discontented Pendulum *and many others, which drew me almost into despair, for I could see their design."*

Joseph Mayett may have been down, but he was not out.

POVERTY

What governed Joseph Mayett's life in Quainton almost as much as the seasonal round in agriculture was the operation of the Poor Law. From the sixteenth century, the parish had become the "natural" unit of local administration as more duties, and especially Poor Law duties, were placed upon the unpaid short-tenured shoulders of the parish officers.

"The poor" are a very difficult group to recapture, because they were a constantly changing population: the Poor Law was a complex system of mutual rights and responsibilities designed to deal with that situation. If we take people like Mayett from an economically marginal group and follow them through their lives, we can see those shifts.

Even in economically favourable circumstances, the pattern in a family economy at the lower end of the social scale would be one of surplus alternating with deficit. A newly married couple might have savings or an inheritance, and possibly a dual income: but the addition of children to the family would tend to depress family wealth, as the mother became economically less productive and the young children's hungry months were a drain upon family resources. As the children grew, so some could contribute to the family economy through their labour, and by leaving home would mean fewer mouths to be fed. By the time the children had all left home the family economy would be in surplus again: but as the parents aged so their earning power would be reduced and they would be forced out of work, eventually to die.

So even in a world of ready employment there would be periods when life for the labouring family was easy, periods when it was hard. The Poor Law provided opportunity for relieving some of that hardship, by providing for families with too many small children or for the orphaned and illegitimate, and by making provision for the elderly and infirm unable to cope for themselves. Assistance might be in the form of occasional or regular maintenance, payment in money or in kind. Parish accounts show the extent of that help: a weekly dole for the aged and infirm, payment of their rents or a place in an alms-house, the purchase of clothing for children, the payment of doctors' bills, and payments for burial. Help was given out of charity and neighbourliness, and the patterns of organized poor relief were instituted to forestall the possibility of mass disaffection. The poor might be helped, but they were expected to be grateful.

Poor relief was therefore another aspect of the "nuclear family" – families did not take in poor relations, and were not expected to care for them without assistance. It was in this context that settlement legislation operated: through a variety of increasingly tightly-defined criteria everyone should have a place to which they "belonged", in which they were legally settled and to which they had recourse when in need. Since this was a mobile society, using birthplace as a criterion of "belonging" would have had little practical meaning: hence all the complicated apparatus for examining paupers on their past lives.

As there were those that received, there were those that gave. Parish assistance, from the seventeenth century and in some places from an earlier date, was usually paid for by parish rates (whereas previously those in need had been licensed to beg from their neighbours). The more prosperous members of the parish were expected to pay; the less prosperous were called upon to pay when they were able or when some greater economic disaster threatened. Administered by local unpaid

THE LIFE OF A LABOURER

CONTENT HAVING FOOD & RAIMENT

John Coulter Pauper two shillings weekly

BEGGARD BY MISGOVERNMENT AND RECEIVING ALMS OF THE PARISH

officials, principally the overseers of the poor, the system could be open to abuse: but there are as many cases of caring and efficient parish authorities as there are of flagrant mismanagement and abuse.

So "the poor" were by no means a monolithic group: even men and women who were once quite comfortably-off could require the attentions of the Poor Law in old age, and certainly some families shifted from giving to receiving poor relief in the event of a personal or more general calamity.

However this rather neat system could not always work smoothly: it was not designed to cater for widespread unemployment and difficulties of the able-bodied and adult. The Poor Laws themselves, of 1597 and 1601, were the general codification of local precedents and experiments in the face of widespread distress; and the seasonal unemployment, wage-cutting and economic difficulties from the 1780s placed enormous strains upon the system. A variety of expedients were adopted: in Quainton as elsewhere farmers were obliged to take a quota of labouring men, and the parish organized work on farms or on the roads. Elsewhere, men received family allowances, or subsidized supplements to their incomes. The cost was substantial: in the years 1816–20 over £7 million per annum, and at about the same level around 1830. The charges to Buckinghamshire were particularly heavy: in 1812 parishes spent on average 22s.9d. per head on poor relief, and 19s.1d. in 1821, compared with national averages in those years of 12s.9d. and 10s.6d. respectively.

Endemic low wages and underemployment in southern agricultural

An early nineteenth century engraved series illustrates the slippery slope of poverty and the Poor Law – the happy labourer pushed into degradation, and met by unfeeling authority.

(Inquire into your distress pho!! nonsense)

PETITIONS.

counties were the cause rather than the effect of a high-cost poor relief system: but this was not clear to the reformers who ousted the Old Poor Law in 1834, ignorant of the growing drift from the land.

"If therefore the allowance system did not find a surplus population it undubitably created it",

declared the Poor Law Report,

"and fixed it to the spot; for on the day the labourer (single or married) accepted parish allowance, he and his became serfs and rooted to the soil."

Mayett tells a different story. Paupers or those in difficulties as Mayett often was knew their rights: on more than one occasion Joseph Mayett demanded fair treatment, appealing to the magistrates (who oversaw the overseers) or confronting the parish overseers head on. Since these were also men who might employ him, he was brave.

In June 1829, for example, Mayett had one of his now-familiar confrontations with authority. He had been thrown out of work, and was forced to apply to the Overseer of the Poor for work organized by the parish.

"At this time there was many men out of work, and the old squire being the chief justice in this part of the country, he took upon himself to reduce every man's pay two shillings per week: and I was allowed only four shillings per week to maintain myself and my wife to pay rent and find fuel unless I could find work, and that I could not do for a constancy. So some of us went to the squire to make our complaint.

But he would not hear a word we had to say, but began to swear and abuse us; and I reproved him for swearing, and told him if he swore again I would make him pay for it. This enraged him to such a degree that, though he took care that he swore no more in my presence, yet he ordered the overseer not to relieve me nor find me a day's work so long as I could get four shillings per week. So when I got a day's work I lived on it until I got another."

There was also self-help. For many years Joseph Mayett had subscribed to a labourers' friendly society in Quainton, and when he was sick he was relieved by the "box". On occasion he received more from the "box" than he could either from labouring or from the parish: but the claims of too many members could place unacceptable strains on the friendly societies' finances. The final sentences in Mayett's autobiography are of his moral victory over those within the society who doubted the extent of his illness:

*"There were some who made their business to inform the club to which I belong that I had carried the bread and wine around [in Quainton's Baptist chapel] in which case they called their committee together to prove me an impostor on the box. But this they could not do without sending a medical to examine me, and [he] returned me in a very dangerous state; so they **could** do me no injury."*

RELIGION AND LITERACY

For us, the significant fact about Joseph Mayett is that a poor labourer with limited horizons and aspirations left for posterity a written autobiography. This book of carefully hand-ruled and written leaves, running to over 100 pages, for all its imperfect and possibly selective memory, shows us a man as he saw himself – rather than, as with almost all others of his class, as others saw them. For Joseph Mayett, the significant fact in writing his autobiography was religion. The book is, above all, the diary of a soul and tells of Joseph Mayett's constant lapses from grace and his wrestling with doctrine and conscience. Although brought up as Methodist, Mayett's family converted to Baptism which was, and remains, strong in rural Buckinghamshire. The late eighteenth-century chapel of which Mayett was an early member still stands at Waddesdon Hill; the successor to the chapel Joseph Mayett helped build in Quainton occupies the ground given to the congregation by a sympathetic gentleman farmer – the Mr Cox whom they did not wish to offend; the pond in which, according to local tradition at least, baptisms took place is still full, and green.

In Mayett's prose there are many echoes, conscious and unconscious, of the great religious adventure story, John Bunyan's *Pilgrim's Progress*. This was for generations the "book of books", with its opening words "As I walked through the wilderness of this world", its worldly traps – Hill Difficulty, Vanity Fair, Doubting Castle, Enchanted Ground – and its aristocratic enemies, "the Lord Carnal Delight, the Lord Luxurious, the Lord Desire of Vain Glory, my old Lord Lechery, Sir Having

Greedy, with all the rest of our nobility." Many like Mayett must have felt themselves to be pilgrims, constantly falling but being rescued by grace. As with *Pilgrim's Progress* itself, and the whole tradition of dissenting literature, this is nowhere better illustrated than in Joseph Mayett's dreams.

"I dreamed that I was in Aldbury in Hertfordshire"

where he had been taken ill at harvest work,

"and entered into a field of wheat which was very strong and green, and the corn in the ear at its full growth but not ripe. And as I stood and viewed it, I perceived a fire on the ground among the wheat, but no flame. I examined the field and found it all alight, and I thought I would stay and see the end of this sight. And as I stood viewing it I perceived a very great cloud of smoke ascend up from among the wheat, so that the sun was darkened with it; but after a little while the smoke vanished away, the sun shone again very bright, and the wheat appeared very ripe. The weeds that grew among the wheat and all the flag that was upon the straw was all consumed by the fire, but not the least stalk of wheat was injured."

God's refining fire would save Joseph despite his afflictions, and his deviations.

Dissent was a way of standing apart, of organizing life *within* the lower end of local society rather than merely bringing up the rear in the parish church. Dissenting congregations were usually not permitted in villages owned and controlled by one or two landowners. But in less "closed" places Dissent could grow, often (as with Methodism) encouraged by evangelical teaching. Primitive Methodism took hold in Myddle as Baptism did in Quainton: the congregations barely numbered dozens, but the fellowship was a powerful bond. The strength of that bond was often dependent on the members' economic well-being. When Joseph Mayett returned to Quainton in 1815 his religious experience – after a largely irreligious army life – was overwhelming.

"A good spirit of hearing prevailed among the inhabitants, so the house began to be too small for the congregation, and almost everyone was willing to contribute to the cause of the Redeemer. This delighted me much, for it was just what I had wished for. For a long time, Religion began to go in his silver slippers, and I fancied myself that it would be summer all the year, and when one Sabbath was over I was eager for the next."

But growing poverty forced even Mayett into a position in which he was unable to afford his contributions to the Church; and, ever able to quarrel, he fell out with each of his brothers in turn over the expense and the theology of the church.

That Mayett was able to write – when most around him could not – was the source of one such grievance. His brother, as deacon, paid for candles to light their chapel: Joseph replaced the candles when required, and perhaps foreseeing what was to come kept an itemized account. When only £8-worth of the £14 collected had been used, the deacons called for a new collection: Joseph's accounts proved that his brother had embezzled the remaining £6. Joseph's literacy drove a wedge between members of the congregation: Mr Cox, "the gentleman who supported the cause" in Quainton, and his brother at Waddesdon Hill had to intervene. The Coxes' conclusion was that

"money was a tempting thing, and oftentimes when it is deposited in the hands of poor people without any account being kept they might be tempted to make use of it at times, thinking to make it up again. But not being able to do it, they might be tempted to embezzle it from time to time until it became habitual to them, without any design to defraud in the first instance."

Thereafter, proper accounts were to be kept.

Should we be surprised that a poor Buckinghamshire labourer, long before the advent of compulsory schooling, was able to read and write, and write well enough to compose a lengthy autobiography?

We should not be surprised at his being able to read. Reading and writing skills were seen as separate, and were taught separately; and a minimal amount of teaching (although sometimes little more than child-minding) was often sufficient to acquire the rudiments of reading. The Devon woman who appeared in court in the 1670s, in a case over a disputed will, cannot have been alone when she declared that she "could not write, nor read but printed". There are three types of evidence to demonstrate, from the seventeenth century onwards, the wide spread of reading skills.

As reading was taught first, then a signature (as opposed to a mark) measures some half-way point in literacy skills. From 1754 all couples had to mark or sign the marriage register, providing a convenient general source of measurement; but before 1754 there were many documents which people from all social groups were required to sign, providing evidence to push the measurements back into the period around 1600.

Secondly, there is the evidence of the bulk of printed material published – without a market, that publication would not have taken place. Thirdly, men such as Joseph Mayett record for us their personal experience in acquiring literacy, reading and of course (given the nature of an autobiography or diary) writing.

The evidence of literacy from marriage registers suggests that in England in the 1750s about 40 per cent of men and 65 per cent of women were unable to sign their name. By 1840 about 35 per cent of men and 50 per cent of women could not sign, and by 1900 this had declined, for both sexes, to just a few percentage points. During the second half of the eighteenth century men's ability to sign their name hardly improved at all, although women were improving their ability throughout.

This of course disguises considerable social variation. Gentlemen and professional men were almost universally able to sign: and as the social scale was descended, so the extent of writing literacy declined. More than 80 per cent of farmers could usually sign their name – and fewer than 40 per cent of labourers. Bedfordshire and Buckinghamshire fell below this national average: Bedfordshire, the worst-ranked county in England for illiteracy, scored 45 per cent able to sign in 1839 compared with 67 per cent nationally. Pushing the picture further back in time produces estimates of male literacy in 1600 of 30 per cent, and female literacy of 10 per cent, and in 1700 of 45 per cent and 30 per cent respectively. In many rural areas of seventeenth century England, labourers were almost without exception unable to sign their name: labourers, and women from most social groups, were always at the bottom of the literacy pile. Joseph Mayett, and his wife Sarah, were therefore unusual.

But an inability to write did not preclude reading. The sheer volume of ephemeral literature published – little chapbooks, ballads and almanacs – testifies to the strength of a reading public, and a public which was reading above all for entertainment and edification.

Before entertainment, there had to be instruction. The *Reading made easy* which was Joseph Mayett's first book is but one instance. *Reading made easy* and *The only method to make reading easy* were published in the 1770s, and by 1839 the latter was in its 72nd edition. They spawned many pirated editions and near-copies: *Real reading made easy* (1782), *Reading made completely easy* (1792), and the Banbury-printed *Reading made most easy* which was probably the one available in Quainton.

Ballads, printed on single sheets and written to well-known tunes, were the first mass-circulation printed material. As their popularity waned in the later seventeenth century, so chapbooks and almanacs replaced them. Both were small books of few pages. Samuel Pepys, who collected these books as part of his great library at the end of the seventeenth century, divided chapbooks into *Penny Merriments*, *Penny Godlinesses*, and the slightly more substantial and expensive *Vulgaria* or *Pleasant Histories*. Almanacs contained astrological predictions, but came to resemble the diary or pocket book we would recognize.

It is impossible to know how many small books were published. But at the height of their popularity, from the 1660s to the 1680s, 400,000 almanacs were published a year – about one for every twelve people in the country. The stock of a London chapbook publisher of the 1660s, bound and unbound, was around 90,000 books: and this man was only one of many. And in the eighteenth century the trade was to grow considerably further.

Until well into the eighteenth century London totally dominated the small book trade. Ballads and books were written there, printed and published there – and were distributed by pedlars, by *chapmen* selling at fairs and markets or door-to-door. Books had not been amongst Mayett's wares when he became a pedlar – by that time shops, especially in Aylesbury, may have catered for a book-buying public. But little books were part of the general stock in trade of the itinerant seller, part of the widespread popular culture of the seventeenth and eighteenth centuries.

This reading matter was seized upon avidly. As a young boy John Clare read all that he could lay his hands on.

"About now all my stock of learning was gleaned from the 6d. romances of 'Cinderella', 'Little Red Riding Hood', 'Jack and the Bean Stalk', 'Zig Zag', 'Prince Cherry' etc. and great was the pleasure, pain or surprise increased by allowing them authenticity, for I firmly believed every page I read, and considered I possessed in these the chief learning and literature of the country."

Mayett and many others read Bunyan: 150 years before, Bunyan himself had come from a small-time farming background, and as a boy his own tastes had been distinctly secular.

". . . give me a ballad, a news book, 'George on Horseback' or 'Bevis of Southampton', give me some book that teaches curious arts, that tells of old fables; but for the Holy Scriptures, I cared not. And as it was with me then, so it is with my brethen now."

The chapbook stories of derring-do appear in religious guise in *Pilgrim's Progress* – and within a few years of publication the process came full circle, as the *Progress* itself began to be published in a highly abbreviated, chapbook form.

The evidence of the autobiographies shows the importance of reading in introducing men (and perhaps less often women) of a lowly status to a world well outside their own. Adventures were retailed in chapbooks; "polite" literature was available in cheaper form; Bibles could be studied, news and gossip was carried through ballads and news-sheets; traditional values were reinforced by printed godly books. In Mayett's day there was the tug-of-war between the tracts of Hannah More and her kind, and the political reformists spearheaded by William Cobbett: Mayett read both, and found them equally unacceptable.

Joseph Mayett stands in a firm and long tradition, of the 'puritan' critical self-examination of the individual's ability to withstand the shocks of life. In the seventeenth century that was the realm in particular of godly men, especially clergy. This included men like the Revd Ralph Josselin of Earl's Colne who prefaced his diary entries each week with "God has been good to me and mine" and then proceeded to itemize all the accidents, disasters and lapses of faith which had occurred during the preceeding seven days. But it also included young men like Josiah Langdale, another farm servant (although from a farming rather than a labouring background) around 1700. He and a labourer on his farm

"would often go on First Day Mornings into the Field, taking a Bible with us. . . . we have sat silent, waiting with Desires in our Hearts after the Lord."

The eighteenth century also saw a growing autobiographical tradition celebrating personal success in acquiring wealth or knowledge (rather than the religious struggle) written by self-made men such as William Hutton who progressed from being a poor apprentice clothworker to one of the leading lights in the political society of Birmingham. That trend

was to become more firmly entrenched in the nineteenth century with the full flowering of the working-class autobiography of *Bread, Knowledge and Freedom*, of self-knowledge and self-help.

Literacy was in very many cases won with considerable personal difficulty, or later in life than one might expect. Joseph Mayett only learned to write properly when he was in the militia, taught by a friendly officer: he first used his newly-acquired skill to write home for money, from the sale of some of his belongings, to enable him to pay off his debts. Writing, when he was ill, allowed him to express his anguish and resentment on paper, to relive the few moments of joy and the many blows, physical and psychological, he had received. But literacy did *not* extricate Joseph Mayett from the social group and the economic predicament in which he found himself, could not propel him towards higher earnings in industrial or service occupations. That may have been the result of a lack of personal ambition and of a failure to recognize opportunity elsewhere: for certainly the drift from the land was underway on a larger scale than ever before, and many who made the move were men like Joseph Mayett. We cannot know: this was an area in which he did not subject himself to self-examination, or self-justification.

Coalbrookdale at night, *de Loutherbourg's classic vision of the early Industrial Revolution. If Mayett and his companions felt the draw of an alternative working life, they neither articulated it nor responded to it.*

Even in the lowest social groups reading was a widespread skill in the eighteenth century; and although the ability to write was much less widespread, there were nevertheless poor, labouring people who could write – state their grievances, keep up a correspondence, draw up accounts, take up new occupations. The speed with which printed material was disseminated, even to distant areas, is further evidence of how much English villages fail to match up to the picture of isolation.

There is nothing else quite like Joseph Mayett's life history, written by a farm labourer, before his time. Since Mayett's autobiography is such a rare, and idiosyncratic, document it is difficult to assess how far he is able to stand as representative of his class and time. We can compare his account with other details about men like him, but writing his life-story places him on his own. On many occasions he stood on his dignity – and in economic terms was the loser. He may have stood alone, but he gives the lie to an unmixed picture of cringing deference and resignation on the farm labourer's part.

What makes Mayett especially interesting is his evocation of the period of intense change through which he was living. Age-old institutions which must have seemed immutable were changing or disappearing, while poverty in agricultural areas became more firmly entrenched. He was not to know that that had happened before, nor to have our benefit of hindsight to know that new trends, a new industrial world, were taking over and breaking England out of those old cycles.

We can understand Mayett: like most individuals he had little or no sense of wider economic trends, of spreading markets and intensifying industrial production. He was concerned for his next shilling and for the next prayer meeting. The statistic has spoken.

Goldsmith published his *Deserted Village* in 1770 as a rhapsody for an agricultural "Golden Age". The perfect happy community had been destroyed to make park and landscape "improvement" for an aggressive and uncaring landowner. Labourers and servants could suffer from the changed perceptions of those who partly or fully controlled their working lives, in "closed" parishes like Ashburnham and in more "open" places like Quainton.

Joseph Mayett has been both a general and particular guide to farm labouring and the position of the lowly in village life. His life story stands at a special point in the history of farm labour. For centuries, labour had grown as small proprietors were swallowed up by their larger neighbours, particularly in periods of economic crisis. Farming was still labour-intensive, and many changes in agriculture were achieved through more efficient labour strategies than through technological change. But the nineteenth century saw the gradual eclipse of the labourer, the twentieth century full-scale decline. The advent of machines and artificial fertilizers, and relative costs of labour, have produced an agricultural world in which hired labour is rare.

The view from below is rather different from that from above. And the

view of the world of above has not been that of received wisdom. Villages, stately homes, landlords and labourers have not matched the general expectations we outlined at the very beginning. There we saw that England before the Victorians was predominantly a rural world, but there was always an urban dimension, and as towns grew so did their contribution to society and to the countryside.

Employers and fellow-labourers of Joseph Mayett lie in the graveyard looking out over the fields and hills of the Vale of Aylesbury.

Pam Williams

─5─
MARKET AND TOWN

So far, we have been concerned with the world of the countryside, with villages and estates, with lords, farmers, labourers and rural industrial workers. Yet, at each turn there have been intimate links with towns: with Shrewsbury, Banbury, Kendal, Lavenham, Hastings, Aylesbury, and for all of our places, London.

The history of the English countryside is incomplete without the history of the town. If, as we have shown, villages were not isolated, "closed" communities, and regions were connected to each other to an extent we may find surprising, then that was achieved above all through towns.

The principal function of a town is centralization, at its most basic a weekly market allowing people from the surrounding countryside to sell surplus produce – and exchange news and gossip. A concentration of people also allows specialization to take place. A small village may only have been able to support a few craftsmen – a carpenter and a blacksmith, say; a larger village might have been capable of supporting more – a shoemaker, a tailor, a farrier in addition. But even small market centres could support a wider variety of craftsmen and artisans: blacksmiths, farriers, coppersmiths, tinsmiths, even silver- and goldsmiths; tailors, shoemakers, hatters, wigmakers; tanners, glovers, saddlers; and, increasingly, shopkeepers – grocers, apothecaries, booksellers. A village could support small alehouses (and often a surprising number of them), whereas a town would have inns, taverns, alehouses (and in the eighteenth century often gin-shops).

Sitting on top of the pile was London, always far and away the largest city in the land, and below the metropolis a hierarchy of towns: the large cities, Bristol, Norwich, York and Newcastle; county and regional centres, Exeter, Gloucester, Ipswich, Shrewsbury; and the variety of smaller towns. In the sixteenth century there were about 750 English markets, and over 850 by the end of the seventeenth century. In late seventeenth century Shropshire, for example, there were markets at Bishop's Castle, Bridgnorth, Church Stretton, Cleobury Mortimer, Market Drayton, Ellesmere, Hodnet, Ludlow, Newport, Oswestry, Shifnal, Wellington, Wem, Much Wenlock and Whitchurch. And in Suffolk, the market towns were Aldeburgh, Beccles, Bildeston, Blythburgh, Brandon, Botesdale, Bungay, Bury St Edmunds, Clare,

Debenham, Dunwich, Eye, Framlingham, Hadleigh, Halesworth, Haverhill, Ixworth, Lavenham, Lowestoft, Mendlesham, Mildenhall, Nayland, Needham Market, Newmarket, Orford, Saxmundham, Southwold, Stowmarket, Sudbury, Wickham Market and Woodbridge. It would be difficult today to classify some of these places as towns – especially Dunwich, which fell into the sea – and the variation in their size was considerable. Ipswich in the late seventeenth century had about 8000 inhabitants (which put it in the top ten places in England), Shrewsbury and Bury St Edmunds had around 6000, whereas the population of many of these market towns numbered fewer than 1000.

This hierarchy was by no means unchanging: some towns prospered, some small markets failed and other towns faltered. Birmingham, Liverpool and Manchester were small towns in the early seventeenth century, with a few thousand inhabitants, and were industrial and commercial giants of 70, 80, and 90,000 respectively two hundred years later. As a counter-example, Salisbury was one of England's largest towns in the sixteenth century (despite its population's fall through that century from 8000 to 6000); by 1801 it was still only 8800.

Towns and villages are therefore usually separated by their size: although some markets were villages only brought to life on a regular market day, most were more permanent residential centres. One essential feature of towns of any size was their inability to maintain their population size without continued injection of numbers from the surrounding countryside: death rates were usually higher than in the countryside, and higher than birth rates. Without immigration town populations would have fallen. When English population growth was high, as it was in the late sixteenth and eighteenth century, towns could siphon off part of the rural surplus; when population growth was low or non-existent, as it was in the late seventeenth century, then towns had to bite quite deeply into the population of the countryside.

Man cannot live by bread alone, and towns did not exist solely for their trading functions. Unlike the medieval and modern periods, considerable manufacturing activity took place in the countryside during the seventeenth and eighteenth centuries; but industry in towns remained important, particularly for the quality market. Laid upon the market and industrial activities of towns was their importance as travelling and social centres: the provision of inns and stabling, the residence of wealthy men and women, and providing entertainment for visitors. Domestic servants were more common, shops more prolific and better-stocked; promenades were walked, and "assemblies" assembled.

Town and country were closely linked: but the gulf between them seemed to grow. The country meant to Lord Ashburnham "Little but certain", the city "greater profit and more danger". Country people were yokels, townspeople sophisticates – or so the townspeople believed. And yet the country came to represent the repository of peace and stability, more natural values as opposed to the hurly-burly and artificiality of the town.

The growth of towns is therefore an important index of change in England. Only in the mid-nineteenth century did England become officially "urban", in the sense that a majority of the people lived in towns. Between the early sixteenth century and the early nineteenth, London grew from little more than 50,000 people to a million, from just over 2 per cent to 11 per cent of the national population (the proportion the capital had held throughout the eighteenth century). Until 1700 large-scale urban growth had been concentrated in London, but thereafter (although London continued to grow massively, nearly doubling between 1700 and 1800) the other urban areas began to take off. In 1670, 4 per cent of the English population lived in the larger towns. In 1700, after thirty years of general stagnation in numbers in England as a whole, that proportion had risen to 5½ per cent. During the period of fairly steady population increase between 1700 and 1750 the proportion grew to 9½ per cent. That is some indication of the degree to which towns were siphoning people out of rural areas: and there is evidence to suggest that a far higher proportion of those migrants from country to town were women than had been the case early in the seventeenth century, drawn into the service and retail occupations.

The nineteenth century "drift from the land" which the 4th Earl of Ashburnham tried to stem, and which placed Joseph Mayett and his kind in an increasingly isolated position, was no novel phenomenon. Bigger towns and urban immigration did not suddenly burst onto the scene with a new industrial age.

Changes in size, marketing, retailing, social life and aspirations marked English towns. And if there is one town exemplifying all these features, it is Bury St Edmunds, in West Suffolk.

BURY ST. EDMUNDS

"Giant Pedantry also will step in. . . and cheerfully apprise you, that this was a very great Abbey, owner and indeed creator of St Edmund's Town itself, that its lands were once a county of themselves, that the monks had so many carucates of land in this hundred, and so many in that, till human nature can stand no more of it. Another world it was, when these black ruins, white in their new mortar and fresh chiselling, first saw the sun as walls."

One of the greatest and wealthiest institutions of medieval England was the abbey of Bury St Edmunds, whose forlorn post-Dissolution ruins chilled Thomas Carlyle. The Saxon King Edmund was martyred in 869 by Viking invaders, and his shrine was one of the great English places of pilgrimage. Supplanting a straggling Anglo-Saxon settlement, the post-Conquest abbot, Baldwin, built a brave new town on a grid-iron of streets focusing on the abbey's great precincts. Just before Henry VIII's wholesale programme of dissolution, Bury St Edmunds was described by one of the earliest of English travel writers, John Leland:

"The sun never beheld a town in a finer situation, on such a gentle hill with a rivulet to the east, or a nobler abbey, whether in view of its endowments, extent or unparalleled magnificence. You would think the abbey was itself a town, so many

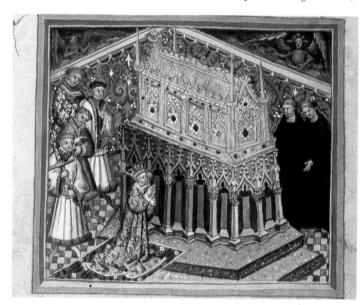

The lavish shrine of St Edmund, NEAR RIGHT, was sacked at the Dissolution. Little remains of the great Abbey but the ruins of the West Front (converted into houses in the sixteenth century), ABOVE RIGHT, and a few forlorn pillars, FAR RIGHT.

gates (some of them brass), so many towers, and a church exceeded in magnificence by none."

Little remains of that magnificence: the antagonism between abbey and town was centuries-old, and the townspeople willingly joined in the toppled tyrant's destruction.

Bury's medieval wealth had been built upon its ecclesiastical and administrative position, its market and its woollen industry. Lavenham, for instance, is only some ten miles south of Bury St Edmunds, and Bury was an important trading centre for cloths from its hinterland as well as a producer in its own right. Many of Bury's citizens were conspicuously wealthy before the near-simultaneous decline of the cloth industry and disappearance of the pilgrimage trade, and their wealth is reflected in the magnificent medieval buildings which remain, and the charitable foundations still bearing their names. Bury's medieval bones are still apparent.

The largest single feature in Abbot Baldwin's planned new town was the market place, a wide open space in the north-western corner of the walled area of the town. The present open market place is but a fraction of the original, which has been built onto and into in a lengthy process of market change.

A walk through the market place would take us through all the stages of that change. The process of increasingly sophisticated and extensive marketing of agricultural produce – grain, animals, butter and cheese, and more recently fruit and vegetables – has meant that at times the physical space itself was important, at other times unimportant except for providing for the most local needs.

The first important move away from the basic, classic face-to-face market was the building of houses or structures which encroached onto the market place, where more private dealings and longer-term storage could take place, often out of the watchful gaze of the abbey authorities and their market tolls. The oldest and longest surviving of these is now known as Moyses Hall, a substantial stone and flint house of the late twelfth century (repaired and restored in the nineteenth). The abbey's chronicler at the time that Moyses Hall was built showed the process of encroachment under way.

"We made complaint to the abbot in his court, saying that the turnover of all respectable towns and boroughs in England was increasing and growing to the benefit of their owners and the prosperity of their lords – all except this town, which pays its £40 and never the slightest increase. And we said the burgesses were to blame, for they had so many and such large encroachments in the market place, in the shape of shops and booths and stalls, with no agreement by the Abbey. . ."

The great angel roof of St Mary's church, OPPOSITE, was installed with the aid of Bury's great woollen mercantile wealth to mark the holding of Parliament in 1446. Despite its size and grandeur, this parish church could still have been fitted into the nave of the Abbey.

In the centuries which followed, it was pre-eminently dealers from and for the ever-growing London market who led change in marketing technique. At times of difficulty, when harvest supplies of grain were inadequate, local and non-local demand were in direct confrontation. In those circumstances, grain dealers and wholesalers were restricted in

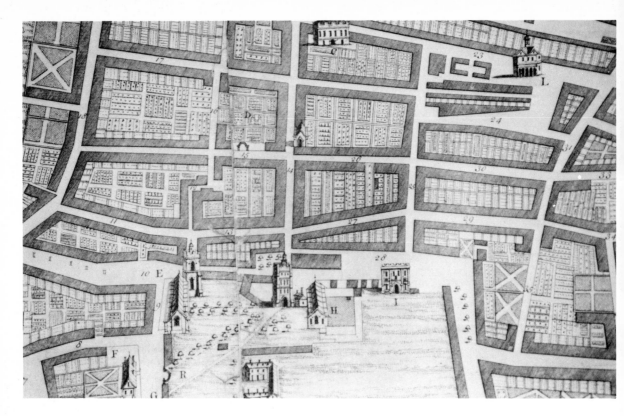

Bury's distinctive Norman gridiron street pattern is clear in Downing's map of 1740, ABOVE. Marked are the parish churches, E and H, the great gateway to the Abbey precincts, I, with the site of Bury Fair on Angel Hill, 28. The Earl of Bristol's town house stands at F, the Guildhall at C, and the pre-Adam market cross at L. All still survive: but not marked and still standing are the great Norman house in the Market Place, Moyses Hall, OPPOSITE, or the grandiose Cupola House.

their activity and local purchasers given protection: in the 1590s and 1620s, both decades of frequent difficulty of supply, the problems appear especially clearly. Marginal areas – the Lake Counties, for example – were hit hard, experiencing famine conditions. Corn was in short supply in most regions, and the demands of a large and potentially rebellious metropolitan population had to be weighed against those of the population in which the produce was actually grown. In such circumstance an unhappy compromise was reached, assisted by grain imports from northern Europe.

In Bury as in many other later sixteenth century towns, the erection of a covered market cross demonstrated the increasing dominance of larger corn-sellers and buyers, and the growing self-esteem of the town. Self-esteem was not quite enough, and in 1583 the town appealed to the villages around for assistance in paying towards its construction:

"Whereas there is now very lately builded in the market place in Bury a very fair large house for cornsellers repairing with their corn out of the country thither, wherein they may stand to their great ease very commodiously in the heat of summer, and also in the time of rainy and cold wet winter, which hitherto they could not do. . . the charge of the building of the said house is much greater than the inhabitants of the said town can well bear. . ."

In the disastrous town fire of 1608, in which 160 houses and 400 outhouses were destroyed, the market cross was burned down; altogether, damage was placed at £60,000, but town and cross were rebuilt.

One of a series of naive paintings of Bury dating from c.1700, this view of the Market Place has all the essential elements: the Cross in the centre with Cupola House to the right, inns with their signs all around and, encroaching into the market area, the butchers' shambles and new rows of shops.

So town and country were interdependent, but obviously the town put its own interests first, particularly through market regulations. These were restrictive, and intentionally so for the protection of the borough's own traders against those from outside. The town's bye-laws of 1607 itemize the rules. Bakers had to mark their loaves with their individual motif, and were to stand in the market in order of seniority; and only bakers were permitted to bake bread for sale. Sellers from outside were not permitted except within the market hours on the appointed days. Those hours were marked by the ringing of a bell.

"Item: that no foreigner [outsider] shall buy any barley in the market of this borough to be converted into malt before one of the clock in the afternoon on the market day nor after three of the clock. . ."

"Item: that no mealmonger [oatmeal-seller] shall put to sale any meal within the said borough but only upon three days in the week, viz Monday, Wednesday and Friday, and that none of them shall sell any meal upon any Monday between the 25th day of March and the 29th day of September after six of the clock in the afternoon, nor upon any Monday between the 29th day of September and the 25th day of March after four of the clock in the afternoon. And that no mealmongers shall upon any Wednesday or Friday put to sale any meal after the hour of eleven of the clock in the forenoon. . ."

Regulations such as these were an invitation to evasion, and more and more grain intended for the wider market was sold in private dealing. The market square in Bury was, and is, ringed with inns: here, as in other towns, buyers and sellers would strike deals, in rooms provided by the landlords, and sometimes using credit facilities also provided by the landlords. In those circumstances, the location was no longer significant:

roadside rather than town centre inns served as well, and were further from the vigilance of market regulators. In certain circumstances sales could take place at the farm gate, or of crops still standing in the fields – one means of farmers avoiding the risk of harvest failure – and certainly samples of grain rather than whole consignments could be brought to sell.

The process was described by Daniel Defoe, the economic journalist and novelist:

"The mentioning of these [corn] factors here naturally brings me to observe a new way of buying and selling of corn, as well as of malt, which is introduced by those factors; a practice greatly increased of late, though it is an unlawful way of dealing, and many ways prejudicial to the markets; and this is buying of corn by samples only. The case is thus: the farmer, who has perhaps twenty load of wheat in his barn, rubs out only a few handfuls of it with his hand, and puts it into a little money bag; and with this 'sample' as it is called in his pocket away he goes to market.
"When he comes thither, he stands with his little bag in his hand, at a particular place where such business is done, and thither the factors or buyers come also; the factor looks on the sample, asks his price, bids and then buys: and that not a sack or a load, but the whole quantity; and away they go together to the next inn, to adjust the bargain, the manner of delivery, the payment etc. Thus the whole barn, or stack, or mow of corn is sold at once; and not only so, but it is odds but the factor deals with him even after, by coming to his house; and so the farmer troubles the market no more."

The spread of these marketing processes was not immediate; but diffusing out from the Thames valley and Home Counties, closest to the London market, so these practices became more widespread.

Market developments were connected with changing specialization in agriculture. Rather than great strides being made in techniques and technology – whether it be seed drills or water meadows, new ploughs or even new crops – agricultural progress in the seventeenth and eighteenth centuries largely came through rationalization. Doing more of the same and so doing it better. With fast-growing numbers of people between 1560 and 1650 grain cultivation was a universal priority; static population and grain prices, growing urban demand and animal production in the century which followed promoted greater regional specialization. Lowland eastern England became more devoted to grain, pastoral areas to animals, both benefiting from what they could produce more efficiently.

This of itself necessitated greater inter-regional trade, of grain to pastoral areas, meat to grain areas, and of both to towns. As a measure of the impact of those changes, the marketable surplus in grain increased by a half between the end of the seventeenth and the middle of the eighteenth century. Supply difficulties in one area could be met from surpluses elsewhere, travelling overland by wagon, or by river and coastal craft.

Of course, this picture is too neat. Agriculture was mixed, and many

The mid-Victorian pomp of the second of Bury's Corn Exchanges, OVERLEAF, proclaims the bounties of a grain-growing heaven.

143

small farmers could only occasionally produce for the market. But small producers were on the whole being squeezed out, over the long run, and specialization undoubtedly increased. In times of difficulty local purchasers could step in and secure what they believed to be their rights: locally-produced grain sold at a fair price. Grain "riots" were frequently fairly orderly affairs, with consignments being taken over and sold by and to local people at a reasonable rather than the inflated price. Local authorities used their powers to restrict malting and thereby inhibit drink production – releasing more grain as food, and forestalling potential dissidence from inns and alehouses, "nurseries of naughtiness" as one magistrate called them.

The ever-greater scale of grain purchasing, and the increase in important purchasers' control of the market, promoted a return to the formal market place. The first Corn Exchange, a regulated and contained official market, opened in Mark Lane, London in the 1740s. Provincial towns followed suit. In Bury St Edmunds, the Market Cross had long been abandoned as an important selling place: it became a theatre in 1734, and in 1775 the old Cross was reclothed in elegant classical style to the designs of Robert Adam. Next to the Market Cross a Bury St Edmunds Corn Exchange was built in 1836. By that time the importance of Bury's Corn market stood out within the whole of East Anglia – so much so that twenty-five years later a new, larger and even grander Corn Exchange was built, by a London architect with London pretensions. Elsewhere, corn exchanges have been bypassed in their turn, and stand empty, or house roller-skating discos or shopping arcades. Bury's Exchange still thrives, the volume of its trade surpassing now the Mark Lane Exchange. True, there are no farmers left, and business is between dealers, but still their pockets contain samples, and still they buy and sell between the hours set by regulation and marked by a bell.

In a row in Bury St Edmunds stand the stages in the wider and larger-scale activity of corn-trading – the open area, the Market Cross, and two Corn Exchanges, ringed by the inns in which dealers and farmers would have done unregulated business. The 1861 Corn Exchange stands on the previous site of the beast market, which had to be moved outside the main market area. Buying and selling of animals follows a broadly similar development of concentration, although not at such a rapid rate. East Anglia was one of the destinations of the cattle drovers from the north and west, often to the great fairs for large-scale selling. The familiar weekly auction is something of a recent development, dating from the middle and end of the last century; previously, bargains were struck on an individual basis between buyer and seller. Other areas in Bury market place were reserved for other commodities, notably cheese and subsequently butter.

Suffolk cheese has long since ceased production – and little wonder, for it is reputed to have been hard-textured and foul-tasting. But until the more intensive production and the safer and cheaper carriage of

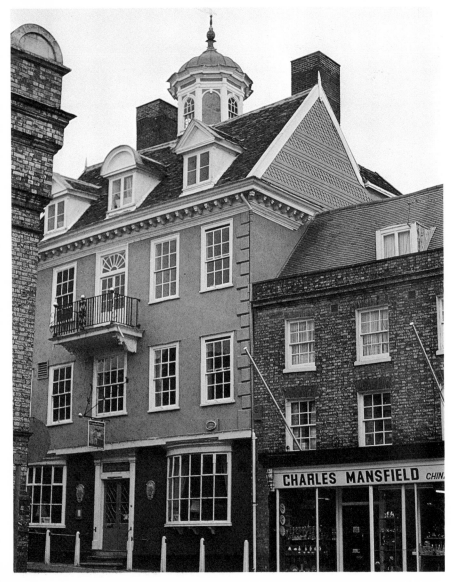

All the fun of the fair, LEFT, and the Assembly Rooms ABOVE, to which the quality retreated away from the crowds.

other cheeses, notably Cheddar and Cheshire, occurred Suffolk cheese with its keeping qualities, production fairly close to London, and naval victualling contracts was an important commodity. Important, that is, until London consumers were able to vote with their tastebuds.

Marketing, on specific days and for particular commodities, is but one aspect of the selling function of towns. Retailing in permanent shops is a subsequent development, but was present in Bury from the later Middle Ages. The rows of shops, forming two streets, which extend into the original market area stand on the site of the semi-permanent butcher's shambles, while the main route down towards the Abbey gate, until the last century known as Cooks' Row, was lined with shops in the seventeenth century if not earlier. One of the many travellers who visited Bury, Thomas Baskerville in the 1680s, reported it to be a "town full of rich shops and tradesmen, the streets spacious and the houses well built." Of course Celia Fiennes came, a few years later, and with her disdain for the old and rapture for the new found at least some things to admire.

"So to St Edmunds Bury. . . the towers and buildings look so compact and well together with the trees and gardens thick about it, the prospect was wonderfully pleasant. . . The Market Cross has a dial and lantern on the top, and there being another house pretty close to it, high built with such a tower and lantern also. With the two churches, towers and some other buildings pretty good made it appear nobly at a distance. This high house is an apothecary's, at least 60 steps up from the ground and gives a pleasing prospect of the whole town that is compact. Several streets but no good buildings except this, the rest are great old houses of timber and mostly in the old form of the country. . . This house is the new mode of building. . .
"There are a great deal of gentry which lives in the town, though there are no good houses but what are old rambling ones. . . It's a very dear place: so much company living in the town makes provision scarce and dear. However, it's a good excuse to raise the reckoning on strangers."

So Bury St Edmunds had markets, inns for traders and travellers, and shops. Although its river transport was not especially good, the river Lark was navigable to Ely, and small cargoes could transfer into the Ouse river system or onto roads to Thetford and Norwich. Roads led to Newmarket and hence to London, while the Stour valley some ten to fifteen miles south gave river access out to Ipswich. By 1637 there was a London carrier service; Bury's first newspaper was started in the 1730s, and a London coach service followed.

What made Bury so attractive?

Bury Fair was an annual commercial and social extravaganza, in England second only to the great Stourbridge Fair held just outside Cambridge, itself one of the premier commercial gatherings in the whole of Europe. Thomas Shadwell's Restoration comedy has had few performances since 1689 when it appeared, but *Bury Fair* captures the essence of the event: sellers and stallholders coming from far away with a great range of goods and wares, the gentry and aristocracy gathering together for a bright social whirl, the townspeople cramming the visitors into their houses and charging handsomely for the privilege.

The Bury Fair of the seventeenth and eighteenth centuries was held around Michaelmas: it was the survivor of a sequence of three or four fairs held in spring and autumn, principally for the sale of cloth and leather. Until the middle of the eighteenth century, fairs were an important focus for itinerant retailers and for large-scale sales of cheese, horses, sheep and cattle: they were the substitute for permanent shops as well as the resort of wholesalers. The 1st Baron Ashburnham, for instance, carefully noted all the fairs held within reach of his Sussex estate of which there were at least thirty, plus the great London and Norwich cattle fairs. Chapmen and pedlars bought and sold at fairs, the staging posts of their long-distance routes.

Vestiges of these great fairs survive, as fun-fairs: the streets throughout the centre of Abingdon, Oxfordshire are filled for a week every year by the substantial remnants of its Michaelmas Fair, and the attractions of Nottingham's Goose Fair remain. Other fairs have long since perished. The great Dorset fair of Woodbury Hill was held on an open site near Bere Regis which is now just fields, and Bury Fair itself closed down in 1871, its social and commercial attractions exhausted.

In the preceding centuries Bury Fair had been quite otherwise.

"I returned north-west. . . to visit St Edmund's Bury, a town of which other writers have talked very largely, and perhaps a little too much. It is a town famed for its pleasant situation and wholesome air, the Montpelier of Suffolk, and perhaps of England. . . it is crowded with nobility and gentry, and all sorts of the most agreeable company; and as the company invites, so there is the appearance of pleasure upon the very situation; and they that live at Bury, are supposed to live there for the sake of it."

Daniel Defoe was another of the travel writers who came to Bury to watch and admire.

"That the ladies round the country appear mighty gay and agreeable at the time of the fair in this town, I acknowledge; one hardly sees such a show in any part of the world; but to suggest they come hither as to a market, is so coarse a jest that the gentlemen that wait on them hither (for they rarely come but in good company) ought to resent and correct him for it.
"It is true Bury Fair, like Bartholomew Fair, is a fair for diversion, more than for trade; and it may be a fair for toys and trinkets, which the ladies may think fit to lay out some of their money in, as they see occasion. But to judge from thence, that the knights' daughters of Norfolk, Cambridgeshire and Suffolk come hither to be picked up is a way of speaking I never before heard. . ."

The open space in front of the abbey ruins, the surrounding streets, were thronged with people and stalls at fair time. Shopkeepers from London and other fashionable places such as Bath set up in Bury for a week or two, renting rooms from local shopkeepers.

151

"To the Ladies: Ward, hairdresser, from Jermyn Street, St James', London is come to Cook Row, Bury during the Fair, and begs leave to inform the nobility and gentry that he has just received the most approved head-dresses and fashions from Paris. . ."

declares one of the many advertisements in the local newspaper. Another eighteenth century visitor observed,

"This Fair consists chiefly of several rows of haberdashers, milliners, mercers, jewellers, silversmiths and toy shops, which make a fine show."

He also described the Fair as

"The Rendezvous *of the* Beau Monde *every afternoon, who conclude their Evenings by the Plays or Assemblies."*

Polite society, attracted to Bury Fair by the town's gentility (and its proximity to the races at Newmarket) felt itself unable to mix with the hurly-burly of the Fair, and the social round was conducted in select, private establishments with only occasional forays to make purchases, to mingle with the common sort, or to promenade in the Abbey Gardens.

Local magnates, such as the Earl of Bristol at nearby Ickworth, had their own town houses in Bury, principally for use at Fair time; and houses around the main area of the Fair were used for private, and increasingly institutionalized "assemblies". The main Assembly Rooms were first built, from a house previously used for private assemblies, in the opening years of the eighteenth century; their successors still stand, with their Adam-style interior decoration of the 1780s. Here public breakfasts were held, together with balls and assemblies, card parties and tea parties, supervised by "marshalls" and "officers" drawn from amongst the local nobles and notables, who included the Duke of Grafton and Lord Cornwallis, as well as the Earl of Bristol.

Touring theatre companies performed at Fair time, in the old and then the new Market Cross; finally in 1819 a new playhouse was opened, the Theatre Royal (recently restored to its Regency elegance). But by the early nineteenth century the glittering social set had deserted Bury Fair: the assemblies were no longer so exclusive; the range of goods and services provided every day in Bury matched those of the Fair, and Bury Fair, once synonymous with gentility and society, was to become noted more for lewdness and cheap entertainment. A jaundiced description of 1847 shows the decline.

"Now a dropsical Mayor, followed by four scarecrows in blue and yellow liveries and preceded by a tame lunatic with a bell, informs the four corners of the town of the opening of the Carnival."

The Home Secretary, as guardian of public morals, finally closed the fair down in 1871.

Even today, Bury St Edmunds has a conspicuous air of Georgian gentility, eighteenth and early nineteenth century façades mixed with a few earlier survivals (and a variety of later structures of widely varying quality). Bury's Georgian appearance is often only skindeep, new fronts placed on older properties. But despite the elegance, Bury St Edmunds has always had to work for its living: as market centre, as retail centre, as purveyor of services to the pilgrim and the gentry, as manufacturer.

Modern Bury St Edmunds, like the old is dominated by towers: but these are the great storage facilities for sugar, from East Anglian beet, and the chimneys of the Greene King brewery complex. Bury continues to fulfil its ancient functions: as a focus for the distribution and processing of the agricultural production of the surrounding countryside, as a centre for shopping, and as a haven for genteel society. Or as Defoe described it in 1724:

"But the beauty of this town consists in the number of gentry who dwell in and near it, the polite conversation among them; the affluence and plenty they live in; the sweet air they breathe in, and the pleasant country they have to go abroad in."

Bury St Edmunds' history is distinctive, but the town shares in trends typical of country towns. The late sixteenth and early seventeenth centuries were difficult times for most urban centres, which experienced some growth but not always of the type they wanted. Instead they became the destination for poor migrants from the surrounding countryside, and often for towns in the south and east of England from the more disadvantaged north and west. It is indicative of the difficulties which town authorities faced that the very first bye-law in the town's new set of regulations in 1607 is "An order to avoid idleness and to relieve the poor". Poverty in towns when harvests were deficient could be acute: a report of that date to Westminster recorded that at Bury

"four millers at the least weekly brought every day in the week three or four horseloads of meal of rye and barley, to the great relief and comfort of the poorest sort of people, who being very many in number, can buy meal of them by the penny and twopence, and employ part to bread, part to make a pudding for the relief of them and their children."

Sixty or seventy years later, there were fewer outcries against immigrants, for they were less likely to be poor and needy, more likely to enter productive jobs, particularly service occupations. Items which had been unknown or London luxuries were more widely available: Bury shopkeepers advertised "Warwick and Cottenham cheese", "colours for house-painters as cheap as at London", "all sorts of school books, books of devotion, history and law", "fenugreek powdered at 8d. a pound, fenugreek whole at 6d. a pound", and "Dr Stephen's acquamirabilis".

The rebuilding of towns in new materials and styles is a notable feature from the 1660s on, with brick and tile squares and terraces, promenades and carriageways: compare most towns of any success with Lavenham, fossilized because it was too poor and insignificant to be rebuilt and recased. The social season was emulated in quite small towns, with their assemblies and clubs.

The pattern we have seen is one of some small market centres reverting to village status, and the survivors more intimately connected by longer-range marketing, to the great provincial centres and to London. Market towns tended to achieve slow and steady population growth: they were bypassed considerably by other towns, heralds of a new commercial and industrial order, the major port and dockyard towns and the new great manufacturing centres. Between 1520 and 1600, the English population grew by 70 per cent, whereas London was the only established town to exceed that rate. Between 1600 and 1700 the national population grew by one quarter, a rate exceeded by all types of town and city. Between 1700 and 1750, and 1750 and 1800, the population grew by 14 per cent and 50 per cent respectively. That was broadly similar to London's growth rate and for the first half of the eighteenth century to some of the 'historic' regional centres, but it was eclipsed by the growth of ports like Hull, Bristol, and Liverpool, and especially by the 'new' manufacturing towns, Birmingham, Manchester, Leeds and Sheffield.

Towns like Bury were by no means stagnant, and were indeed quite affluent: but they were far outstripped by competitors. In the mid and late seventeenth century Bury was one of the top twenty or so English provincial towns, at least in terms of size – by 1800 it was way down the league table. But even by 1800 the gap between numbers 1 and 2 at the top of the table was immense. From the mid-seventeenth century London was never less than a *hundred* times the size of Bury St Edmunds, and from the mid-sixteenth century until well into the nineteenth never less than *ten* times larger than its nearest rival.

London was not just a city, it was a phenomenon.

THE METROPOLIS

Around 1670 Ned, a Somerset yokel from the Vale of Taunton, visited London.

"Than goin on, London zity zdid view:
And when zdid zeet, schoor aready to spew.
Whaat with the neezz and what with the zmoake,
Twas death in my ears, and schoor aready to choake.
And how all the coaches did vly up and down.
Iz thought the whoale world waz here in this town."

The country bumpkin coming to town is one of the most enduring jokes: against the slowness and simplicity of country life stands the haste and hurly-burly of the city. A rather more sophisticated Scotsman, James Boswell, captured the complexity of the metropolis.

"I have often amused myself with thinking how different a place London is to different people. They, whose narrow minds are contracted to the consideration of some one particular pursuit, view it only through that medium. A politician thinks of it merely as the seat of government in its different departments; a grazier, as a vast market for cattle; a mercantile man, as a place where a prodigious deal of business is done upon 'Change; a dramatick enthusiast, as the grand scene of theatrical entertainments; a man of pleasure, as an assemblage of taverns, and the great emporium for ladies of easy virtue. But the intellectual man is struck with it, as comprehending the whole of human life in all its variety, the contemplation of which is inexhaustible."

Dr Johnson had put it more succinctly.

"Here malice, rapine, accident conspire,
And now a rabble rages, now a fire;
Their ambush here relentless ruffians lay,
And here the fell attorney prowls for prey;
Here falling houses thunder on your head,
And here a female atheist talks you dead."

For historians as much as contemporaries, London has been too much, too big to comprehend all at once: we probably know more in detail about many provincial towns' histories than we know about London. So much was recorded – and yet, given the rate of metropolitan growth, so much more went unrecorded.

OVERLEAF
An early eighteenth century map shows the area of our initial interest. In the open area at the bottom stand St Bartholomew's and Smithfield, while Charterhouse, St John's and the burgeoning area of Clerkenwell are all marked.

155

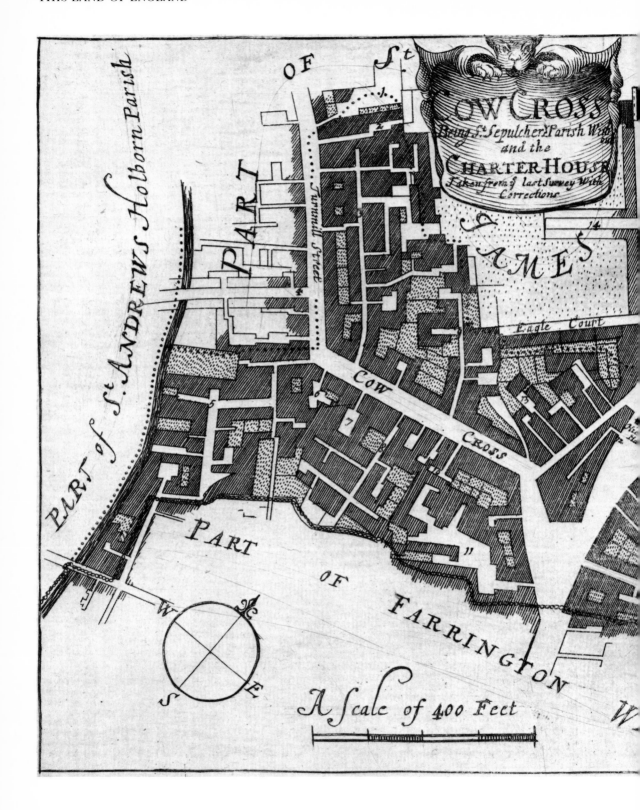

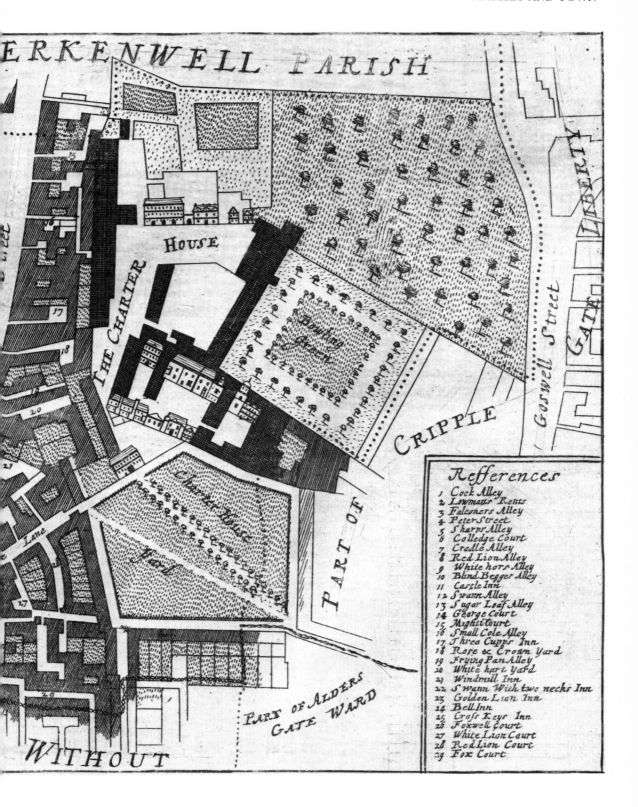

ERKENWELL PARISH

HOUSE

THE CHARTER

Bowling Green

CRIPPLE

PART OF

Charter House

Yard

Lane

WITHOUT

PART OF ALDERS
GATE WARD

Goswell Street

GATE LIBERTY

157

Small may be beautiful, but for London bigger was better. Although London was probably static and in some decay in the early sixteenth century, from the late sixteenth century until the mid-twentieth London never stopped growing, often at a pace difficult to comprehend.

To understand the complex character of the metropolis, perhaps we should put a toe in the water, and take one part of London, seeing the ways in which all these elements connected together and changed over time, before plunging into the full bath. That part is the city's north-western edge, centred upon the market at Smithfield.

Smithfield is synonymous with meat; from the early Middle Ages the great open space outside the City walls was used for animal markets, and for public spectacles – military exercises, fairs, executions. Apart from the unhygienic days of the mid-nineteenth century, when the market moved a few miles north for two decades, this has always been the premier meat market. To Smithfield were driven cattle, and sheep and even poultry from all over England, from Wales, Ireland and Scotland, for sale to the London butchers. Even today, although animals are no longer on the hoof, large refrigerated trucks bring meat from Ireland, Scotland and the Continent.

Produce funnelled towards London and its markets, and the city streets were thronged with sellers. In Shadwell's *Bury Fair*, the country recluse Lord Bellamy declared,

"I view my stately fields and meads, laden with corn and grass; my herds of kine and flocks of sheep; my breed of horses: my delicate gardens full of all sorts of fruits and herbs; my river full of fish, with ponds, and a decoy for water-fowl, and plenty of game of all kinds in my fields and woods; my park for venison; my cellar well furnished with all variety of excellent drinks: and all my own, Ned."

But Ned Wildish, the London sophisticate, had his answer ready.

"All these things have we at London. The product of the best cornfields at Queenhithe; hay, straw, and cattle at Smithfield; with horses too. Where is such a garden in Europe, as the Stocks Market? Where such a river as the Thames? Such ponds and decoys, as in Leadenhall Market, for your fish and fowl? Such game as at the poulterer's? And instead of parks, every cook's shop for venison, without hunting, and venturing neck or arms for it. And for cellars, from Temple Bar to Aldgate; and all that I have use of, my own too, since I have money."

Just as in Bury, and other market towns, the original wide open trading space of Smithfield was encroached onto from the earliest days: large religious and charitable institutions were founded; inns and alehouses built for the meat traders' accommodation and convenience; residential properties developed. Immediately facing onto Smithfield was the Priory of St Bartholomew the Great, founded in 1102, beside it the Hospital of St Bartholomew founded for the poor soon after and maintained by the begging of the clergy in the market. Beyond lay the great contemplative Carthusian monastery Charterhouse, founded in 1349 after the great plague mortality of the Black Death, and a little

Cheek by jowl stand the ancient gateway of Charterhouse and the elegant front of one of the few surviving houses of the eighteenth century Charterhouse Square.

further north the Priory of the Knights of St John and the convent of the "black nuns" at Clerkenwell. The edges of the city had a number of these great religious houses, together occupying a large area of land. The churchyard of St Bartholomew the Great was occupied every August by the most important of the London fairs, Bartholomew Fair – a major venue for cloth-trading and for horses and cattle, as well as for entertainment, trinkets and luxury goods.

The Dissolution of the Monasteries by Henry VIII released a huge amount of land onto a market which, in the early sixteenth century was not buoyant. The Augustinians at St Bartholomew gave up with little difficulty, the prior receiving a fat pension for being so pliable; the Carthusians held out against the royal command, and suffered for it. The last abbot at Charterhouse was hanged; his arm was hacked off and nailed to the gate of his dissolved house.

The disappearance of the religious houses therefore had a significant impact on the look and the topography of the city. The hospital of St Bartholomew was re-endowed, and survived as a secular institution to become one of the premier hospitals in our, medical, sense. The adjacent priory was bought by Sir Richard Rich: he demolished most of the building, keeping the chancel as a parish church, and converting the Lady Chapel, transepts and cloisters into houses. These fine houses were

by the next century converted into industrial premises: the Lady Chapel became a printing works, the cloisters a stable, the transept a smithy. Only in the past hundred years have all these parts been welded together into a proper church again, with extensive restoration and reconstruction – a testimony to the skills of Sir Aston Webb as much as to its Norman builders.

Charterhouse was quite a different story. The Privy Councillor, Sir Edward North, subsequently Lord North, acquired the property from the Crown some time after the Dissolution, and he and the property's second owner, the Duke of Norfolk, had converted the Charterhouse into a fine aristocratic town house by 1571. Part of the lay brothers' lodgings and the kitchen were retained, but almost all of the great monastic church, the cloister area and the monks' cells were destroyed. In their place, a new court was built, with a great hall, grand staircase, and saloon chamber. Charterhouse is a hotch-potch of styles, from the fourteenth century to the twentieth. In 1609 the house was refounded by Thomas Sutton as a charitable institution, a school for poor boys and a hospital for decayed gentlemen. Like many public schools, Charterhouse soon left poor boys behind, and in this century the school moved out into the country, leaving the decayed gentlemen behind as well.

The Priory of St John of Jerusalem in England, the greatest English house of the Knights of St John – and now restored to their refounded successors, and headquarters of the Ambulance Brigade – was almost totally destroyed in the reign of Edward VI. Most of the stone went to help build the new Renaissance mansion, Somerset House, on the Strand. The great gateway, dating from 1504, survives. This was at various times a storeroom and an alehouse, but from 1731 was the place from which the *Gentleman's Magazine* was published by "Sylvanus Urban" – his name as well as his journal linking country and town. Over the site of St John's Priory, and the nearby convent of Clerkenwell, residential development took place, obliterating the sites of the great religious houses which had previously stood there.

Back on Smithfield, the annual Bartholomew Fair had to vacate the great churchyard which had been its traditional site, and move out onto the large open area, since the churchyard was built over, the rows of genteel houses replacing the rows of stalls; only 'Cloth Fair' and the other street names recall the district's previous incarnation. Bartholomew Fair remained until the eighteenth century London's premier fun fair, as well as a leading annual trading event: it, and St Faith's Fair near Norwich, were the only two events outside his immediate area which the 1st Baron Ashburnham noted in his 1690s accounts.

This very varied experience can be replicated all over London. In a few cases the great religious institutions remained little changed, notably at Westminster; many were obliterated; some, such as the Priory of Holy Trinity Aldgate, were made into great houses which, by the end of the sixteenth-century, had been converted into tenement slums. There is a

The great gateway of St John's Priory, OPPOSITE, is almost all that survived the Dissolution, serving its turn as a printing and publishing works, tavern and house for the watch, and headquarters of the revived Order of St John.

161

parallel with post-World War II London, with its bomb sites progressively being built upon, sometimes used for temporary purposes until more buoyant demand turned them into prime locations. For in the early and mid-sixteenth century pressure upon these ex-religious sites, which had taken up so much land, was limited. But the massive and rapid population growth from the mid-sixteenth century made them prime targets for rebuilding and development. Within the walls and without, building carried on apace and overcrowding became acute.

John Stow, the great chronicler and gazetteer of late-sixteenth century London, recorded this process with a mixture of wistfulness for what had gone and admiration for what had come. Of the area around Smithfield he recorded:

"[Long Lane] is now lately built on both the sides with tenements for brokers, tipplers, and such like; the rest of Smithfield from Long Lane and to the bars is enclosed with inns, brewhouses, and large tenements."

Since the fifteenth century, "the building there hath so increased that now remaineth not one tree growing" in an area in Stow's day still called The Elms. And a little further west,

"On the right hand or north side, at the bottom of Holborn Hill, is Gold Lane, sometime a filthy passage into the fields, now both sides built with small tenements. Then higher is Leather Lane, turning also to the field, lately replenished with houses built. . ."

When Stow was writing, this was all on the edge of the built-up area: massive surburban growth in the centuries which followed made it into a very central location. Even today, the area has a highly mixed character. City office workers going to work pass buckets of pigs' heads and cross over with meat market traders on their way home; the accusing and the accused at the Old Bailey cross the paths of the caring and cared for at Barts; and the clock and watch makers of Clerkenwell fashion time as the 'Brothers' of Charterhouse while it away. The Fleet River has long since been covered over, and runs as a closed sewer where once it was an open sewer, gathering all the refuse of the area as celebrated in *The Tatler* in 1710.

"Now from all parts the swelling kennels flow,
And bear their trophies with them as they go:
Filth of all hues and odours seem to tell
What street they sailed from, by their sight and smell.
They, as each torrent drives, with rapid force,
From Smithfield or St Pulchre's shape their course,
And in huge confluent joined at Snow Hill ridge
Fall from the conduit prone to Holborn Bridge.
Sweepings from butcher's stalls, dung, guts and blood,
Drowned puppies, stinking sprats, all drenched in mud,
Dead cats and turnip tops come tumbling down the flood."

All this was within or immediately adjacent to the City of London ward of Farringdon Without. As London grew so it expanded: the area became more built up, the poorer areas became more overcrowded and the wealthier and more socially elevated owners of the largest houses moved west. It is a pattern which is repeated in every district of London's ancient core.

In the early sixteenth century, London was a puny city by international standards, with its 55,000 inhabitants; yet by 1800 a million Londoners made it the largest city in the world. During the sixteenth century London had quadrupled in three generations; in the seventeenth century the metropolis trebled in population, in the eighteenth century it nearly doubled. Whereas Italian towns had led in Europe in the sixteenth century, and Dutch towns in the seventeenth, nothing matched London's overall expansion. Paris, London's nearest rival in scope and scale, was overtaken towards the end of the seventeenth century.

Since town and city populations could not replace themselves, for death rates were usually well above birth rates (at least until late into the eighteenth century), the populations could be maintained and could grow only through immigration from outside. Gregory King, the late seventeenth century pioneer demographer, concluded:

"The reason why each marriage in London produces fewer children than the country marriages seems to be,
from the more frequent fornications and adulteries;
from a greater luxury and intemperance;
from a greater intenseness of business;
from the unhealthfulness of the coal smoke;
from a greater inequality of age between the husbands and wives."

Lower fertility and higher mortality produced a vacuum into which people were sucked. Estimates for the end of the seventeenth century suggest that 6000 people a year were needed to come to London simply to maintain the population: and many more than this were needed to produce its fast growth. Given the movement *away* from London as well as *towards* it, perhaps one-sixth of the English population had had some experience of life in the metropolis – a far cry indeed from the imagined immobile world of the past.

In the sixteenth century it appears that a majority of those moving into London came from the northern half of England, and that there was a marked predominance of men amongst the migrants. There were fewer competing attractions in the north; it was comparatively more disadvantaged than it was to become, and manufacturing and trading dominated the metropolitan economy and hence the demand for labour. Through the seventeenth century that southwards movement became less important: London was from then on to draw people mostly from the south and east, keeping population levels well down in the Home

Counties. But always London was a magnet for men and women from far away. In the sixteenth century Welshmen arrived in large numbers, as well as many Protestant refugees from the Low Countries. Later, there were large-scale movements of the Scottish and Irish into London; while after Louis XIV's Revocation of the Edict of Nantes in 1685, Huguenots came to London in their tens of thousands. Some 20,000 Jews (principally from Spain and Portugal) settled in the East End of eighteenth-century London. But the great majority of those coming to London were from England. They were attracted by the prospects of higher wages and of varied or specialist employment; the number of households and crafts requiring servants and apprentices was a great draw. In the mid-eighteenth century 215 occupations were listed in London – and nearly 500 different occupations were known by the end of the century.

In the late sixteenth century there was a considerable migration "push" of people out of poorer areas into a central place which could maintain them – later, it was the "pull" of the metropolitan life that produced the high levels of immigration. At the end of September 1686 Sir John, later Baron, Ashburnham, noted in his diary,

"This day John Jordan the gardener went away from my service, the dairy maid Nan Syvyer fell in love with him and went with him to Battle, in order to go with him to London."

Opportunity beckoned – and exploitation and crime flourished. *The Tricks of the Town Laid Open* warned its readers in 1699 that London was a "kind of large forest of wild beasts", a metaphor employed in 1751 by Henry Fielding, *Tom Jones'* author but also a leading magistrate.

"With the great number and irregularity of the buildings, the immense number of lanes, alleys, courts and by-places, the whole appears as a vast wood or forest in which the thief may harbour with as great security as wild beasts do in the deserts of Arabia and Africa."

Guides to London warned of the traps into which newly arrived girls might fall, to be whisked off into the white slavery of prostitution, and the nights held terrors of assault and mugging:

"fear that their hats and wigs should be switched from their heads or their swords taken from their sides, or that they may be blinded, knocked down, cut or stabbed."

London provided a galaxy of opportunities, moral and immoral, proper and improper, commercial, social and political.

'London' is something of a misnomer. The story of London is really a tale of two cities, London and Westminster. The growth of political and legal institutions, the establishment of the royal Court more firmly in London, and the social expansion of the West End placed Westminster in an ever firmer position. In 1500 the vast majority of the metropolitan population lived within the walls of the City, and still a great proportion

164

lived there in 1600. But by 1700, when the metropolis was a city of 575,000 people, the City within the walls held 80,000 people; by 1750 the ratio was 675,000 to 87,000 and by 1800 950,000 to 78,000. The ancient core came to represent only a tiny fraction of the whole.

However far London has now grown to both north and south, the great pull has always been between east and west. The River Thames has always been the artery shaping London's linear growth: parallel to it are the ancient axis of Fleet Street and the Strand between London and Westminster and the rather more recent Holborn-Long Acre link. Only within the past hundred years have many significant north-south routes been reconstructed. The seventeenth and eighteenth century metropolis spread eastwards downriver – Aldgate Without, Spitalfields, Shadwell and Wapping – to cater for both land and river transport; and London spread westwards into Bloomsbury and Covent Garden, St James's, Mayfair and the Grosvenor estates. Northern development was far more marked in the nineteenth century than before, but growth immediately south of the river was astonishing from the late sixteenth century onwards. Until 1749 London Bridge was the only dry crossing of the Thames, and Southwark was the gateway to the south.

Docks and quays catered for the massive shipping traffic up and down the Thames, large inns for the considerable road traffic converging on, and fanning out from, London. Even in the middle of the seventeenth century there were 900 carrier services a week to and from London.

The growth, diversity and traffic of London is nowhere better shown than in the series of great panoramic views of London from the south, drawn or painted many times from the sixteenth century to the nineteenth. The first of these to achieve widespread circulation was drawn by Visscher and published in 1616. In this view Southwark lies along the south bank of the Thames; the river both above and below London Bridge was crowded with ships and boats; London Bridge itself was built up on both sides of the roadway; and London stretched out on the other side of the river.

The skyline was dominated by the towers and spires of the City churches: medieval London had 107 parishes which in an area of little more than a square mile was a formidable concentration – a church on almost every street corner – and although some were suppressed, post-Reformation City churches were still numerous. Above them all stood Old St Paul's, without the spire which had burned down in 1561 and which, at 489 feet, had made the cathedral England's tallest building.

Following the panorama from east (right) to west (left), that being the main thrust of the city's expansion, the great Norman stronghold of the Tower stood downstream of London Bridge. Between the two were a cluster of docks and quays, of which Billingsgate was by far the most important. Not until later was Billingsgate exclusively devoted to fish; at this time, its principal commodity would have been grain. Lion Quay is also marked; the third quay from the Custom House – the central place

Visscher's 1616 panorama of London, ABOVE. The City on the far bank is a forest of towers and spires, a maze of streets, courts and alleys. The crowded thoroughfare of London Bridge provides access to that packed world of quays, shops, guilds, tenements and palaces.

The crowded quayside of Boitard's engraving, FAR LEFT, is a satire on the taste for imported luxuries and for anything French. A Sussex shopkeeper visiting London in 1767 reflected on the Royal Exchange, NEAR LEFT, that the "sole cause of that vast concourse of people, of the hurry and bustle they were in, and the eagerness that appeared in their countenances, was the getting of Money."

for monitoring and registering trade and shipping – towards Billingsgate was Wiggins Quay. This too was principally a grain quay. During the second half of the seventeenth century, when the volume of the goods going through the Port of London doubled, Wiggins Quay traded with east coast and Kentish ports, in the grain coming from regions increasingly specialising in its production. Boats came from King's Lynn, Great Yarmouth, Spalding, Wisbech, Hull, Ramsgate, Sandwich, Deal and Margate; they returned with some of the goods traded from overseas or elsewhere in England for which demand, especially town demand, was growing.

On the waterfront above the bridge stood the livery company hall of the Fishmongers, and in the midst of the built-up area behind, the provisions market of Leadenhall. Lining the river were the many wharves, quays and stairways; behind Coleharbour (the name speaks for itself) the city's central civic institution, the Guildhall. The Steelyard was the centre for the merchants trading from northern Germany, which reached its height in the fifteenth century. The complex of buildings included warehouses and housing, cranes and wharves, wine taverns and shops. The water equivalent of a taxi rank operated from the bottom of the stairs down to the water's edge.

In from the Steelyard stood the Eleanor Cross on Cheapside, the last but one of the markers on the medieval queen's funeral procession route which, like Banbury Cross further back along the route, was destroyed in an outburst of iconoclastic zeal. Cheapside was the prime retailing street in the City, lined with the shops and stalls of goldsmiths and other high-quality craftsmen and dominated by the greatest of the city parish churches, St Mary-le-Bow. Cheapside led to the greatest of the English cathedrals, St Paul's.

Below the Cathedral's grandeur were the crowded industrial and commercial areas of the Three Cranes, Paul's Wharf and above all Queenhithe, the most important of the upstream docks and quays, especially for corn. Visscher's panorama suggests a similar physical layout at Queenhithe, Steelyard and Billingsgate: a square dock in the case of Queenhithe and Billingsgate, a wharf and cranes in the case of Steelyard, with open arcades on the western range. These doubtless functioned as open market halls – sales areas, temporary storage areas, a place for the examination and quality control of the goods.

On the other side of the river, Southwark housed many of the most entertaining and least entertaining aspects of London life. Until their suppression in 1546 this was the site of the Stews, the public brothels. The Bear Gardens were there, as were the most important of the theatres of Shakespeare's day – the Globe and the Swan. Here also were the main London prisons, the Clink and the Marshalsea.

From this point up, the character of the built-up area and the waterfront of around 1600 changed. The half-ruined Barnard's Castle, a sometime royal palace, and beyond it Bridewell, again a one-time royal palace but subsequently the main poorhouse of correction, marked the edge of the city itself. Between the Strand and the river stood some of the great noble and episcopal palaces, with their stairs as access to the river: Somerset House, the great neo-classical house built from the stone of St John's Priory, Burleigh House and on the other side of the Strand, Bedford House, Durham House, York House, and at the end of the panorama the straggle of the great royal and administrative complex of Whitehall. Beyond that lay the Palace of Westminster: but none of that is shown by Visscher. This is a panorama of the significant commercial and residential area. When the Court was in residence, and during the sessions of Parliament and the Law Terms, the population of Westminster increased with those directly or indirectly involved in those activities. But the City was still the hub.

But above all the panorama catches the city in the throes of rapid change. The City had always been a great jumble, with aristocratic houses and tenement houses in close proximity. The City was divided into rich and poor areas, but there was a much more varied mixture than in the cities we know. A common pattern was for the grander or more expensive properties to face onto the street, with courts or lanes running down at right angles from the street. The deeper into the court, the poorer and denser was the housing. The astonishing population growth of London produced considerable overcrowding in these poorer areas, as individuals and families crammed into subdivided houses and often single rooms. And overcrowding bred disease. London was prone to major and devastating outbreaks of epidemics, of which the bubonic plague was the most spectacular. The Great Plague of 1665, in which perhaps 70,000 people died, was probably not the most severe such epidemic the capital had seen, but it was the *last*. In such circumstances, the victims' beds in some areas were barely cold before newcomers moved into them – sometimes to succumb in their turn. But these great crises were only a temporary setback to growth, and in a few months or years the tide of immigrants made up the shortfall.

The great change of the seventeenth century was the rapid development of the West End towards and around Westminster, and the architectural revolution which accompanied it. Revolution is not too strong a term. In place of the crowded streets, and the jumble of buildings, of the ancient city, uniformity was the keynote, in squares and terraces and in planned developments. Of course, the planning was largely confined to the buildings intended for the more polite levels of society, and the housing in the poorer areas which sprang up to service and provide the labour for the wealthier areas was far from ordered and sophisticated. Rich and poor are not unconnected: for the supreme native achievement of English town architecture is surely the *terrace*. Whether it be grand or lowly, the world sees a regular, uniform facade – behind which all manner or virtue, vice and lack of uniformity might hide.

The astonishing "helicopter view" map of West Central London, drawn by Wenceslaus Hollar around 1660, conveys the impression of a

*The Stocks Market,
ABOVE, was one of the
City's ancient produce markets,
but was ousted by the building
of the Lord Mayor's Mansion
House in 1739. Through the
preceding century the westward
expansion of London resulted in
the replacement of many of the
great aristocratic houses on the
Strand, OPPOSITE, by new
development, the West End
building of the kind depicted in
Hollar's map, of which this is
a detail. (see pp. 196–197).
New Square, ABOVE RIGHT,
next to and now part of
Lincoln's Inn, was just one of
the elegant and ordered
additions to the townscape.*

newer, ordered world. Apart from the great houses along the Strand and
the Inns of Court, almost all of what is shown here had been built in the
preceding sixty years. At the centre is Covent Garden and the Bedford
Estate. This was one of the first developments to succeed in breaching
the building regulations which were the vain attempt to contain the
physical growth of London. Before the Reformation, the area had been
the produce garden of Westminster Abbey – hence the name, Co[n]vent
Garden, and had been granted by the Crown in 1553 to Sir John Russell.
The Russells became Earls, and later Dukes of Bedford, and the safari
parks and slot-machine arcades at modern Woburn are but the
continuation of a lengthy tradition of entrepreneurship and innovation.
The Earl of Bedford engaged Inigo Jones, the great early Stuart court
architect, to build a grand square on the Italian model, with a *piazza* and
colonnaded arcades. On the south side stood the Tudor pile of Bedford
House, and the centrepiece of the west side was the new church of St
Paul Covent Garden, built as "the handsomest barn in England". New
residential streets focused upon the square at the heart of the Bedford
estate.

The 4th Earl of Bedford could claim proudly, "If London is the ring,

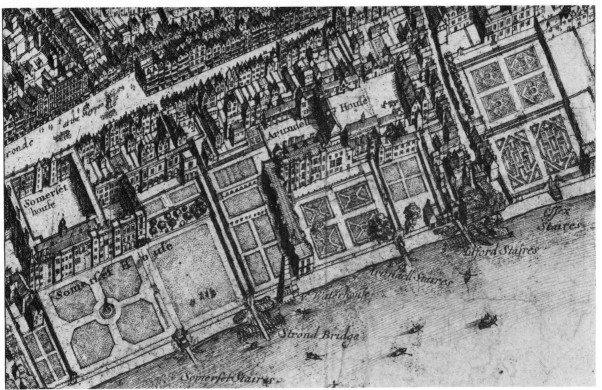

Henry Fielding's magistrate's journal for Covent Garden in 1752, some fifteen years after Balthazar Nebot painted this view of the square and its market, gives a different perspective on the women who traded there. On two market-

women brought before him, one *of no crime but poverty had*
"*in a dreadful condition from* *money given her to enable her to*
the itch was recommended to the *follow her trade in the*
overseers; another who pleaded *market.*"

then Covent Garden is the jewel of that ring." Jewel indeed: the square attracted the right type of aristocratic and gentry residents, at high rents. In the 1630s and 1640s, the Fiennes' were only one of the grand families who chose Covent Garden as their new London home. In 1704 Bedford House was demolished when the Russells moved to their new residential development a little further north in Bloomsbury, and Tavistock Street and Southampton Street were built, linking the squre with the Strand. It was to Southampton Street that the 1st Baron Ashburnham had moved shortly before his death. But already Covent Garden was on the way down: a produce market had been officially established in the square in 1670, the Bedfords putting empty space to profitable use. That had the effect of driving out the well-to-do, who were in any event attracted by newer houses north and west; and Covent Garden became the great haunt of prostitutes and their customers. The innuendo-filled pages of *The Tatler*, and the more direct descriptions of sexual excess in James Boswell's *Journals*, show how far the eighteenth-century Garden had fallen.

East of the Covent Garden development stands Lincoln's Inn, one of the Inns of Court, training and housing lawyers. In the sixteenth and seventeenth centuries a period at one of the Inns was as much a part of a gentleman's training as a period at Oxford or Cambridge, or as the Grand Tour was later to become. The Inns included not only those which have survived to our day – Lincoln's, Gray's and the Inner and Middle Temple – but others such as New Inn and Clement's Inn, both shown on the map, which have failed to survive (though some of the latter's buildings still stand). Hollar's map shows the fifteenth and sixteenth century buildings of Lincoln's Inn, most of which are there today, and the early seventeenth century chapel. Under construction was the second great square, Lincoln's Inn Fields, with the architecturally innovative Lindsey House its showpiece (and now the only surviving building of the original square). Lincoln's Inn had objected to the land being built upon – but by 1687 they had relented sufficiently to allow Henry Serle to build the grand New Square immediately next to the Inn, (and later to incorporate the square into the inn itself, thereby preserving it in its entirety).

By the end of the seventeenth century, the remaining undeveloped areas on this Hollar map had been built over. The tiny figures shown squelching across the marshy St Giles' Fields were succeeded by carriages bowling along Monmouth Street and Earlham Street, and later by the inhabitants of the notorious "rookeries" of Seven Dials. Residential expansion further west was well under way: Leicester Square was laid out in 1670, St James's Square from the 1660s, Piccadilly and the streets running north later in the seventeenth century. Along the river front further development was taking place. The Duke of Buckingham's mansion had been built in 1626, on the site of the house of Archbishop of York, (and before 1556 of the Bishop of Norwich). All that survives is the Water Gate, now marooned hundreds of yards in

Two faces of London life: ABOVE, a Fleet wedding. Until 1753, the Fleet liberty was one of the main centres for clandestine marriages, where couples could marry without consent, banns or licence. The coffee house, RIGHT, pictured at the very end of the seventeenth century, is a place of smoke, drink and talk – "where muddling muck-worms were as busy as rats in a cheese-loft."

*Two faces of grand life:
ABOVE, St James's Square,
heart of the later-seventeenth
century aristocratic quarter,
and RIGHT, what little is left
of the Adam brothers' Adelphi.*

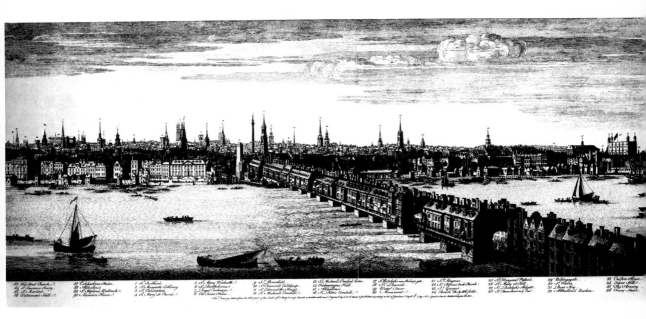

from the water after the Victorian construction of the Embankment. In 1676 the palace had been demolished, and on its site a new estate was built, commemorating the previous ownership in its street names: George Street, Villiers Street, Duke Street, Of Alley, and Buckingham Street. (In its wisdom, the City of Westminster has renamed Of Alley York Place.)

Every spare corner was being taken over for building works, and still London grew. Daniel Defoe was, as ever, impressed by the fine new growth.

"The increase of the buildings here in the last thirty years is really a kind of prodigy. The new westward addition is more in built than the cities of Bristol, Exeter and York if they were all put together – and all was mere fields of grass employed only to feed cattle."

Within a century the division between City and West End was clear. *Town-Talk*, Steele's short-lived successor to the *Tatler* and *Spectator*, captured that division.

"As the Exchange *is the Heart of* London; *the great* Hall, *and all under the contiguous roofs, the Heart of* Westminster; *so is* Covent Garden *the Heart of the* Town. *What happens to be in Discourse or Agitation among the Pleasurable and Reasonable People is what shall make up the* Town-Talk... *It is in this Spirit, that when the Streets and Houses are full, it is often very justly said there is no Body in Town. And when the Men of Business are at a loss, it is dictated by us who are in Town what they should do, and we say,* the Town will have it so and so."

From Aldgate and the Tower in the east, the mid-eighteenth century panorama of London moves up-river, past wharves and quays, the still-crowded London Bridge, and the densely-packed City, its skyline punctuated by Wren's myriad churches.

177

The gulf between City and West End is the organizing principle of Defoe's novel *Roxana, or The Unfortunate Mistress*: the heroine, to escape her dissolute past, moves just two miles further east to the other side of the City.

> *"I was now in a perfect Retreat indeed; remote from the eyes of all that ever had seen me, and as much out of the way of being ever seen or heard-of by any of the Gang that used to follow me, as if I had been among the Mountains in Lancashire; for when did a Blue Garter, or a Coach-and-Six come into a little narrow Passage in the Minories or Goodman's Fields?"*

The eighteenth century saw that division become clearer still. The trading heart and the social centre of the capital remained distinct and apart. In the great panoramic view of London drawn by the brothers Samuel and Nathaniel Buck in 1749, the engraving is twice the length of that drawn by Visscher at the beginning of the previous century: the western extension could no longer be excluded. Travelling its length gives an even clearer picture of London than did the Bucks' predecessors.

We begin again at the Tower. Downstream, the East End was growing fast; so was the shipping on the water. The value of London's overseas trade between the 1690s and 1790s grew from £10 million to £23 million, of which imports were usually a little under half. London's trade was between two-thirds and three-quarters of all English overseas trade, a very marked concentration in one place. Daniel Defoe in the early eighteenth century was as ready as ever to extol the virtues of English trade.

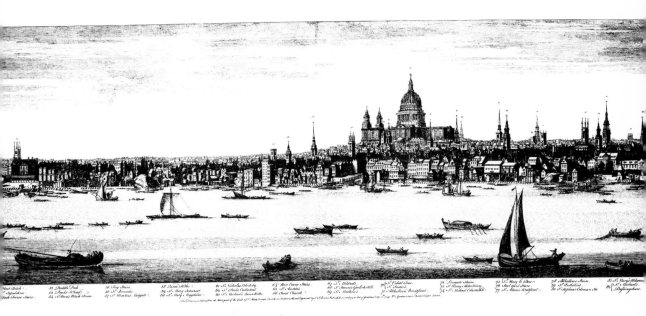

"As to our product for exportation, 'tis all our own, or of our colonies, which is the same thing, such as

Corn	Lead	Alums	Cotton
Coal	Fish	Sugar	Molasses
Salt	Drugs	Tobacco	Ginger
Malt	Copperas	Peltry (Furs)	Indigo etc. . .
Tin	Rice	Flesh	

We import Gold, Silver, Wine, Brandy, Hemp, Pitch, Tar, Flax, Wax, Oil, Iron, Steel, Fruit, Wool, Silk, Hair, Drugs, Dye stuffs, Saltpetre, Tea, Coffee, Timber, Spice: all these and many more. But these are all the Growth and Produce of the Lands, not the Manufacture and Workmanship of foreign countries."

The panorama continues up-river, past St Paul's and the jumble of wharf facilities, massive dung piles and waterfront building development, the entrance of the canalized Fleet, the legal enclaves of the Middle and Inner Temple, and thereafter the new residential areas alongside Fleet Street and the Strand.

Eighteenth-century English trade was the world leader, exporting manufactured goods and *re-exporting* colonial produce: and London was the centre which in spite of the resurgence of other ports – Bristol, Liverpool, Dublin – remained pre-eminent.

As the wharves and quays were thronged with goods and men, so the financial and commodity exchanges were equally packed. Sir Thomas Gresham had established the Royal Exchange in 1566, and that building's fourth incarnation still stands, and once more a trading centre, in the heart of the City. Celia Fiennes' description is typical of her breathless excitement, that "the Royal Exchange's middle space was designed and is used for the merchants to meet to create their business and trade and bills. . ." But Ned Ward as *The London Spy* was considerably more jaundiced in his description.

"We marched towards the Royal Exchange, to which traders were trotting in as

179

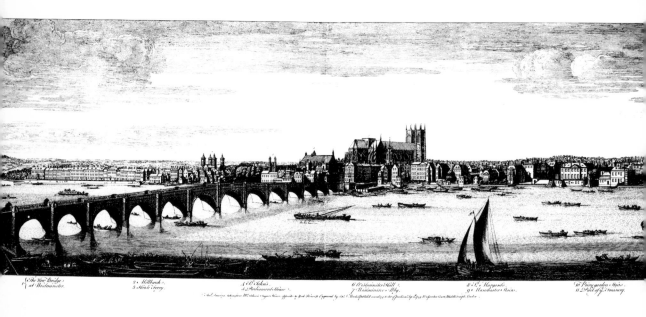

*much haste as lawyers to Westminster or butchers to Smithfield. . . We went on to the
'Change, jostled in amongst a parcel of swarthy buggerantoes who would ogle a
young man with as much lust as a whoremaster would gaze upon a beautiful virgin.
Advertisements hung thick round the pillars of each walk, the wainscot was adorned
with quacks' bills. We passed by them, and squeezed amongst coasters and English
traders who were as busy in outwitting one another as if plain-dealing was a crime
and cozenage a virtue."*

Commerce and trade, like London itself, were all things to all men.
Upon this subject, there was no more spirited contemporary of Celia
Fiennes and Ned Ward than Daniel Defoe. "The Merchant", he
concluded,

*"makes a wet Bog become a populous State, enriches Beggars, ennobles Mechanics,
raises not Families only but Towns, Cities, Provinces and Kingdoms."*

He defended the acceptable face of capitalism:

*"O Money, Money! Thous art the Test of Beauty, the Judge of Ornament, the
Guide of the Fancy, the Index of Temper, and the Pole Star of the Affections. Thou
makest Homely Things Fair, Old Things Young, Crooked Things Straight."*

Money had not been able to make the crooked streets and narrow alleys
of the City straight and wide. The principal difference between the
panoramic view and the earlier one is the wholesale rebuilding as a
result of the Great Fire. The "most horrid, malicious, bloody flame" of
the Great Fire devastated most of the area of the City in September
1666. Although the City was rebuilt, in brick, stone and tile, and in a

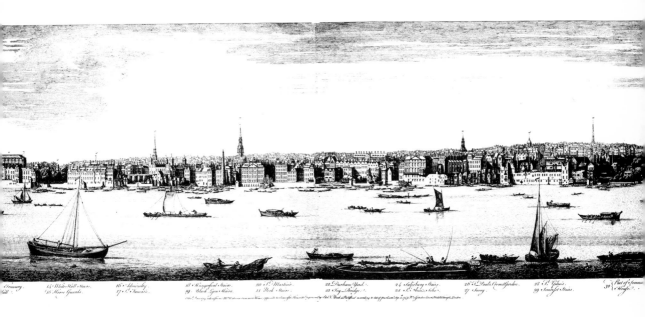

self-consciously new style, the plans of Sir Christopher Wren and others to replace the old layout with a new regular streetplan with a gridiron of streets transected by grand avenues linking St Paul's, the Exchange and the Monument built to commemorate the Fire, came to nothing. The many vested interests meant that the old street pattern was largely replaced intact. The density of housing decreased, the intensity of business increased, and civic and business institutions took on a grander appearance, but this was still recognisably the same city. The great church rebuilding programme undertaken by Wren and his assistants provided a skyline as dramatic as that before the fire, and all continued to be dominated by the massive pile of St Paul's, the new baroque cathedral completed in 1711 and Wren's masterpiece.

In contrast with the heavenly and commercial aspirations of the skyline, the water's edge showed the more basic aspects of London life. At the aptly named Dung Quay, Puddle Dock and at Whitefriars Stairs the huge mountains of dung, animal and human, awaited the boats to take the refuse of the city upstream to the market garden areas of Pimlico and beyond. The intensive horticulture provided fruit and vegetables for the London markets, and so the cycle continued. Further along, at the western edge of the City, the Fleet Ditch debouched into the Thames, carrying the "Sweepings from butchers' stalls, dung, guts and blood, Drowned puppies, stinking sprats. . ." of John Gay's poem. The Fleet had been planned after the Fire as a ship-carrying canal, dug out to a width of forty feet with quays up to the bridge at Holborn. The width of the tributary, the bridge over it and the surrounding houses and courts had a Venetian air: but by 1760 the Fleet had been paved over to

The great noble houses which Wenceslaus Hollar drew had been for the most part demolished, replaced by estates of houses. Behind the chaotic jumble of Whitehall and Westminster Palaces stretched the new streets and squares of the West End. And as the panorama began with the old world of London Bridge, so it ends with the new world of Westminster Bridge and the prospect of further development upstream.

provide the access to the new Blackfriars Bridge. Today the only signs that this was a heavily trafficked river are the steep slopes of the 'dry' valley and street names leading away from the line of the old river, Sea Coal Lane and Newcastle Street, for the collier ships from Tyneside.

Between the Fleet and the Temple – central to both City and West End – was one of the capital's most notorious areas, the resort for footpads and pickpockets, highwaymen and murderers. London was always filled with those contrasts: the havens of the law and of lawlessness stood side by side.

Upriver from this point the new housing developments of the later seventeenth century predominated. On the site of the old Arundel House were residential streets – some shockingly jerry-built – while the stout walls of the medieval Savoy palace still withstood the developers. Where the old Durham house had once stood the Adam brothers, John, Robert, James and William, were to build their adventurous Adelphi between 1768 and 1772, declaring their objections to the classically pure Palladianism of the previous generation. They replaced the pre-existing blocks with their great river-front palace decorated with "a beautiful variety of light mouldings, gracefully formed, delicately enriched" – a palace composed of individual houses which in the end proved difficult to sell and were disposed of by lottery. In from the river and *avant garde* gestures, residential properties in the once very fashionable areas around St Paul Covent Garden, St Anne Soho and St James Piccadilly, all shown on the panorama, were easier to let and sell.

From housing to government: immediately next to the riverside properties the panorama shows Whitehall, with its state offices, the Treasury and Inigo Jones' Banqueting House standing proud over the general muddle of buildings of varying age and degree of architectural pretension. Beyond the Palace of Whitehall was the Palace of Westminster: Westminster Hall, housing the great law courts, and the Houses of Commons and of Lords. Still recognizable is Westminster Abbey; and occupying the prominent position in the front of the picture is Westminster Bridge – still in fact undergoing construction when the Bucks were drawing. The Bridge marked the emergence of the West End, as only the second metropolitan crossing of the Thames. Clearly not to the liking of the watermen, who were the only upriver link as they ferried across people and goods, the bridge was a spectacular success, wide and without the line of decaying houses along each side as at the ancient crossing. Other bridges across the river followed, and London Bridge itself was reconstructed, without its houses and with a wider thoroughfare.

Only a little beyond Westminster, the built-up area began to dwindle, although the "upturned-table legs" of the church of St John Smith Square marked an area already in the throes of expansion. In contrast with the earlier panorama, only here does the countryside begin to appear. Meadows and market gardens lined the river up to the village of Chelsea. They too were soon to be gobbled up.

By the time the Bucks drew their panorama the puny London of two centuries before had become the greatest city in the world. And England, one of the least urbanized western countries, had become the most urbanized. London led – what London spent money on today, Bristol or Norwich would purchase tomorrow, Bury St Edmunds or Shrewsbury the next day, Quainton, Myddle and Hawkshead in the days that followed.

To take the example of tobacco to illustrate that process of diffusion and change may seem perverse, but it embodies in miniature all these features. Tobacco has many qualities favouring rapid and easy distribution: it is high in value compared to its weight, and it is addictive. Forget Sir Walter Ralegh being doused by his servant; the weed was introduced to England in the 1580s from contraband trade with Spanish colonies in South America, and Trinidad alone may have supplied 60,000 pounds of contraband tobacco in the boom years after 1600. Retailing at a high price, it was a fashionable commodity in London. Pipe-smoking was a running joke in *Bartholomew Fair*: Mistress Overdone exhorts her unheeding hearers, "Thirst not after that frothy liquor, ale. . . Neither do thou lust after that tawney weed tobacco." The termination of the illicit trade after 1610 coincided with the introduction of tobacco growing to the new English colonies in Virginia and then the West Indies. As their production increased so the price fell dramatically; and as prices fell and more could purchase tobacco, so they were hooked. Annual English imports of tobacco from Virginia and Maryland reached a million pounds in weight by 1640, fifteen million pounds by the late 1660s, and fluctuated around thirty million pounds by the early eighteenth century. At least in the beginning almost all came through London. Once London had been bitten by the smoking bug, tobacco was sold more and more widely, first in the larger towns, then the smaller towns and larger villages, and finally even in the smallest hamlets. And first in the south and west, later in the north. By mid-seventeenth century, no part of the country was free. So when in 1633 the Government tried the revenue-raising device of getting tobacco suppliers to obtain licences, almost every part of the country had tobacconists and apothecaries supplying their neighbourhood. From London and from the provincial towns pedlars carried tobacco to alehouses and inns for their customers' pleasure; in the eighteenth century, with growing integration in the victualling trade, breweries began supplying their clients with tobacco, just as tobacconists became involved in the gin trade. Price and availability made England a smoking nation.

London has a unique place in the history of English countryside. It *created* the countryside as much as it was created *by* the countryside. As the fattest belly in the land, London needed feeding: and as it grew, so its tentacles stretched further. The scale of the trade with London made organization necessary – through efficient markets, transport facilities, specialist traders. The demand from London, and in the eighteenth century from other rapidly growing towns, helped persuade farmers to become more specialist, concentrating more on what they could do best.

Similarly, as an industrialist market, so much was concentrated in London. A mid-seventeenth century commentator, for example, described the central place of London in the woollen industry.

"Great store of wool is brought to London to be sold, and the same wool carried again into the country to and fro, perhaps to different places, to be carded, spun and weaved into stuffs, and these stuffs brought up to London again to be sold."

Only with the rise of other important centres, beginning to compete with the capital, did this degree of concentration upon London in metalwares, pottery, glass and much else besides wool, begin to diminish. The cost of production in London itself, with its high wages, gave the impetus for industries to quit London for lower-wage areas elsewhere in the country. London had once produced pins and needles in vast quantities, for example: by the late seventeenth century the industry had largely transferred to the West Midlands. Whereas weaving had been an employer of large numbers in sixteenth-century London, that became either a highly specialised occupation, especially in silk, or a poor man's work in impoverished eastern and southern suburbs. Silk weaving followed other industries in quitting London, for Essex, the East Midlands and the North West.

Alongside the traffic in food and goods, information and gossip flowed back and forth – what London had to offer in the way of employment and wages, what the best-dressed men and women were wearing, what Robin Hood did to the Sheriff of Nottingham, what was the *Town Talk* of the moment. A ballad of 1634 – to be distributed through the provinces by itinerant traders, and to be pasted up on alehouse walls and sung with the standard liquid accompaniment – set out the attractions of metropolitan life, to the tune *Hyde Park*.

> *All you that delight in pastime and pleasure*
> *Now list to my ditty wherein I will show*
> *In London they'll say there is a good store of treasure*
> *And that for a certain there is many doth know,*
> *Great store of gold and silver you may see,*
> *With all things as pleasing as ever can be:*
> *There are fine shews and glistering sights,*
> *Then come to the City for your delights.*

The propaganda really did say that the streets of London were paved with gold.

On the economic front, the importance of London can hardly be over-estimated. Through the later years of the sixteenth century and the early years of the seventeenth, London's growth was phenomenal, whilst urban growth elsewhere was limited. People and resources were being concentrated in London, a city with ten times more people in the reign of James II than in the reign of Henry VIII, and considerably more than ten times the wealth. Concentration in London produced change elsewhere: that in turn led to the growth of other urban centres which could begin to compete with London – with its manufacturing and wholesaling functions, as with Birmingham; with its port and dock facilities, as with Liverpool; with its social pretensions, as with Bath. London may have sucked in people, and disposed with many of them very rapidly: but without the "engine" of London, England would have been a very different place.

London was not simply an economic centre. The key to its overwhelming importance was that almost every aspect of life had its centre in the capital. The law, government, administration, finance and genteel society were all part of London: there was not a separate place for Court and Government as was instituted with Louis XIV's Versailles; trade and government were not separated as were Seville and Madrid; supremacy was not shared in the way that Amsterdam, Rotterdam and The Hague shared it. England, moreover, did not have separate, largely antonomous regions: from the early sixteenth century it was a politically and, broadly speaking, fiscally united country. James VI and I had complained, "Soon, London will be all England" – growth was so fast that it had to be contained. Attempts to curb the capital's growth were of little use: and in many senses London *was* all England in the extent and the depth of its penetration into life elsewhere.

As town life attracted many, it repelled some. The Somerset yokel Ned was horrified by London: the pies for sale were hardly edible, the prostitutes' charges were extortionate (apparently, Somerset girls obliged for a pint of wine), people laughed at his accent and tried to con him, there were people, horses and buildings as far as the eye could see. Ned for one turned tail and fled.

Town and country were, and are, seen as opposites – the growth of the image of the country bumpkin is but one part of that. In William Wycherley's Restoration comedy, *The Country Wife*, written at almost exactly the same time as the poem recounting Ned's adventures, Pinchwife's new wife is a model of rustic virtues:

"she has no beauty, but her youth; no attraction, but her modesty; wholesome, homely and housewifely, that's all."

He tries to keep her from being contaminated by London ways, and from being seduced by his London friends: metropolitan manners appear to win the day, but the country wife has inner strengths. Country and town are on a more equal footing, are more closely tied, than might appear.

When Wycherley was in town, he lived in the new West End, worshipping in a fashionable church. When he visited the small country estate he had inherited, the church he attended on Sunday was less fashionable, but his position more familiar to us. He sat in the pew immediately behind Richard Gough's in Myddle church, the seventh pew on the right hand side of the north aisle.

We come full circle

—6—
THIS LAND OF ENGLAND

Two phrases have found many echoes in this book: the title, 'This Land of England', and L.P. Hartley's epigram, "The past is a foreign country: they do things differently there." But the echoes – as echoes do – have shifted emphasis and changed meaning. We have been less concerned with the *foreignness* of the past than with its *familiarity*, have dealt less with the *land* than with *England*. There is relatively little here on the detail of landholding or on the practicalities of farming; but much on movement and social structure, on cohesion and integration. And we have used landscape and buildings as a constant source of reference, not for themselves but for what they tell us of the people who lived and worked in them.

The altered emphasis has drawbacks. There is not much sense here of muddy boots or tired backs; and it all smells more of the study than the farmyard. But the loss of feeling, we hope, is outweighed by the gain in understanding. For the pecularities of the past lay not so much in the parts – in the developments of leasehold tenure, or crop rotation, or fen drainage – as in the whole, and that England *was* a whole. More than any other West European country it makes sense to talk of England as a unit. We have talked in particular of the degree of economic integration and showed how different parts of the country were tied together in so many ways. But one really stands for all: the increased penetration of the market economy. Here there is a paradox. The market began with the differences between regions, and as it developed it enhanced the degree of local specialization in agriculture and industry. But specialization meant exchange, and exchange meant contact. The twin elements of population dynamics and urban growth were prime factors in promoting change, just as London, the largest and usually the fastest growing town, was a prime agent.

On the other hand, there is an understandable tendency to believe that England was, and still is, a highly regionalized place: that Yorkshiremen are innately different from Lancastrians, as they are from Kentishmen and Men of Kent. They sound different, sometimes they look different – and if that is so now, surely it must have been more pronounced before. That belief is understandable, but it should not be taken too far. Differences there may have been, but they were often of emphasis rather than of substance.

This sense of muted difference is best seen in English population trends, moving in the same direction at the same time. If illegitimacy and pre-marital pregnancy were low in late-seventeenth century Essex, they were also low in Yorkshire and Devon; if population growth was high in sixteenth-century Somerset and Wiltshire, it was so too in Sussex, Shropshire or Westmorland. The basic economic and demographic institutions were the same throughout: in every part of the country there were farm servants and farm labourers; the nuclear family and later ages at marriage were the norm; mobility was a common feature of life. Certainly the pace of regional population change was not uniform. In the seventeenth century, the rate of population increase was higher in pastoral farming regions than in arable, and in the eighteenth century gains in northern populations, with increasing industrial employment, were greater than in southern. Nevertheless, basic relationships persisted, and regional demographic behaviour was not in opposite directions as it was often, say, between northern and southern France.

Although we have chosen to concentrate upon the economic and demographic varieties of integration in England, they were not the only ways in which England was welded together as a country. The thing which all Englishmen shared, and share, is English. A sense of national identity and of the closeness of the various regions was possible because linguistic barriers did not exist. If central authorities sent out instructions or Parliament passed laws, they were transmitted or interpreted in English. The same joke books could be read by gentlemen or by husbandmen – and, at least in the earlier part of the period we have been concerned with, often were. Searching for a pre-literate English popular culture is difficult, for the roots of the surviving oral culture are usually to be found in printed and widely disseminated material. When Cecil Sharp, Ralph Vaughan Williams and the other English folklorists went out collecting folk songs, following the example of Continental scholars, they were in for a surprise. Instead of strong regional variation and English "Songs of the Auvergne", they found the same basic songs and rhymes in many parts of England. England was a cultural as well as an economic unity, and through the same mechanism of the market and London. Most songs and ballads were actually written (or rewritten) in London, and for most of the time all, including those produced in the regions, were printed and published there. Then, from St Paul's Churchyard – the Wardour Street of its day – they were distributed throughout England by the trading network.

On top of these varieties of social integration, England can also be considered as a politically and legally unified nation. "Everybody in England", it was already a commonplace in the fourteenth century, "was bound by what was done in parliament because everybody was present there, either in person or by their representative." So there was one law – that decided in Parliament – and one system of taxation – that levied in Parliament. The contrast with pre-Revolutionary France, say, where the different provinces had their own systems and forms of taxation, could not be greater. But it was not only a unity of rules, but of place also. Parliament met at Westminster; the law courts sat in Westminster Hall; taxation was paid into the Exchequer at Westminster; and above all, the King held court there, at Whitehall and later at St James's. So London–Westminster was the political as well as the economic capital. And just as London had no rivals in size or trade, it had none politically either. England did not have, as France had (and still has) great provincial cities that were regional capitals with all the buildings and trappings of a real capital: a *salle des états* for the provincial parliament; a *palais de justice* for the provincial courts; and a *chambre des comptes* for the provincial treasury.

To explain why not would take another book as long as *This Land of England*. But like *This Land of England* it would have a dominant theme. Economically England was integrated by the market; politically it was united by its kings. The long lines of Henrys and Edwards forged the most impressive apparatus of government in medieval Europe, while the Tudors broke the independent power of the nobility – the only group strong enough to challenge the monarchy. The identification between the authority and unity of the state and the monarchy was complete, and though Parliament and the Army might cut off the King's head in 1649 they soon put his crown back on the coat of arms of the Commonwealth and on its coinage, and in 1660 on the head of his son. Shakespeare of course put it more grandly. In John of Gaunt's speech in *Richard II* (from which our title itself is derived) he hails England as "This royal throne of kings, this scepter'd isle". Grand indeed, but in a real sense no more than a summary of England's political history. King and Kingdom were one, and it was the crown that made England one.

But if the kings were strong, so were the challenges they faced. Four English monarchs were murdered or killed in battle, and almost all were confronted by rebellion or protest at some time in their reigns. The challenges to social and political integration were just as powerful as the forces promoting it. Over time regions became progressively more connected one with another. The connections were particularly important in periods of bad harvest and dearth, yet these were also the times when the movement of grain was most likely to arouse vigorous, and often effective, popular protest. Again, villagers were highly mobile over their lifetime. But that did not prevent them from erecting mental and legal barriers to outsiders, particularly undesirable outsiders, to exclude them. While certain individuals went unhindered, others were treated harshly as vagrants. The Kentish girl who was arrested in Bedfordshire in 1742, and who confessed

"that she was persuaded by strollers to travel a strumpet abroad, being a pleasant life, and has got ill distemper and forced to beg"

did not only offend public morals but also tried to place a claim upon purses to which she was not entitled. Her mobility did not offend, her begging did.

By all accounts, early modern England was not a violent society; and yet the threat of violence simmered just below the surface. Those in authority strove to avert the threat of disorder, or else permitted protest in a contained form. But threatened violence could become actual in full-scale riot or rebellion. Almost exclusively, however, rebels were revolutionary only in wanting to turn the clock back, not forward: back to a period when life was more stable and simple. That stability was when small landholders were not being squeezed out by their larger neighbours; when more familiar religious forms had not been ousted by novelties; when ministerial advice to the Crown was benevolent rather than malevolent, or when the gulf between rich and poor was either not as acute or even non-existent. Thus the men of East Anglia in Kett's Rebellion of 1549 wanted "unreasonable rents" put back to the levels of "the first year of King Henry VII", while the followers of Wat Tyler in the Peasants' Revolt of 1381 took an even longer perspective. "When Adam delved and Eve span, who was then the gentleman?" Almost universally at times of difficulty, the past came, and comes, to represent a Golden Age.

Preconceptions about the past, whether it was a golden or an iron age, need constant testing. For historians do not just "find out about the past"; they think and rethink how the rich but fragmentary evidence of the past can be assembled and reassembled. Nowhere have we attempted to give a broad description of "this land of England". Instead we have looked in detail at a single place, like Myddle or Bury St Edmunds, or a single family like the Fiennes or the Ashburnhams, or even at a single individual like Joseph Mayett. This kind of "thick description", as it is now often called, can provide an otherwise unobtainable view of the past: it is like opening a door in an empty room and suddenly finding all its old life on the other side. But it is life in the raw, and who is to say it is typical of anything but itself? That requires comparison with other research, which is nowadays often of a statistical nature. The ideal is when the two – the fact and the figures – blend seamlessly and, as with Joseph Mayett, a statistic speaks.

But at least "thick description" preserves the form, if not the content, of the older narrative history. More radical is the historian's search for *patterns* of behaviour: the "streamlined" nuclear family and its effect upon social institutions, the relationship between population behaviour and wage levels (and *vice versa*), processes of the accumulation of wealth and its dissipation, the performance and growth of market towns compared with industrial or port towns, or of metropolitan compared with non-metropolitan growth. Traditional history was concerned with change in time, but these sorts of patterns – which embrace many of the basic institutions of social and family life – altered comparatively little over long periods, and such change as there was (and in some cases still is) turns out to be episodic rather than decisive. The result is a conscious rejection of history written in terms of the Victorian vision of progress, ever onward and ever upward. No longer does the past matter only as a formative influence upon the present; no longer even is the present necessarily an improvement on the past.

So it is with the information and interpretations we have offered here. We began with a common sense of the past: that there was a relatively straightforward and essentially unchanging time "back there" that was suddenly torn apart by change. Old patterns of life were overwhelmed by modern industrial, urban and economic growth, and old values swamped by the rising tide of consumer society, with its avidness for new tastes and untried experiences. That was how we began. Indeed no one can deny that we occupy a very different world. But the old certainties about the absolute nature of the differences have gone; and so too have the old views about how the differences came about.

Where for example are the old heroes of the "Agricultural Revolution", beloved still of the school textbooks? If there is one 'certainty' in English agricultural history, it is that Turnip Townshend introduced the turnip and the Norfolk four-course rotation to help revolutionize grain-growing and eighteenth century English agriculture. But the real certainty is that turnips were introduced into East Anglia a century before Townshend, as was clover – and they were intended to improve animal feed and not grain output. Jethro Tull and his seed drill, and Coke of Norfolk with his Holkham estate improvements, are two other famous examples of the same phenomenon: a keen eye for self-publicity but without matching real success. Agricultural change came much more slowly, through intensification rather than innovation, specialization rather than mechanization. Whereas difficulties of grain supply in the early seventeenth century were often acute, by the mid-eighteenth century England was an exporter of grain. And yet, in the period of rapid growth of population in the early nineteenth century and the attendant difficulties of wartime, food shortage and economic crisis loomed. Deep and lasting agricultural change came later in the nineteenth century.

If the idea of the classic "agricultural revolution" has gone, historians' perceptions of the "industrial revolution" are also changing. Recent estimates of economic growth place the onset of rapid change further into the nineteenth century. Large-scale factory industry, even in the leading sector of cotton, was still quite rare by the 1840s. The industrial labour force in the 1830s was still relatively small – although its contribution to national income was increasingly important. None can deny the tremendous and rapid impact of change in nineteenth century England, "the first industrial nation"; but we can deny the belief that change sprang upon an unprepared world, and that it smashed apart an England which had hitherto existed little-changed and which was never to be the same again.

So, we can speak of "this land of England" because England, although composed of many and varied landscapes, was a single political nation and a country with deep internal cohesion in terms of culture, economy and population. In *This Land of England* we have tried to steer a course between the Scylla of structure and the Charybdis of change. The world of the sixteenth, seventeenth and eighteenth centuries had broad, enduring features, and it knew change within those features.

Take farm service. Young people left home and went to live as servants in other households for a number of years, leaving service usually when they married. Service was a characteristic of medieval society, and in some areas still a characteristic of twentieth-century society. Above all, service had an important part in preserving the *status quo*. Service was enduring but not unchanging: the proportion of young people becoming servants varied from period to period, as did the length of time they spent in service. Only with the demise of the *status quo* did the institution of service die, as its system of mutual rights and responsibilities withered.

Take mobility. The myth of the never-moving English peasant has been dumped into history's dustbin, for we know that English men and women moved frequently in the past. The person who was born, married, lived a lifetime in the same place was so rare as to be an oddity. An early seventeenth-century villager may well have moved more often than his twentieth-century counterpart. Much of that movement would have been local, over short distances, which did not necessarily change anything. What it did do was to put people and work or housing together within a local economy, an economy which was far wider than a single village. Change occurred with movement further afield, to larger towns. Sometimes, as in the 1580s and 1590s, that was to alleviate local pressure of numbers. But at other times, as in the 1680s and 1690s, the incentive of living in town was greater, and the economic impact larger.

Take the aristocracy. Peers and their families were a tiny elite at the top of the landowning hierarchy: peers had great political and economic control. But rather than being a monolithic group, the peerage was constantly shifting as lines died out or distant relations succeeded to titles, or as political disgrace removed magnates from the scene. Without new creations, the peerage could not have survived. On the other hand, the peerage was not an "aristocracy of all the talents" in which successful men were rewarded for their industrial and entrepreneurial achievements. The peerage was a fairly closed group of landowners and political operators (and usually the two went hand in hand). And only with the late nineteenth-century creations of the "beerage" and "racketeerage" was the grip of the old order broken. It was the *norm* for families and lines to be extinguished, even when wealth, land and political influence were at stake.

The history of Myddle's parishioners tells a similar story on a more lowly level: families and individuals came and went; "dynasties" were established only to be broken apart; farmers descended into poverty and the lucky hard-working few could ascend into large-scale farming. But the great majority remained within the group and at the level from which they came. Social mobility was there – it had to be – but it was usually constrained.

These seem to be paradoxes: social flexibility with inflexibility, high mobility in a slow-changing environment, a far-reaching and integrating market for agricultural and industrial products in a low-technology and labour-intensive world. The paradoxes are not designed to confuse but to illuminate. The past *was* different, and yet knowing more about it makes it feel closer to us. So many things which are commonly assumed to be the product of a new industrial and urban order can be shown to be forerunners of it or to have survived through it. The degree of difference depends, like perspective, upon the point of view of the observer.

If we return to those images of the rural pastoral world in the opening chapter, our perceptions will have changed. The painting of the haymaking at Dixton depicts a group of workers differentiated by sex rather than status, watched by the family owning all that they, and we, could see. But this seeming dual division of status does not bear investigation, for the workers in the fields would have perceived great social distinctions amongst themselves, from yeoman or yeoman's wife to labourer or labourer's wife. The man on horseback may have been less conscious of those divisions than of the separate strata amongst the landowners – gents, baronets, barons, viscounts, earls, marquises and dukes. But to one of the men mowing, a gent was a gent and a lord was a lord.

A map, on the other hand, may be more than a map. The plan of landholding at Ashburnham was not just an attractive *aide mémoire*, but an instrument of estate policy. Farms could be expanded and contracted, or more efficient or lucrative tenancies instituted, on the basis of such a record. And the area covered by the map was a building block, the centre from which Ashburnham wealth and enterprise was to be expanded through the acquisition of many such areas elsewhere, recorded on similar maps and papers – and the centre to which the Ashburnham estate was to contract.

In the family's last phase, Ashburnham was turned into the microcosm of an ordered rural world. But at "The door of a village inn", all is not as well as at first appears. The woman giving the rider the drink scowls rather than smiles; the little girl is poorly clad, and there is none of the jolliness of "Mine Hostess" traditionally associated with hostelries. The enigma is the man at the side, lighting a fire; he has turned his back upon the more affluent visitor, ignoring him. Whether the fire has a deeper symbolism we cannot know, but the veneer of deference is very thin.

Finally, the earthly paradise of Great Cheverell appears so benevolent only in comparison. Other places experienced bastardy and drunkenness, not Great Cheverell: such immoral behaviour was deliberately excluded, and doubtless any such sign of a separate popular culture was vigorously stamped upon. The poor were well cared-for; but they were visible in their reception of help. As the elderly paupers lined up to receive their annual dole, so their neighbours, friends and relations who provided the assistance could watch, self-satisfied.

Any historical phenomenon or artefact is capable of bearing a wide range of interpretations. It is part of the satisfaction of history to replace one, selected interpretative note with the more realistic many.

That makes it sound a private matter. But perhaps there is a public dimension. For too long we have looked to the past only for explanation of our national decline. That decline, however, is both recent and catastrophic. Until the mid-nineteenth century, at least, England's story is one of success, not unqualified of course, but still striking. And that earlier success matters as much as present failure. Indeed in the perspective of world history it matters much more. *This Land of England* deals with this age of success, and it offers some explanations for it. Whether they have any moral for the present the reader must judge.

Over a period of some years in
the 1650s, Wenceslaus Hollar
surveyed and drew this intricate
map of the growing West End
of the metropolis. London
sucked in people and produce,
sent out ideas and fashions. Its
tentacles reached into the
darkest corners of the land.
London was as much a part of
the countryside as the labourer,
the landowner or the landscape.

197

BIBLIOGRAPHY

This is both a list of archives, books and articles which have been important in the writing of this book, and a guide to further reading. The bibliographies and footnotes of these works will provide a much fuller guide to the literature than is available here.

There is now available a variety of general books on English social and economic history. Hutchinson is publishing a social history series, which includes the most valuable early modern general book so far, Keith Wrightson, *English society 1580–1680* (1981), plus Robert Malcolmson, *Life and labour in England 1700–1780* (1981) and Pamela Horn, *The rural world 1780–1850* (1980). Penguin has embarked upon a new social history series, Joyce Youings, *English society in Sixteenth century England* (1984) and Roy Porter, *English society in the eighteenth century* (1982), the latter with a useful compendium of tables.

Peter Laslett's *The world we have lost*, now in its 3rd, *Further explored* edition (Methuen, 1983), stands in a class of its own, as does the still highly controversial Alan Macfarlane, *The origins of English individualism: the family, property and social transition* (Basil Blackwell, 1978).

Amongst the economic histories covering the period of this book, the most widely useful are Donald Coleman, *The economy of England 1450–1750* (Oxford University Press [UP], 1977), Roderick Floud and Donald McCloskey (eds.), *The economic history of Britain since 1700*, vol. 1 (Cambridge UP, 1981), and Peter Mathias, *The first industrial nation*, 2nd ed. (Methuen, 1983).

On buildings, the county volumes of Nikolaus Pevsner's *Buildings of England* (Penguin) are invaluable gazetteers, while W.G. Hoskins, *The making of the English landscape*, 2nd ed. (Hodder and Stoughton/Penguin, 1970) is a fascinating guide.

There are many travellers' accounts of England between the sixteenth century and the nineteenth, including L. Toulmin Smith (ed.), *The itinerary of John Leland 1535–43*, 5 vols. (1907–10), Thomas Wilson, *The state of England AD 1600*, ed. F.J. Fisher (Camden Society, 1936), Christopher Morris (ed.), *The journeys of Celia Fiennes* (Macdonald/Webb & Bower, 1982), J. Byng, *The Torrington diaries*, ed. C.B. Andrews, 4 vols. (1934–8), and Christopher Morris (ed.), *William Cobbett's Rural Rides 1821–32* (Webb & Bower, 1984).

Howard Newby's *Green and pleasant land?* (Penguin, 1980) is a stimulating book about attitudes to the modern countryside. Raymond

Williams, *The country and the city* (Chatto & Windus, 1973) is equally stimulating on literary interpretations.

In addition are particular works which have bearing upon the particular chapters in this book.

Richard Gough's *History of Myddle* was first published in 1834, and published in full (with an index) in 1875, but is most accessible (although without an index) in David Hey's edition (Penguin, 1981). The original is in the Shropshire Record Office. There is a fuller study of Myddle in David Hey, *An English rural community: Myddle under the Tudors and Stuarts* (Leicester UP, 1974). Other good local studies are Margaret Spufford, *Contrasting communities: English villagers in the sixteenth and seventeenth centuries*(Cambridge UP, 1974), and Keith Wrightson and David Levine, *Poverty and piety in an English village: Terling 1525–1700* (Academic Press, 1979). These books deal with Cambridgeshire and Essex respectively, and Alan Macfarlane *et al.*, *Reconstructing historical communities* (Cambridge UP, 1979) describes the sources available for the authors' intensive study of another Essex village, Earls Colne. That study is enlivened by Alan Macfarlane (ed.), *The diary of Ralph Josselin 1616–83* (British Academy, 1976). These village studies are far less common for the eighteenth century, but another journal, David Vaisey (ed.), *The diary of Thomas Turner 1754–65* (Oxford UP, 1984), of a village shopkeeper in East Hoathly, Sussex conveys a vivid impression. Many authors have been concerned with social structure: see, for example, David Cressy, *Literacy and the social order: reading and writing in Tudor and Stuart England* (Cambridge UP, 1980), Geoffrey Holmes, 'Gregory King and the social structure of pre-industrial England', *Transactions of the Royal Historical Society*, 5th ser., 27 (1977), Gordon Mingay, *The gentry: the rise and fall of a ruling class* (Longman, 1976), Ann Kussmaul, *Servants in husbandry in early modern England* (Cambridge UP, 1981), and Peter Laslett, 'Clayworth and Cogenhoe' in Laslett, *Family life and illicit love in earlier generations* (Cambridge UP, 1977).

The history of the Fiennes and their titles is told in brief in G.E.C[ockayne], *The complete peerage*, 14 vols. (1910–65; repr. Alan Sutton, 1982), and at length in the unpublished work of David Fiennes. Harry Gordon Slade, 'Broughton Castle, Oxfordshire', *Archaeological Journal*, 135 (1978) lays bare the history of the house, various articles in *Cake and Cockhorse* (the journal of the Banbury Historical Society), and in the *Victoria County History, Oxfordshire*, vols. 9–10 (Oxford UP, 1969, 1972), illuminate other aspects; Conrad Russell, *The crisis of Parliaments: English history 1509–1660* (Oxford UP, 1971) provides a political framework for understanding the 1st Viscount, and John Cannon, *Aristocratic century: the peerage of the eighteenth century* (Cambridge UP, 1984) is a brave new look at that subject.

The computer files of the ESRC Cambridge Group for the History of Population and Social Structure, the probate archives in the Lancashire Record Office, and the resources of the Centre for North-West Regional

Studies, University of Lancaster provided the raw material for studying Hawkshead. Of the publications of John Marshall, 'Agrarian wealth and social structure in pre-industrial Cumbria', *Economic History Review*, 2nd ser., 33 (1980) is the most useful here. He and Colin Philipps, 'The Cumbrian iron industry in the seventeenth century' in W.H. Chaloner and B. Ratcliffe (eds.), *Trade and transport: essays in economic history in honour of T.S. Willan* (Manchester UP, 1977), follow in the way led by Henry Swainson Cowper, *Hawkshead (the northernmost parish of Lancashire)* (1899). Andrew Appleby, *Famine in Tudor and Stuart England* (Liverpool UP, 1978) is primarily concerned with Cumbria; E.A. Wrigley and Roger Schofield, *The population history of England and Wales 1541–1871: a reconstruction* (Edward Arnold, 1981) is one of the most important works of the current historical generation.

There is no proper history of either the de Vere or the Ashburnham families. The de Veres feature in K.B. McFarlane, *The nobility of later medieval England* (Blackwell, 1973), some of their properties in Norman Scarfe, *The Suffolk landscape* (Hodder & Stoughton, 1972), and *Lavenham: 700 years of textile making* by David Dymond and Alec Betterton (Boydell Press, 1982) is a study of their proudest possession.

The considerable archives of the Ashburnham family are principally housed in the East Sussex Record Office, and a catalogue was published by Francis Steer in 1955. Other family archives are held by the National Library of Wales and by Suffolk Record Office, Ipswich; other material came from the archives of Hoare's Bank in Fleet Street.

Lawrence Stone and Jeanne C. Fawtier Stone, *An open elite? England 1540–1880* (Clarendon Press, 1984) joins Lawrence Stone, *The family, sex and marriage in England 1500–1800* (Weidenfeld & Nicholson, 1977) as a controversial study of elite life. Gordon Mingay, *English landed society in the eighteenth century* (Routledge & Kegan Paul, 1963), Michael Thompson, *English landed society in the nineteenth century* (Routledge & Kegan Paul, 1963), and Heather Clemenson, *English country houses and landed estates* (Croom Helm, 1983) are useful introductions to the thorny problems of landed wealth past and present. Mark Girouard, *Life in the English country house,* (Yale UP, 1978) takes us inside stately homes, through the ages. Miriam Slater, *Family life in the seventeenth century* (Routledge & Kegan Paul, 1984) studies the copious papers of the Verney family, not without controversy as in *Past & Present*, 85 (1979). Brian Outhwaite (ed.), *Marriage and society* (Europa, 1981) is a comprehensive collection of essays. The particular enterprises of the Ashburnhams are illuminated by such works as Ernest Straker, *Wealden iron* (1931; repr. David & Charles, 1969), Michael Flinn, *The history of the British coal industry, vol. 2: 1700–1830* (Clarendon Press, 1984), Michael Flinn, *Men of iron: the Crowleys in the early iron industry* (Edinburgh UP, 1962), P.G.M. Dickson, *The financial revolution in England 1688–1756* (Macmillan, 1967); Ross Wordie, *Estate management in eighteenth century England* (Royal Historical Society, 1982) and Mary Finch, *The wealth of five*

Northamptonshire families 1540–1640 (Northamptonshire Record Society, 1956) are valuable case studies.

The autobiography of Joseph Mayett is in the Buckinghamshire Record Office, ref. D/X 371. Ann Kussmaul's edition for the Buckinghamshire Record Society is in press. Her book on *Servants in husbandry* is complemented by Alan Everitt, 'Farm labourers' in Joan Thirsk (ed.), *The agrarian history of England and Wales, vol. 4: 1500–1640* (Cambridge UP, 1967). David Robinson (ed.), *John Clare: autobiographical writings* (Oxford UP, 1984), Donald Woodward (ed.), *The farming and memorandum books of Henry Best of Elmswell, 1642* (British Academy, 1984), and Fred Kitchen, *Brother to the ox* (Dent, 1940; repr. Penguin, 1984) are all cited in the text. Margaret Spufford, *Small books and pleasant histories: popular fiction and its readership in seventeenth century England* (Methuen, 1981), Victor Neuberg, *Popular literature* (Penguin, 1977), David Vincent, *Bread, knowledge and freedom* (Methuen, 1981), and Roger Schofield, 'Dimensions in literacy', *Explorations in economic history*, 10 (1973) all consider literacy and autobiography.

Poverty is now attracting academic interest again. Such works as Dorothy Marshall, *The English poor in the eighteenth century* (Longman, 1926) have now been joined by such as John Marshall, *The Old Poor Law*, 2nd ed. (Macmillan, 1985), Keith Snell, *Annals of the labouring poor* (Cambridge UP, 1985), Tim Wales, 'Poverty, poor relief and the life cycle: some evidence from seventeenth century Norfolk' in Richard Smith (ed.), *Land, kinship and life cycle* (Cambridge UP, 1984), and John Barrell, *The dark side of the landscape: the rural poor in English painting 1730–1840* (Cambridge UP, 1980). B.A. Holderness, '"Open" and "close" parishes in England in the eighteenth and nineteenth centuries', *Agricultural History Review*, 20 (1972) looks at varieties of villages, Robert Malcolmson, *Popular recreations in England 1700–1850* (Cambridge UP, 1973) at people letting their hair down, Eric Hobsbawm and George Rudé, *Captain Swing* (Lawrence & Wishart, 1969) at rural incendiarism. Howard Newby, *The deferential worker* (Penguin, 1977) is an important work on recent and modern farm workers. Michael Anderson, *Approaches to the history of the western family 1500–1914* (Macmillan, 1980) is a judicious introduction to a new and growing subject. Joseph Mayett's forms of religion are discussed in M.R. Watts, *The dissenters* (Oxford UP, 1978), and James Obelkevich, *Religion and rural society: South Lindsey 1825–75* (Oxford UP, 1976) is a valuable study incorporating insights into local society and religion.

Urban history has been a growing specialization in recent years. The town records of Bury St Edmunds in Suffolk Record Office, Bury, the map and picture collections of St Edmundsbury Borough, and the Crace collection in the British Museum were especially useful here.

Peter Clark and Paul Slack, *English towns in transition 1500–1700* (Oxford UP, 1976) and Penelope Corfield, *The impact of English towns*

1700–1800 (Oxford UP, 1978) are general surveys, while many important articles are reprinted in Peter Clark (ed.), *The early modern town: a reader* (Longman, 1976). Internal trade and marketing are examined in Alan Everitt, 'The marketing of agricultural produce' in Joan Thirsk (ed.), *Agrarian history of England and Wales, vol. 4: 1500–1640* (Cambridge UP, 1967), John Chartres' article of the same title in *vol. 5, 1640–1750* (Cambridge UP, 1985), and in John Chartres, *Internal trade in England 1500–1700* (Macmillan, 1977). Rural-urban migration is studied in Peter Clark, 'The migrant in Kentish towns 1580–1640' in Peter Clark and Paul Slack (eds.), *Crisis and order in English towns 1500–1700* (Routledge & Kegan Paul, 1972), and David Souden, 'Migrants and the population structure of late seventeenth century provincial cities and market towns' in Peter Clark (ed.), *The transformation of English provincial towns 1600–1800* (Hutchinson, 1984). E.P. Thompson, 'The moral economy of the English crowd in the eighteenth century', *Past & Present*, 50 (1977) is a classic study of food riots. Peter Clark, *The English alehouse: a social history 1200–1830* (Longman, 1983) studies places of liquid refreshment.

Of the many studies of London, the most important additional items here have been C.L. Kingsford (ed.), *Stow's Survey of London*, 2 vols (Oxford UP, 1908), Dorothy George, *London life in the eighteenth century* (1925; Penguin, 1965), John Summerson, *Georgian London* 3rd ed. (Penguin, 1978), and John Schofield, *The building of London from the Conquest to the Great Fire* (British Museum, 1984). E.A. Wrigley, 'A simple model of London's importance in changing English economy and society 1650–1750' repr. in P. Abrams and E.A. Wrigley (eds.), *Towns in societies* (Cambridge UP, 1978) is a wide-ranging synthesis and analysis.

INDEX

Figures in **bold** at the end of an entry refer to an illustration on that page.

PICTURE CREDITS

We wish to thank the following for permission to reproduce pictures or items used here as illustrations:

Revd J. Bickersteth, pp. 4 (bottom), 87.
British Library, 111 (top), 136.
British Museum, *viii*, 85, 166, 167, 170, 175, 176 (top), 196–7.
Cheltenham Museum and Art Gallery/Bridgeman Art Library, 3.
Country Life, 35, 36 (left), 69 (bottom), 90.
Emmanuel College, Cambridge, *Frontispiece*, 36, (right), 74 (top left and right), 80, 81, 111 (bottom left and right), 119, 148.
ESRC Cambridge Group for the History of Population and Social Structure, 47 (top).
Greater London Council, 166–7, 177–81 (top).
Mansell Collection, 122–3.
National Monuments Record, 25 (top), 99, 102, 104, 139.
St Edmundsbury Borough Council, 140, 142.
Science Museum, 129.
Tate Gallery, 4 (top), 172–3.

The watercolours on pp. *xvi*–1, 8–9, 50–1, 96–7, 132–3 were painted by Pamela Williams.

The photographs on pp. *v*, *xiii*, 5, 12, 16, 17, 20, 25 (bottom), 32, 33, 39, 47 (bottom), 53 (bottom right), 54, 55 (top), 57, 59 (top), 72, 73, 74 (bottom), 88, 99, 100, 101, 103, 141, 144–5, 147, 149, 186–7 were taken by Peter Anderson.

The photographs on pp. 40, 44, 53 (left and top right), 55 (bottom), 59 (bottom), 69 (top), 89, 91, 94, 105, 131, 137, 159, 160, 171 (top), 176 (bottom) were taken by David Souden.